T0305296

Elgar Introduction to Organizational Discourse Analysis

ELGAR INTRODUCTIONS TO MANAGEMENT AND ORGANIZATION
THEORY

Series Editors: Cary L. Cooper, *Alliance Manchester Business School, University of Manchester, UK* and Stewart R. Clegg, *School of Management, University of Technology, Sydney, Australia*

Elgar Introductions to Management and Organization Theory are stimulating and thoughtful introductions to main theories in management, organizational behaviour and organization studies, expertly written by some of the world's leading scholars. Designed to be accessible yet rigorous, they offer concise and lucid surveys of the key theories in the field.

The aims of the series are two-fold: to pinpoint essential history, and aspects of a particular theory or set of theories, and to offer insights that stimulate critical thinking. The volumes serve as accessible introductions for undergraduate and graduate students coming to the subject for the first time. Importantly, they also develop well-informed, nuanced critiques of the field that will challenge and extend the understanding of advanced students, scholars and policy-makers.

Elgar Introduction to Organizational Discourse Analysis

Marco Berti

Lecturer, UTS Business, University of Technology Sydney, Australia

ELGAR INTRODUCTIONS TO MANAGEMENT AND ORGANIZATION THEORY

 Edward Elgar
PUBLISHING

Cheltenham, UK • Northampton, MA, USA

Published by
Edward Elgar Publishing Limited
The Lypiatts
15 Lansdown Road
Cheltenham
Glos GL50 2JA
UK

Edward Elgar Publishing, Inc.
William Pratt House
9 Dewey Court
Northampton
Massachusetts 01060
USA

A catalogue record for this book
is available from the British Library

Library of Congress Control Number: 2016949967

This book is available electronically in the **Elgar**online
Business subject collection
DOI 10.4337/9781784717056

ISBN 978 1 78471 704 9 (cased)
ISBN 978 1 78471 705 6 (eBook)

Typeset by Columns Design XML Ltd, Reading

Contents

Figures and tables

FIGURES

TABLES

Introduction: the aim and structure of the book

The fundamental importance of communication for organized action has been acknowledged since the early days of management studies. In his seminal work, Fayol (1916 [1949]) stated that well-developed organizational communication systems are essential for command and control. The foundational role of communication for modern organizations is evident in the pragmatist philosopher Dewey's assertion that communication "is a means of establishing cooperation, domination and order" (Dewey 1925 [1958], p. 202). A "linguistic turn in organizational studies" (Alvesson and Kärreman 2000), which was preceded by the seminal work conducted in the early 1970s by Silverman (1970) and Clegg (1975 [2013]), but which only became mainstream in the 1990s, claimed that discourse is substrative for organizations. According to this more radical view language is a shaping force that produces knowledge, understanding, norms and behaviour, thus making it constitutive of, rather than merely instrumental to, organization.

The central premise of contemporary organizational discourse analysis (ODA) is that language is not a neutral medium, a tool used to communicate ideas and intentions. By structuring coherent systems of meaning, coalescing in stable (but not immutable) patterns, it shapes reality and subjectivity. It becomes 'discourse'. The opportunities offered by this perspective to organizational studies are evident. It is possible to investigate the specific ways of representing and communicating information that emerge in a given organizational setting, but it is also possible to examine how ordinary ways to describe phenomena or to 'talk about things' shape knowledge and action in an organized setting. The appeal of the notion of organizational discourse rests on its promise to reveal a complex of subliminal messages and suggestions that shape the perceptions, interpretations and actions of organizational members. By uncovering the dense lattice of textual references used to describe and prescribe events and things it becomes possible to predict and explain regularities in behaviours, and even to prescribe effective ways to regulate identities (Alvesson and Willmott 2002).

However, the linguistic substrate that produces these different meanings is also elusive. While the idea of discourse analysis seems to suggest that discourses have sufficient material consistency to be anatomized and scrutinized, their ontological status is, at best, uncertain. As a consequence, discourse risks assuming the same role in sociological theory that the *Luminiferous Aether* had in 19th-century physics. As Aether was the postulated medium enabling the propagation of light, so discourse becomes the made-up intermediary for justifying the existence of power/ knowledge effects. In this regard, its widespread invocation evokes the notion of *culture*, an analogous concept that it is considered both omnipresent and difficult to encapsulate in description.

Discourse is even more insubstantial than culture. The latter is merely *hidden* in the folds of social action, propagating through narratives and artefacts, and through a partial codification in explicit codes and taboos (Schein 1985 [2004]). Discourse, on the other hand, can be considered as the very *fold* of social action; it is what gives meaning and poignancy to stories; it is the underlying cognitive framework that gives sense to rules. Most of this constitutive role of organizational discourse is indeed invisible, because taken for granted. It appears only 'natural' that corporations are hierarchically structured, led by a professional management and devoted to maximizing efficiency and profit. Modern bureaucracies are indeed founded on the notion of instrumental rationality, whereas "expectations are used as 'conditions' or 'means' for the attainment of the actor's own rationally pursued and calculated ends" (Weber 1922 [1978], p. 24). As such they are not a neutral technology but a powerful discourse producing subjects and meanings: contemporary 'rational' organizations are predicated on a model of self-imposed discipline based on the fundamental principles of control through constant hierarchical observation and the fitting of individual diversity into normalized roles (Foucault 1979). To use a contemporary pop culture reference, discourse is like the *Matrix*, a world that has been weaved around us by the 'machines' created by humans (ideologies, architectures, social roles, languages, etc.) that now entrap us in an illusory but seemingly truthful reality.

A supplementary pragmatic hurdle for those who intend to employ the lens of discourse to understand organization is the impossibility of capturing the idea of discourse in a single, comprehensive, commonly accepted definition. Many different 'flavours' of discourse are in use in organizational studies such that, coming across this label, one cannot ever take for granted what concept the author has in mind. Discourse is also frequently used as a trope, to manifest allegiance to a post-structuralist paradigm. The organizational student or practitioner who tries to approach this fascinating perspective is faced by the daunting task of making sense of an enormous variety of different approaches to 'organizational discourse'. For any neophyte, trying to approach the debate on organizational discourse is like entering a jungle of divergent interpretations of what organizational discourse is (or is not). Points and counterpoints are intertwined like lianas and vines making the travel arduous, and finding the way is challenging because of an undergrowth of divergent definitions.

Yet the risk of objectifying discourse is intrinsically connected with any univocal statement about it. Citing the famous Foucauldian statement, according to which discourses "systematically form the object of which they speak" (Foucault 1979, p. 49) it is easy to assume that discourses are a clearly delimited subject, performing actions ('speaking'), even performing specific functions or at least having the intent of 'forming objects'. One might choose a more 'concrete' perspective, considering discourse "to cover all forms of spoken interaction, formal and informal, and written texts of all kinds" (Wetherell and Potter 1987, p. 7). Even in this case the desire to offer useful methods to analyse, measure, compare different discourses in order to understand social interactions can also lead to a reification of the concept. If discourse is reduced to some of its vehicles (the 'texts') or to its ideal content ('statements') we risk overlooking some fundamental characteristics and implications of discourse, such as the role of symbolic practices in its constitution and reproduction, its relationship with power and knowledge and its organizing function.

It is neither practical nor advisable to devise an 'ultimate definition' of what organizational discourse *is*, and of the 'one best way' in which its analysis should be performed. It is rather more important to become acquainted with a ragged jungle of disparate interpretations, methodologies and practices. Discourse is better treated as a Kantian noumenon, a *Ding an sich* that can be imagined but not reduced to a set of sensible quantifications.

This book provides a succinct but wide-ranging introduction to organizational discourse. It does not attempt to offer a 'map of the jungle' since doing so would be highly impractical because organizational discourse may be thought of through the simile of a conceptual rainforest, a living organism, constantly changing and growing in unexpected directions, offering a set of ideas that can help understand the diverse but interconnected nature of this theoretical ecosystem. The book offers a *phenomenology of discourse*, considering the idea of discourse as an epistemological device to explore how symbolic practices become patterned and routinized, producing widespread ways to make sense of events and offering specific modes of organizing.

In order to compare and contrast different views on discourse and to explore the implications of applying a discursive perspective to the study of organizations and organizing I explicitly harness the power of metaphors attempting to provide a rich and – at the same time – approachable set of descriptors that can be used to study and investigate discourses. Vivid, shared images can help discussion and reflection on concepts that are too complex or vague to be contained in a univocal designation, enabling us to extend our conceptual grasp. They have an *indexical* value (Garfinkel 1967), in the sense that they allow us to explore and better understand certain features of an otherwise too abstract or exoteric concept by pointing us to a tangible object that is closer to our everyday reality. Metaphors can be useful heuristic tools, enabling the emergence of new meaning and new insight, thanks to the juxtaposition of ideas from different domains (Cornelissen 2005).

Each of the 'images of organizational discourse' that I propose, is used as an interpretative device to shed light on different attributes of discourse and to connect several research perspectives that share discursive roots (e.g. organizational culture, organizational identity, organizational fashions, organizational rhetoric, etc.).

I commence the book positioning discourse analysis in the broader paradigm of studies that examine the linguistic and cultural aspects of organizing (Chapter 1); then I review alternative attempts to provide taxonomies of varieties of ODA and discuss some of the ontological and epistemological challenges encountered by discourse analysts (Chapter 2). I subsequently describe how the use of metaphors can be useful to reflect on the issues surrounding discourse analysis (Chapter 3). Three different metaphors are employed to connect several approaches to organizational studies that have their conceptual roots in discourse, with the purpose of extending the readers' awareness of the various implications of ODA: discourse as a map, discourse as an organizing device, and discourse as a mask (Chapters 4–6). In lieu of a conclusion, Chapter 7 provides a concrete exemplification of the application of ODA, in which the heuristic potential of the approach is employed to critically describe a complex interorganizational field of practices that underlies the global institution of business education. Applying a discursive lens to this specific object is of particular interest and not just because of the dimension and complexity of the phenomenon, or thanks to the richness of the empirical textual material, constituted by a large corpus of literature presenting the history of business education and discussing avenues for its future reform. The relevance of this discussion resides in the mutually constitutive relationship that business education, seen as a global, paradigmatic discourse, has with all possible local forms and manifestations of organizational discourses. Despite their attempts to project an image of themselves as neutral, scientifically-driven knowledge brokers, business schools' discursive practices are neither value free nor immune from the rhetorical and ideological undercurrents that affect their objects of study. Moreover, education is obviously a discursive practice, based on symbolic performances and aimed at disciplining learners (Foucault 1979), and by training generations of aspirant and practising managers and entrepreneurs business schools have a remarkable influence on the (re)production of organizational discourses. This exemplification highlights the interpolation of the symbolic and pragmatic side of social life, bringing to life the issue of power and its constitutive effects, and thus showing the potential for a productive (of ethical awareness, positive innovation and managerial reform), rather than merely descriptive, use of ODA.

REFERENCES

Alvesson, M. and Kärreman, D. 2000, 'Taking the Linguistic Turn in Organizational Research: Challenges, Responses, Consequences', *The Journal of Applied Behavioral Science*, vol. 36, pp. 136–58.

Alvesson, M. and Willmott, H. 2002, 'Identity Regulation as Organizational Control: Producing the Appropriate Individual', *Journal of Management Studies*, vol. 39, pp. 619–44.

Clegg, S.R. 1975 [2013], *Power, Rule and Domination*, Routledge, Oxon.

Cornelissen, J.P. 2005, 'Beyond Compare: Metaphor in Organization Theory', *The Academy of Management Review*, vol. 30, pp. 751–64.

Dewey, J. 1925 [1958], *Experience and Nature*, vol. 1, Dover Publications, New York.

Fayol, H. 1916 [1949], *General and Industrial Management*, Pitman, London.

Foucault, M. 1979, *Discipline and Punish: The Birth of the Prison*, Vintage Books, New York.

Garfinkel, H. 1967, *Studies in Ethnomethodology*, Prentice Hall, Englewood Cliffs, NJ.

Schein, E.H. 1985 [2004], *Organizational Culture and Leadership*, 3rd edn, Jossey-Bass Publishers, San Francisco, CA.

Silverman, D. 1970, *The Theory of Organisations: A Sociological Framework*, Heinemann Educational, London.

Weber, M. 1922 [1978], *Economy and Society: An Outline of Interpretive Sociology*, University of California Press, Berkeley, CA.

Wetherell, M. and Potter, J. 1987, *Discourse and Social Psychology: Beyond Attitudes and Behaviour*, SAGE Publications, Newbury Park, CA.

1. Language and organization

THE CENTRALITY OF LANGUAGE

Can you imagine a human organization without a name? This simple thought experiment reveals how language and organization are intrinsically connected. Organizing implies the development and maintenance of regular patterns of interaction, and the conceptual and material activities involved in planning, acquiring resources, negotiating with internal and external stakeholders, coordinating action, etc. that constitute any contemporary organization, would not be possible in the absence of a sophisticated communication system. Any activity performed in a contemporary organization, be it a government agency, a corporate body, or a not for profit organization, demands the agency of language. In the absence of place names, signs, written policies, rules, procedures and a myriad of oral performances any organization would become effectively mute. It is only through linguistic construction that we can, individually and socially, make sense of the phenomena that we label 'organized activities'. While simple communicative interactions (expressing threats or friendliness, conveying elementary meaning, etc.) do not require a codified language to be performed, organized behaviour is founded on the use of a sophisticated sign system, allowing the transfer of articulated meanings.

The relationship between communication and language is not one of one-directional causation: as organizations are a product of language, so in the modern world language embeds organizations. A precondition for conceiving and understanding ideas that we consider commonplace, such as 'rule', 'money', 'market', 'sport', 'authority', is the tacit acknowledgement of a multiplicity of organizations. Taken-for-granted actions such as boarding a train, sitting in a lecture or attending an event imply the active participation of the subject in a complex network of organized actions involving a multitude of human and non-human agents (Latour 2005). Consequently the specific ways of organizing transactions of a given human society define the way in which we talk about and understand things. Even an apparently simple idea such as 'buying lunch' for a friend, could never be conceived by a member of a hunter-gatherer tribe, where commerce, market transactions, specialization of work do not exist. As language makes organizations possible so different organizational contexts attribute dissimilar meaning to words, including concepts that appear to be firmly grounded in our experience. For instance, the idea that something is 'urgent', or needs to happen 'immediately', can assume completely different connotations and bring about totally different behaviours, on a trading floor, in an accounting department or in a R&D department.

In order to comprehend the nature of this relationship between language and organization we need to elucidate the meaning of these two entities. The problem is that there is quite a chasm between 'lay' and academic research-informed characterizations of organization and language. Dictionary definitions are a good starting point to determine general consensus, in the mundane sense, about concepts. According to the *Oxford Dictionary of English* an 'organization' is "an organized group of people with a particular purpose, such as a business or government department", whereas 'organized' means "arranged or structured in a systematic way" while 'language' is defined as "the system of spoken or written communication used by a particular country, people, community" (*Oxford Dictionary of English* 2011). These definitions privilege an essentialist view of the described objects and emphasize their instrumental functions: while such views are commonplace, they are problematic and they fail to incorporate a more nuanced and sophisticated understanding of these phenomena.

The traditional view of communication conceptualizes it as a linear transmission of contents from a sender to a receiver, using a coherent system of symbols which refer to objective phenomena. Contemporary organizational communication studies take a different perspective, looking at how the vocabulary in use shapes the reality of the situation, framing personal interaction (Ashcraft, Kuhn and Cooren 2009). Language is neither a discrete object made of utterances nor it is a representational instrument: it "is not only content; it is also context and a way to recontextualize content. We do not just report and describe with language; we also create with it" (Boje, Oswick and Ford 2004, p. 571).

Analogously, contemporary organizational scholarship rejects both reification and naïve teleological explanations of organizations. While the purposeful nature of organizations is not in doubt, their goals are contested and plural. Rather than providing a shared purpose, they act as sets of common constraints for individual actors (Simon 1964). More importantly, organizations are better understood as "islands of fabricated coherence in a sea of chaos and change" (Chia 2002, p. 866). Rather than stable objects, embodied in buildings and formal structures, they are a "momentary apprehension of an ongoing process of organizing" (Clegg, Kornberger and Rhodes 2005, p. 158). Their endurance is the outcome of a constant labour of re-production of routines, structures and relationships. A well-established stream of contemporary organization scholarship is indeed devoted to investigating how this 'organizing phenomena' produce and maintain the illusion of stability that we recognize as tangible and persistent institutional entities (see for instance Weick 1969 [1979]; Chia 2002; Tsoukas and Chia 2002; Clegg et al. 2005; Hernes 2007; Czarniawska 2008a, 2008b).

Shifting from a simplistic view of language and organization has fundamental implications for the notion of *organizational discourse*. Organizations are not just a stage for discourses, or their 'manufacturers', they are discursive products, kept together by rhetoric, narratives, speech-acts. Equally, language is not a mere instrument used to convey those orders and instructions that are necessary for cooperation. For any form of collaborative action to occur actors need to develop a common understanding of their situation. As such, language empowers cooperation not just by exchanging information useful to coordinate action but also by producing a coherent model of meaning making, enabling individuals to build a common frame of reference. Words such as 'manager', 'meeting', 'incentive', 'process', 'promotion', 'policy', are not describing natural objects but they activate, make possible, organizational action and define expectations, roles and relationships.

Organizing is founded on a collective attribution of meaning, a "sense-making" process (Weick 1969 [1979], 1995) through which the multiple actors who participate in the organization share coherent processes to identify, describe, catalogue and interrelate their perceptions:

> every perception is dependent on the conceptual apparatus which makes it possible and meaningful as this conceptual apparatus is inscribed in language. Talk and writing are thus much more than the means of expression of individual meanings: they connect each perception to a larger orientation and system of meaning. The conceptual distinctions in an organization are inscribed in the systems of speaking and writing. (Deetz 1982, p. 135)

The existence of these common patterns of meaning attribution is predicated on the existence of shared communicative codes. By labelling specific segments of our experience according to standardized conceptual descriptors we are separating and recombining in an intersubjectively intelligible picture an otherwise anarchical multiplicity of viewpoints. There is therefore a close interrelation between use of language and *organizing*. The ordering enacted in a given organization is as much a narrative and ideal reconstruction as a pragmatic arranging of words, bodies and actions towards an end (Rhodes 2001; Clegg et al. 2005). In Weick's word, organizing is "a consensually validated *grammar* for reducing equivocality by means of sensible interlocked behaviours" (1969 [1979], p. 3; emphasis added). This process involves selecting elements regarded as salient, ignoring others, clustering elements into discrete items and 'events', and attributing causal relationships (Weick 1969 [1979], pp. 148–9). Organizations are thus created and reproduced by linguistic means: discourses which articulate the flow of experience in a collectively meaningful and consistent picture. In this activity, material, performative ordering and cognitive sensemaking are mutually constitutive, since the former requires the latter for its execution. Both linguistic and organizational sensemaking thereby involve a process of mutual *enactment* through which they impose order on a more or less incoherent stream of random stimuli (Weick 1969 [1979]) that facilitates the emergence of practical objects and practices.

The intricate relationship between organizing and discourse will be the subject of Chapter 5; for the moment, it is important to clarify how language is not simply used to generate and convey meaning but also to 'order', in the dual meaning of 'arranging' and 'commanding'. A uniform, a workspace layout, a spreadsheet, contribute to articulate meaning and to offer a specific frame that regulates social behaviour through the explicit or implicit exercise of power. Deetz provides us with a vivid example:

> the accountant's report invisibly creates the "visible" organization as a financial entity and provides a language for corporate self-understanding. Accounting is a disciplinary power that colonises the organization by creating newly internalized facts and vocabularies that are constitutive of organizational reality in a way that suppress potential conflict over its mission. (1992, p. 280)

What this author means is that by choosing to discuss an organization in terms of 'assets', 'liabilities', 'depreciation', 'cash flow', etc. and representing its complexity in simple mathematical figures a whole range of issues is silenced and interests ignored or treated as subordinate to financial outcomes. Even when the espoused intent of an accounting practice is that of safeguarding nature and society, as in the case of 'triple bottom-line', the attempt to capture the complex impact of a company on its environment in a single figure or to consider it in a short-term perspective produces spurious results (Norman and MacDonald 2004). The quantitatively based discourses of financial audit, quality control and risk management become therefore generative mechanisms that establish and legitimize the power of specific expert groups (Reed 2000, p. 529).

Using a discourse analysis perspective involves investigating three roles of language: the constitutive (of meaning), the productive (of identity) and the regulative (of behaviours). Rather than seeing these different outcomes of symbolic practice as 'functions' of language, which would convey an idea of agency and rational purpose, I prefer to define them as a consequence of our 'symbolic work'. An agent can use language strategically to pursue specific interests and goals (as happens for instance in the case of rhetorical statements); nonetheless, the disciplinary use of discursive elements is very often tacit. For instance, the accountants working for a university will certainly employ quantitative metrics to define and assess their organizational performances and in doing so they are actively supporting a managerialist view that privileges the commercial over the social role of academia, one that subordinates academic authority to bureaucratic direction (Parker and Jary 1995; Pfeffer and Fong 2004; Parker 2014). However, this behaviour is implicitly assumed as a 'normal' default way of performing their job, rather than a strategy instrumental to reinforcing their administrative power. The interpretive patterns are routine and applied unthinkingly (Luckmann 2008). Equally, the same academics who would have a vested interest in resisting the erosion of their professional autonomy actively participate in competitive benchmarking activities measuring their output by means of accounting measures, in accordance with the same discourse.

What emerges from these examples is the ambiguous separation between symbolic and material elements in any real setting. Tangible objects and concrete actions, even embodied, emotional reactions, are entangled with symbolic meanings; therefore symbolic practices are not merely representational but productive of meaning and action. Before investigating further the relationship between material and symbolic practices, we need to expand our understanding of the latter. To do so, I will devote the next section to a reflection on the attributes of language.

LANGUAGE AND MEANING MAKING

A fundamental set of questions regarding language concerns the topic of *semantics*, which covers two separate matters: first, understanding what is the meaning of this or that symbol for a particular group and, second, describing the set of conditions that have generated that meaning (Lewis 1970). Applied to the field of organizational studies this corresponds to two alternative research questions: to investigate what exactly a term, such as 'leadership' or 'strategic planning', refers to in different organizational settings; versus questioning why and how these different ways of constructing the notion of leadership or strategy have emerged in those contexts. Without entering into the complex and highly debated field of alternative theories of language and of semiotics it is useful to quickly outline the genealogy of the most widespread set of concepts currently informing the 'linguistic turn' in organizational studies.

Of foundational significance is the thought of de Saussure (1916 [1966]), who posited that words and symbols are mere signifiers – that is, totally arbitrary – that acquire meaning when combined with a mental image (a 'signified'). The notion of the whimsicality of language was not original: more than a century before, Fichte defined language as "the expression of our thoughts by means of arbitrary signs" (Fichte 1794 [1995], p. 120). The truly revolutionary value of the Saussurean lesson is to break completely with a "referential theory of meaning – i.e., the idea that language is a nomenclature which is in a one-to-one relation to objects" (Laclau and Mouffe 1987, p. 89), thus understanding language as a social phenomenon. Language is expressed in speech acts (*parole*) that are a concrete expression of an underlying system of differences, the language (*langue*); in terms of analogy, a specific game of chess is but one of the quasi-infinitely possible games that can emerge from the application of the rules of chess.

Even if one assumes that the purpose of verbal communication is to convey ideas and emotions faithfully, the relationship between signifier and signified is not just arbitrary but it is complicated by various factors. When pigeon-holed in word sequences, complex and fluid ideas are degraded, and any attempt to escape this verbal straightjacket by using linguistic or material tropes will have the consequence of emphasizing connotative meanings that exist only in the eye of the beholder. For instance the word 'family' has a very intelligible meaning for any English speaker; yet, any two individuals will probably append different connotations and references to the word, depending on their context and personal experience. To paraphrase Tolstoy, "all idealized families are alike; each experienced family is different in its own way".

The observation of this trade-off between clarity and comprehensibility led Bateson and Ruesch (1951, pp. 170–71) to describe two alternative coding modalities for human communication – digital and analogical. The former involves the type of arbitrary signification that Fichte mentions, for instance the use of the word 'sadness' to represent an emotion, while the latter entails representing an event in a socially recognizable way, using posture and gesture that convey that feeling, or evoking the emotion by means of metaphors or music. Analogical communication is easier to understand, because it "can be more readily referred to the thing it stands for" (Watzlawick, Jackson and Bavelas 1967, p. 62) but this broad intelligibility comes at the expense of precision, exactness of meaning and economy of expression. For instance, while gesturing sadness comes easily to an accomplished actor or mime such as Marcel Marceau, one needs to resort to a digital language to argue the distinction between sadness and depression or their performance as theatre. The problem with these 'digital idioms' is that in the attempt to enhance accuracy and rigour they become esoteric and impenetrable for the uninitiated, so that the version of English language used by a British post-modern sociologist can be so different to that of an American economist as to render their texts mutually unintelligible. The range of 'digital languages' is at any rate enormous, since 'natural languages' and their idiomatic variations do not exhaust the possibilities of symbolic practice. Any symbolic system shared by a community, and which uses signs and rules to order it in order to communicate meaning, can be defined as a language, including mathematics, logic and musical notation, to name just a few. Therefore communication involves not only using language but also choosing among available languages, a choice that is often tacit but never unimportant or inconsequential.

The relationship between cognition, symbolic representation and communication has indeed been hotly debated by linguists, philosophers and psychologists. Divergent answers have been offered to questions on the innate or acquired structure of language, or on whether language determines our way of thinking. A substantial consensus has emerged, however, on the existence of a strong mutual relationship between language and production of meaning.

The gist of the matter is that "meaning [...] is not a quality inherent to certain experiences emerging within our stream of consciousness but the result of an interpretation of a past experience looked at from the present" (Schütz 1945, p. 535). Language enables knowledge in two manners: by offering a repository of these 'past experiences' that we use to interpret our present ones; and by expanding our possibilities of knowledge, surpassing the limits of our direct private experience to include "knowledge by description" (Russell 1912 [2004]).

Even if one accepts the position that sees language structures and grammars as (at least partially) innate and constitutive of the human mind, thus considering language as an "organ" (Chomsky 2000), the way in which language is used and performed remains culture and context specific. The importance of context can never be underestimated, not just because any interpretation of the text is context dependent but also because the same may be said of human rationality (Wittgenstein 1958).

The idea of language as a repository of culturally specific experiences, interpretations and truths is connected to the notion of *intertextuality,* or how any text is a link in a chain of texts (Hardy 2001). This is an idea originally put forward by Kristeva (1980), who summarized and expanded the Saussurean idea that signs derive their meaning within the structure of the text, explaining how the meaning of a text is not directly and univocally transferred from a writer to a reader, but is mediated by the ideas that they both received from other texts. In other words, "all texts, whether they are spoken or written, make their meanings against the background of other texts and things that have been said on other occasions" (Paltridge 2012, p. 11). This sequence of references is what makes them intelligible, and recognizable, and constitutes a repository of "past interpretive acts that had been performed by innumerable other people, in short, a social stock of knowledge" (Luckmann 2008, p. 285).

The obvious question that emerges is then: to what extent a specific language, with its baggage of preconceived ideas, intertwined references, and idiosyncratic punctuation of infinitely nuanced phenomenological life-experience, constrains reasoning? The once-fashionable principle of linguistic determinism or Whorfian hypothesis (Whorf 1956 [1998]) predicates that the structure of a language determines (or at least influences) its speakers' cognition, a notion based on the observation of the characteristics of different linguistic communities. For instance, it was observed that a rich vocabulary to describe different types of snow enabled Inuit to perceive subtle differences in their environment that would be lost to a non-Inuit, and that the specific structure of tenses in Hopi language provided them with a peculiar notion of time. The validity of some of this empirical evidence has been contested (Malotki 1983; Pullum 1991), and more importantly the causal direction of the relation has been put in discussion: critics argue that it is not language that 'forces' individuals to think in specific terms but rather that specific contextual conditions determine the development of particular distinctions (Pinker 2008). Yet, differences in the languages used by different groups can make visible some historically developed cultural assumptions. As a matter of fact "the world can be conceptually partitioned in endless different ways" (Wetherell and Potter 1987, p. 25) as different languages are. For instance, in English a distinction is made between mutton and sheep, which has no parallel in French. Conversely, in Italian the difference between romantic love (*amare*) and friendly or parental affection (*voler bene*) is clearly articulated, whereas an English speaker would use the same expression 'I love you' for a partner or for a sibling. An examination of the Whorfian hypothesis in the perspective of cognitive psychology reaches the conclusion that different languages pose different challenges and opportunities for cognition, rather than determining them (Hunt and Agnoli 1991).

These differences in the performance of a language can enable speakers to sharpen their perception or at least their capacity to communicate subtle distinctions: for instance French speakers can more readily distinguish between different shades of brown having two terms (*brun* or *marron*) at their disposal. These differences can bring crucial capabilities, as demonstrated in the case of Guugu Yimithirr speakers. In their talk about location and motion these Indigenous Australians from Far North Queensland do not use their body as a point of reference (using left/right/front/back) but always refer to inflected forms of the four cardinal directions (north/south/east/west), which provides an exceptional ability to find their bearings (Haviland 1993; Levinson 1997). This does not necessarily imply linguistic determinism or that language determines cognition or social practice (since the opposite can be also be true) but rather that they influence each other. An example in point is offered by the perception of different types of (mild) medical conditions in different cultural contexts. Germans feeling dizzy and light-headed (i.e. having a funny turn) will describe their condition in much more serious terms as a 'circulatory collapse' (*kreislaufkollaps*); French speakers often complain of a circulatory condition known as 'heavy legs' (*jambes lourdes*), that is unknown outside France; Italians customarily attribute musculoskeletal aches to having been 'hit by air' (*colpo d'aria*) (Webb 2015). In each of these contexts these ailments are well recognized by laypeople and medical personnel alike and it is the existence of a specific terminology that enables the emergence of this intersubjective agreement and – most importantly – of a related set of diagnostic and preventative practices.

From this point of view, languages are sensemaking devices which provide their users with shared ways of 'punctuating' the stream of events into meaningful sequences and producing recognizable contexts (Bateson 1972, p. 166). As organizing tools, they enable individuals to position themselves in relation to events, consider their options, rank priorities, and identify problems and solutions. "Language does not 'simply' constitute reality, but also connects, frames and instructs" (Alvesson and Kärreman 2011, p. 1141). In sum, languages are not neutral vehicles for concepts. The difficulty of transmitting meanings in a social setting transcends the mere difficulties of 'diffusion', where the information spread by virtue of an intrinsic inertia is only opposed by resistance offered by the medium or by the receiver (Latour 1986). In order to convey ideas we need to translate them into a code, a process in which any translation is also a transformation, hence an alteration, of original meaning (Latour 2005).

Dismissing the notion of language as reflecting an external independent reality and highlighting its role in the process of sensemaking leads to a form of linguistic idealism, the view according to which "what appears to us, or what we experience or what we are aware of, is a function of the language we use" (Rorty 1970, p. 116). This does not necessarily imply a radical form of constructionism, assuming that there is no objective reality independent from the observer:

> The fact that every object is constituted as an object of discourse has nothing to do with whether there is a world external to thought, or with the realism/idealism opposition. An earthquake or the falling of a brick is an event that certainly exists, in the sense that it occurs here and now, independently of my will. But whether their specificity as objects is constructed in terms of "natural phenomena" or "expressions of the wrath of God", depends upon the structuring of a discursive field. What is denied is not that such objects exist externally to thought, but the rather different assertion that they could constitute themselves as objects outside any discursive condition of emergence. (Laclau and Mouffe 1985, p. 108)

This implies that language (and discourse) do not 'create' the world but make it meaningful (Cederström and Spicer 2014), which enables us to transcend the subject–object dualism, exploring how "experiences and objects are constituted in dialectical relationship to one another" (Mumby 2011, p. 1149). This idea can be explained by the case of the long search for a cure for scurvy. A potentially fatal degeneration of the connective tissues caused by a lack of vitamin C, scurvy became common among sailors during the Age of Sail, when it has been estimated that it killed more than two million sailors (Bown 2005). Ocean-crossing seamen were particularly affected by the disease because they had very limited access to fresh food, rich in vitamin C. In addition to human suffering, this 'occupational hazard' had important strategic consequences, limiting the operational capabilities of navies and affecting the wealth and capacity to project power for seafaring nations. Various empirical methods to stave off this hideous ailment – all based on the consumption of vitamin C-rich food – had been empirically discovered since the 16th century by a number of sailors and surgeons (Bown 2005). Nevertheless, all these effective remedies were overshadowed by other dubious, if not outright pernicious, 'cures' (including the swallowing of sulphuric acid or mercury) that appeared to be consistent with the dominant paradigm of Hippocratic medicine, according to which all illnesses stemmed from an imbalance in 'body fluids' or from noxious vapours. Lacking an appropriate conceptual (and linguistic) framework to distinguish scurvy from other ailments affecting mariners, to assess the validity of the claims of the many who insisted to have developed an effective remedy, but also to make sense of the therapy, understanding the reasons of its success, the medical establishment failed to acknowledge the empirical know-how of experienced sailors such as James Cook. "Scurvy could not be cured or prevented as long as it was not understood" (Bown 2005, p. 86), with the consequence that effective prophylactic measures were not implemented on a large scale by the navy until the 19th century.

Scurvy has a reality that transcends language: it can affect us equally regardless of whether we call it a 'grey killer' and attribute it to sloth or 'blocked spleens', or if we recognize it as a nutritional deficiency, where our body cannot produce collagen because of the lack of ascorbic acid. However the capacity to recognize its causes and to prevent and cure the disease is contingent on the availability of the development of a specific discursive apparatus. Other than clarifying the relationship between language and (perceived) reality, this example stresses the performative implications of language, indicating how our symbolic practices have a concrete impact on social action. The next section will explore this notion.

LANGUAGE AND (SOCIAL) PERFORMANCES

The 'ordering' work of language is not exclusively performed through an abstract process of meaning making, by which the available vocabulary and syntax shape our experience. Language has both an ostensive quality (ideal, conjectural, notional) and a performative quality (producing action, thinking and feeling) (Latour 1986), and language and society are intrinsically associated: "linguistic phenomena are social phenomena of a special sort, and social phenomena are (in part) linguistic phenomena. Linguistic phenomena are social in the sense that whenever people speak or listen or write or read they do so in ways which are determined socially and have social effects" (Fairclough 1989, p. 23).

There are various ways in which language is connected to action, becoming constitutive of social relationships. In the first place language can be used to negotiate the social relationship between the speaker and the audience, performing social tasks and achieving a *phatic* function (Malinowski 1923; Jakobson 1960), that is, acting as a 'social lubricant'. This form of communication, which includes courtesy formulas, etiquette, small talk, etc., conveys information about interlocutors' social identities with the intent of creating the conditions for an effective verbal exchange. The emphasis is on establishing and maintaining a relationship, rather than the content of what is said (Watzlawick et al. 1967).

Moreover language can be used to bring about change, by expressing ideals and visions, appealing for support, setting rules or bargaining deals, performing a political function (Sillince 1999, pp. 488–90). Rhetorical uses of language are a case in point. Rhetoric is not just about persuading, it is also a means of identifying the self in relation to a particular issue, and of using that self-identification persuasively (Sillince 2005; Jarzabkowski, Sillince and Shaw 2010). In this regard rhetoric is both constructive of and constitutive of individual and organizational identity, being employed to resolve and retain the tension between different identities which are often at odds (Hartelius and Browning 2008). This role is performed especially by organizational rhetoric, which is usually directed at many different internal and external audiences, with the intent of projecting the desired organizational identity among many available ones (Sillince 2006).

It is however the interconnection between speech and action on which these social and political uses of language are predicated. The idea of the language as made of ostensive acts – that is, connecting words and objects by pointing to examples ('this is a cat') – is quite familiar but it is limited. Language is more than an ordered catalogue of symbols establishing an unambiguous semantic relationship between a sign and an object. As Wittgenstein (1958, §38) points out "naming appears as a queer connexion of a word with an object", whereas "countless different kind[s] of use" are possible (Wittgenstein 1958, §23). Wittgenstein introduced the concept of "language-game" to highlight that "the speaking of a language is part of an activity, or of a form of life" (Wittgenstein 1958, §23). As a consequence, speech is interwoven with action, whereas "an utterance is itself an act" (Medina 2005, p. 13) structured by local rules and aimed at accomplishing a specific goal: a move in a language game. Through use of words life is injected in otherwise "dead" signs (Wittgenstein 1972, p. 4).

While action gives life to language, the opposite is also true, in a mutually constitutive relationship. Language also acts as a typifying medium for creating knowledge (Schütz 1953, p. 10), and the consequence of language games is thus the production of a "life-world" (Husserl 1935 [1965]), where the sedimentation of linguistic meaning and resources is used by social actors to structure the world into objects (Habermas 1984). Social reality is thus constructed through the use of a language that is, in turn, generated by social performances, in a recursive, iterative process.

Through the notion of language games it is possible to draw attention to the ways in which different communities use specialized forms of discourse to pursue their purposes and address various concerns (Astley and Zammuto 1992). The uses, or performances, that give life to language by fixing its meaning have both a normative dimension, specified by rules of intelligibility, as well as a contextual dimension that situates a concept within a particular environment that activates a context-specific meaning (Whiting 2010). Rather than conflating multiple meanings in an attempt to establish the 'correct' way of labelling a concept, the notion of language games accepts that actors can leverage various meanings of a term to accommodate the specific dynamics, interests and issues that characterize their contexts. Thus "to imagine a language means to imagine a form of life" (Wittgenstein 1958, §19).

For Wittgenstein (1958, §85), the rules that characterize language games function as signposts providing direction, purpose and therefore meaning to action and understanding. These rules do not require enforcement by some external actor charged with their application. Rather their power is expressed implicitly, through acquired customs and taken-for-granted assumptions.

Organizational sensemaking, as a precondition for organized action (Weick 1969 [1979]), can therefore be seen as constituted by a series of interrelated language games, used to position, explain and justify actions and establish meaning. An effective demonstration of the way in which specific language games produce an organizational identity and culture, also defining "appropriate patterns of activity" (Astley and Zammuto 1992, p. 449), is offered by a classic study by Van Maanen:

> Customers at Disneyland are, for instance, never referred to as such, they are "guests." There are no rides at Disneyland, only "attractions." Disneyland itself is a "Park," not an amusement center, and it is divided into "back-stage," "on-stage," and "staging" regions. Law enforcement personnel hired by the park are not policemen, but "security hosts." Employees do not wear uniforms but check out fresh "costumes" each working day from "wardrobe." And, of course, there are no accidents at Disneyland, only "incidents." (Van Maanen 1991, pp. 65–6)

Here the choice of terminology is not simply a marketing device but defines the identities of the employees and their relationship with other agents, and provides clear expectations about their performances and behaviours.

Consequently language is not a neutral medium but constitutes facts (Astley and Zammuto 1992, p. 445) thus becoming a source of identity. In this regard is possible to state that language is at the same time the instrument and the outcome of a process of social construction of reality, since it is on the one hand the essential vehicle for the social interaction that constitutes and maintains 'common-sense' knowledge (Berger and

Luckmann 1967 [1990]) while, on the other hand, it reflects such social understandings.

As communication and language are constituted and maintained by performative acts, material elements also, such as the technologies in use, and the medium of communication, can play an active role in modelling the subjectivities of users and the ways in which they organize their activities and interactions. For instance, as mobile communication devices and portable computers have dramatically increased our capacity to 'stay connected', so the barrier between work and life has become increasingly permeable, making it customary for many of us to receive and send work-related communicatons at any hour of the day, irrespective of rest hours. In this case it is not the language but rather the medium which transforms organizing practices and shapes expectations and performances (McLuhan 1964 [1994]).

Despite the virtual impossibility of summarizing in a few pages the vast multidisciplinary debate on the philosophy, psychology and sociology of language, this brief (and unavoidably skewed) outline of the literature highlights some essential features that appear to characterize this bundle of complex phenomena.

- Language is instrumental to social action, as such it is the basis of any form of organization.
- Language is not merely representational but also interpretative, producing meaning.
- Language is plural: there are many possible modes of symbolic communication that can be either rigorous or broadly intelligible and that are grounded in different cultural contexts.
- Language is given consistency and coherence by communicative actions, and has an essential performative component.

The entanglement between action and communication and between social activities and sensemaking that characterize linguistic performances, together with the plurality of available idioms, suggest that it would be better to refer to *symbolic practices* rather than 'languages'. The concept of *practice* has been used in sociology and organizational studies to maintain that human actions are always situated, drawing meaning and substance from their embeddedness in a social and material network that they contribute to reproduce, thus overcoming dualisms between body and mind, individual and society, organism and environment (Bourdieu 1977, 1990; Gherardi 2000; Knorr-Cetina 2001; Savigny, Schatzki and Knorr-Cetina 2001; Raelin 2007; Corradi, Gherardi and Verzelloni 2010; Feldman and Orlikowski 2011; Gherardi 2012). Practices incorporate both explicit and 'tacit knowledge' (Polanyi 1966); they are "inscribed in bodies, and bodies are therefore the artefacts through which people know and work" (Gherardi 2012, p. 61); they include material objects ('the tools of the trade'); they are inscribed in, and enabled by, an institutional system (Gherardi 2006, p. 35); they include routines and improvisation.

The term *discourse* is therefore used to account for how particular symbolic practices (constituted of narratives, ways of talking, media, contexts, institutions, etc.) implicitly enable and foster specific patterns of meaning and action and influence our way of thinking and feeling; for instance, how prevalent ways of representing organizational leadership or discussing employment relationships, subtly define expectations, benchmarks and identities.

In this sense, discourse can be seen as an "interpretive repertoire" of social practices situated in a specific context, based on the use of linguistic elements but oriented to action (Potter et al. 1990). In the next chapter this concept will be 'unpacked', accounting for the many different notions of discourse that have been developed in social studies and that find application in the study of organizations.

REFERENCES

Alvesson, M. and Kärreman, D. 2011, 'Decolonializing Discourse: Critical Reflections on Organizational Discourse Analysis', *Human Relations*, vol. 64, pp. 1121–46.

Ashcraft, K.L., Kuhn, T.R. and Cooren, F. 2009, 'Constitutional Amendments: "Materializing" Organizational Communication', *The Academy of Management Annals*, vol. 3, no. 1, pp. 1–64.

Astley, W.G. and Zammuto, R.F. 1992, 'Organization Science, Managers, and Language Games', *Organization Science*, vol. 3, pp. 443–60.

Bateson, G. 1972, *Steps to an Ecology of Mind: Collected Essays in Anthropology, Psychiatry, Evolution, and Epistemology*, Intertext, Aylesbury.

Bateson, G. and Ruesch, J. 1951, *Communication, the Social Matrix of Psychiatry*, Norton, New York.

Berger, P.L. and Luckmann, T. 1967 [1990], *The Social Construction of Reality: A Treatise in the Sociology of Knowledge*, Anchor Books, New York.

Boje, D.M., Oswick, C. and Ford, J.D. 2004, 'Language and Organization: The Doing of Discourse', *Academy of Management Review*, vol. 29, no. 4, pp. 571–7.

Bourdieu, P. 1977, *Outline of a Theory of Practice*, trans. R. Nice, Cambridge University Press, Cambridge.

Bourdieu, P. 1990, *The Logic of Practice*, Basil Blackwell, Cambridge.

Bown, S.R. 2005, *Scurvy: How a Surgeon, a Mariner, and a Gentlemen Solved the Greatest Medical Mystery of the Age of Sail*, St. Martin's Press, New York.

Cederström, C. and Spicer, A. 2014, 'Discourse of the Real Kind: A Post-foundational Approach to Organizational Discourse Analysis', *Organization*, vol. 21, no. 2, pp. 178–205.

Chia, R. 2002, 'Essai: Time, Duration and Simultaneity: Rethinking Process and Change in Organizational Analysis', *Organization Studies*, vol. 23, pp. 863–8.

Chomsky, N. 2000, 'New Horizons in the Study of Language and Mind', in A. Arnove (ed.), *The Essential Chomsky*, Palgrave Macmillan, New York, pp. 285–99.

Clegg, S.R., Kornberger, M. and Rhodes, C. 2005, 'Learning/Becoming/Organizing', *Organization*, vol. 12, pp. 147–67.

Corradi, G., Gherardi, S. and Verzelloni, L. 2010, 'Through the Practice Lens: Where is the Bandwagon of Practice-based Studies Heading?', *Management Learning*, vol. 41, pp. 265–83.

Czarniawska, B. 2008a, 'Organizations as Obstacles to Organizing', paper presented to the Nobel Symposium Foundations of Organization, 28–30 August, 2008, Stockholm, accessed 1 March 2012 at http://bit.ly/Zo2fcx

Czarniawska, B. 2008b, 'Organizing: How to Study it and How to Write about it', *Qualitative Research in Organizations and Management: An International Journal*, vol. 3, pp. 4–20.

de Saussure, F. 1916 [1966], *Course in General Linguistics*, McGraw-Hill, New York.

Deetz, S.A. 1982, 'Critical Interpretive Research in Organizational Communication', *Western Journal of Speech Communication*, vol. 46, pp. 131–49.

Deetz, S.A. 1992, *Democracy in an Age of Corporate Colonization: Developments in Communication and the Politics of Everyday Life*, SUNY Press, New York.

Fairclough, N. 1989, *Language and Power*, Longman, New York.

Feldman, M.S. and Orlikowski, W.J. 2011, 'Theorizing Practice and Practicing Theory', *Organization Science*, vol. 22, pp. 1240–53.

Fichte, J.G. 1794 [1995], 'On the Linguistic Capacity and the Origin of Language', in J.P. Surber (ed.), *Language and German Idealism: Fichte's Linguistic Philosophy*, Humanities Press, Adantic Highlands, NJ, pp. 117–44.

Gherardi, S. 2000, 'Practice-based Theorizing on Learning and Knowing in Organizations', *Organization*, vol. 7, pp. 211–23.

Gherardi, S. 2006, *Organizational Knowledge: The Texture of Workplace Learning*, Blackwell, London.

Gherardi, S. 2012, *How to Conduct a Practice-based Study: Problems and Methods*, Edward Elgar Publishing, Cheltenham, UK and Northampton, MA, USA.

Habermas, J. 1984, *The Theory of Communicative Action*, Beacon Press, Boston, MA.

Hardy, C. 2001, 'Researching Organizational Discourse', *International Studies of Management & Organization*, vol. 31, p. 25.

Hartelius, E.J. and Browning, L.D. 2008, 'The Application of Rhetorical Theory in Managerial Research', *Management Communication Quarterly*, vol. 22, no. 1, pp. 13–39.

Haviland, J.B. 1993, 'Anchoring, Iconicity, and Orientation in Guugu Yimithirr Pointing Gestures', *Journal of Linguistic Anthropology*, vol. 3, no. 1, pp. 3–45.

Hernes, T. 2007, *Understanding Organization as Process: Theory for a Tangled World*, Routledge, London.

Hunt, E. and Agnoli, F. 1991, 'The Whorfian Hypothesis: A Cognitive Psychology Perspective', *Psychological Review*, vol. 98, no. 3, p. 377.

Husserl, E. 1935 [1965], *The Crisis of European Sciences and Transcendental Phenomenology: An Introduction to Phenomenological Philosophy*, trans. Q. Lauer, Harper & Row, New York.

Jakobson, R. 1960, 'Linguistics and Poetics', in T.A. Sebeok (ed.), *Style in Language*, The MIT Press, Cambridge, MA, pp. 350–77.

Jarzabkowski, P., Sillince, J.A.A. and Shaw, D. 2010, 'Strategic Ambiguity as a Rhetorical Resource for Enabling Multiple Interests', *Human Relations*, vol. 63, pp. 219–48.

Knorr-Cetina, K. 2001, 'Objectual Practice', in E.V. Savigny, T.R. Schatzki and K. Knorr-Cetina (eds), *The Practice Turn in Contemporary Theory*, Routledge, New York, pp. 184–97.

Kristeva, J. 1980, *Desire in Language: A Semiotic Approach to Literature and Art*, Basil Blackwell, Oxford.

Laclau, E. and Mouffe, C. 1985, *Hegemony and Socialist Strategy: Towards a Radical Democratic Politics*, Verso, London.

Laclau, E. and Mouffe, C. 1987, 'Post-Marxism Without Apologies', *New Left Review*, no. 166, p. 79.

Latour, B. 1986, 'The Powers of Association', in J. Law (ed.), *Power, Action and Belief*, Routledge and Kegan Paul, London, pp. 264–80.

Latour, B. 2005, *Reassembling the Social: An Introduction to Actor-Network Theory*, Clarendon, Oxford, UK.

Levinson, S.C. 1997, 'Language and Cognition: The Cognitive Consequences of Spatial Description in Guugu Yimithirr', *Journal of Linguistic Anthropology*, vol. 7, no. 1, pp. 98–131.

Lewis, D. 1970, 'General Semantics', *Synthese*, vol. 22, no. 1, pp. 18–67.

Luckmann, T. 2008, 'On Social Interaction and the Communicative Construction of Personal Identity, Knowledge and Reality', *Organization Studies*, vol. 29, no. 2, pp. 277–90.

Malinowski, B.K. 1923, 'The Problem of Meaning in Primitive Languages', in C.K. Ogden and I.A. Richards (eds), *The Meaning of Meaning. A Study of the Influence of Language upon Thought and of the Science of Symbolism*, Harcourt, Brace & Company, New York, pp. 451–510.

Malotki, E. 1983, *Hopi Time: A Linguistic Analysis of the Temporal Concepts in the Hopi Language*, Walter de Gruyter, Berlin.

McLuhan, M. 1964 [1994], *Understanding Media: The Extensions of Man*, The MIT Press, Boston, MA.

Medina, J. 2005, *Language: Key Concepts in Philosophy*, Continuum Books, London.

Mumby, D.K. 2011, 'What's Cooking in Organizational Discourse Studies? A Response to Alvesson and Kärreman', *Human Relations*, vol. 64, pp. 1147–61.

Norman, W. and MacDonald, C. 2004, 'Getting to the Bottom of "Triple Bottom Line"', *Business Ethics Quarterly*, vol. 14, no. 2, pp. 243–62.

Oxford Dictionary of English 2011, 3rd edn, Oxford University Press, Oxford.

Paltridge, B. 2012, *Discourse Analysis: An Introduction*, Bloomsbury Publishing, London.

Parker, M. 2014, 'University, Ltd: Changing a Business School', *Organization*, vol. 21, no. 2, pp. 281–92.

Parker, M. and Jary, D. 1995, 'The McUniversity: Organization, Management and Academic Subjectivity', *Organization*, vol. 2, pp. 319–38.

Pfeffer, J. and Fong, C.T. 2004, 'The Business School "Business": Some Lessons from the US Experience', *Journal of Management Studies*, vol. 41, pp. 1501–20.

Pinker, S. 2008, *The Stuff of Thought: Language as a Window into Human Nature*, Penguin, London.

Polanyi, M. 1966, *The Tacit Dimension*, Routledge & Kegan Paul, London.

Potter, J., Wetherell, M., Gill, R. and Edwards, D. 1990, 'Discourse: Noun, Verb or Social Practice?', *Philosophical Psychology*, vol. 3, no. 2-3, pp. 205–17.

Pullum, G.K. 1991, *The Great Eskimo Vocabulary Hoax and Other Irreverent Essays on the Study of Language*, University of Chicago Press, Chicago.

Raelin, J.A. 2007, 'Toward an Epistemology of Practice', *Academy of Management Learning & Education*, vol. 6, p. 495.

Reed, M. 2000, 'The Limits of Discourse Analysis in Organizational Analysis', *Organization*, vol. 7, no. 3, pp. 524–30.

Rhodes, C. 2001, *Writing Organization: (Re)Presentation and Control in Narratives at Work*, vol. 7, John Benjamins Publishing, Amsterdam, NL.

Rorty, R. 1970, 'In Defense of Eliminative Materialism', *The Review of Metaphysics*, pp. 112–21.

Russell, B. 1912 [2004], *The Problems of Philosophy*, Project Gutenberg Literary Archive Foundation, Salt Lake City, UT.

Savigny, E.v., Schatzki, T.R. and Knorr-Cetina, K. 2001, *The Practice Turn in Contemporary Theory*, Routledge, New York.

Schütz, A. 1945, 'On Multiple Realities', *Philosophy and Phenomenological Research*, vol. 5, pp. 533–76.

Schütz, A. 1953, 'Common-Sense and Scientific Interpretation of Human Action', *Philosophy and Phenomenological Research*, vol. 14, pp. 1–38.

Sillince, J.A.A. 1999, 'The Role of Political Language Forms and Language Coherence in the Organizational Change Process', *Organization Studies*, vol. 20, pp. 485–518.

Sillince, J.A.A. 2005, 'A Contingency Theory of Rhetorical Congruence', *The Academy of Management Review*, vol. 30, pp. 608–21.

Sillince, J.A.A. 2006, 'Resources and Organizational Identities: The Role of Rhetoric in the Creation of Competitive Advantage', *Management Communication Quarterly*, vol. 20, pp. 186–212.

Simon, H.A. 1964, 'On the Concept of Organizational Goal', *Administrative Science Quarterly*, vol. 9, pp. 1–22.

Tsoukas, H. and Chia, R. 2002, 'On Organizational Becoming: Rethinking Organizational Change', *Organization Science*, vol. 13, pp. 567–82.

Van Maanen, J. 1991, 'The Smile Factory: Work at Disneyland', in P. Frost, L. Moore, M. Louise, C. Lundberg and J. Martin (eds), *Refraining Organizational Culture*, SAGE, Newbury Park, CA, pp. 58–76.

Watzlawick, P., Jackson, D.D. and Bavelas, J.B. 1967, *Pragmatics of Human Communication: A Study of Interactional Patterns, Pathologies, and Paradoxes*, Norton, New York.

Webb, R. 2015, 'You Are What You Speak: How Your Mother Tongue Shapes You', *New Scientist*, 15 December 2015, accessed at https://goo.gl/EUVPjJ

Weick, K.E. 1969 [1979], *The Social Psychology of Organizing*, 2nd edn, Addison-Wesley, Reading, MA.

Weick, K.E. 1995, *Sensemaking in Organizations*, SAGE Publications, Thousand Oaks, CA.

Wetherell, M. and Potter, J. 1987, *Discourse and Social Psychology: Beyond Attitudes and Behaviour*, SAGE Publications, Newbury Park, CA.

Whiting, D. 2010, 'Introduction', in D. Whiting (ed.), *The Later Wittgenstein on Language*, Palgrave-Macmillan, New York.

Whorf, B.L. 1956 [1998], *Language, Thought, and Reality: Selected Writings of Benjamin Lee Whorf*, The MIT Press, Cambridge, MA.

Wittgenstein, L. 1958, *Philosophical Investigations*, trans. G.E.M. Anscombe, Blackwell, Oxford.

Wittgenstein, L. 1972, *The Blue and Brown Books – Preliminary Studies for the Philosophical Investigation*, 2nd edn, Blackwell, Oxford.

2. The discourse of organizational discourse

DO WE REALLY NEED TO PUT ORDER IN THE VARIETY OF DISCOURSES?

When approaching the subject of organizational discourse the reader is likely to feel overwhelmed by the staggering assortment of definitions and alternative approaches: "it is perfectly possible to have two books on discourse analysis with no overlap in content at all" (Wetherell and Potter 1987, p. 6). It has been lamented that the concept is poorly defined, embracing too many approaches (Iedema 2007a) and "continues to be used in vague and all-embracing ways" (Alvesson and Kärreman 2011, p. 1121).

While such a plurality of perspectives denotes the fecundity of the idea, it can at the same time produce confusion and ambiguity, with the consequence that, in the organizational literature, "discourse may mean almost everything" (Alvesson and Kärreman 2000, p. 1127). There is for instance no consensus on what are the boundaries of discourse, with the consequence that inclusion parameters can be as restrictive as confining it to spoken language or texts or so inclusive that they incorporate language, cognition and material aspects (Keenoy, Oswick and Grant 1998, pp. 1–2). Such an overabundance of meanings is frequently attributed to the diversity of theoretical antecedents of the approach; there are indeed "many conflicting and overlapping definitions formulated from various theoretical and disciplinary standpoints" (Fairclough 1992, p. 3), including sociology, psychology, anthropology, linguistics, philosophy, etc. (Grant et al. 2004, p. 1). The diversity of approaches demonstrates the vitality of the discussion and the plasticity of the concept, but the disciplinary parochialism of researchers can also lead to a dysfunctional compartmentalization of the field (Phillips and Oswick 2012).

Whenever an intellectual field is populated by a variety of non-overlapping designations there will be scholarly attempts to inscribe order in the field, offering some neat taxonomy to organize the conceptual hodgepodge. Indeed, so many alternative ways to classify approaches to discourse analysis have been proposed (Phillips and Oswick 2012) that the taxonomies themselves contribute to the conceptual 'noise'.

There is always the temptation of producing yet another meta-categorization, offering a more comprehensive account, putting order in the semantic clutter, but I believe doing so would only further complicate matters. The problem is that there is no unique system of categories into which matters of discourse can be logically sorted, since "any entity can be situated in more than one mental context" (Zerubavel 1993, p. 121). A classification is a construct based on certain epistemological and ontological assumptions of the observer (Lakoff 1987). Different classifications choose to attend to some features, discarding others, thus reducing the complexity of phenomena to a few characteristics. "Classifying is a normative process (…) [based on] 'rules of irrelevance' that specify which differences are salient" (Zerubavel 1993, p. 78).

Considering alternative classifications is therefore a suitable way to enrich our understanding, since it involves comparing alternative accounts which are based on highlighting different elements. By juxtaposing several different classifications of approaches to organizational discourse, we can obtain a more inclusive view of the original phenomenon, discourse, while revealing (and accepting) its intrinsic "fuzziness" (van Dijk 1997, p. 1).

SOME ALTERNATIVE ACCOUNTS OF THE VARIETIES OF DISCOURSE

Alvesson and Kärreman (2000) produced one of the most influential taxonomies of discursive approaches to organizational discourse by ordering different "varieties of discourse" along two dimensions. The first refer to what they define as the *muscularity* of the discourse; that is, how powerful are symbolic practices in producing meaning and social reality. A stream of research (directly inspired by Foucault) considers discourse as producing meanings and subjectivity, viewing it as a powerful and authoritative force (both in terms of legitimacy and in terms of authoring) shaping practices and beliefs. On the opposite end of the spectrum we find "fragile" discourse (Alvesson 2004), considered as a purely linguistic performance distinct from cognition, feelings and practices.

The second ordering dimension refers instead to the *formative range* of discourse, which can vary from a micro-discourse (with a small 'd'), produced and consumed within a specific local context, to a grandiose, macro-Discourse (with a capital 'D'), which is wide-ranging, encompassing multiple social realities. The researchers interested in close-range discourse will be more attentive to the detail, emphasizing the local social context of language use (e.g. within a specific site or group), while those who try to reveal an overarching grand Discourse (e.g. of human resources management, strategy or managerialism) will look for regularities and will try to abstract from special cases.

By crossing these two dimensions it is possible to identify four different research approaches or interests (see Figure 2.1).

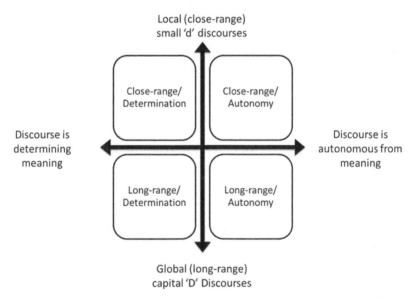

Source: After Alvesson and Kärreman 2000.

Figure 2.1   A classification of approaches on organizational discourse

Close-range/autonomy studies examine language in use in a specific context, to understand how this produces a specific account of social reality. Long-range/autonomy investigations expand the context of the analysis to determine whether certain utterances are part of a repertoire that is shared by a broader community (which might include an entire professional group, an industry, or a type of organization). Close-range/ determination approaches "assume that discourses offer important clues to other kind of practices than pure language use" (Alvesson and Kärreman 2000, p. 1137) showing for instance how appropriate identities are constructed in that particular organizational context (Alvesson and

Willmott 2002). Finally, long-range/determination studies are interested in exploring how broader social meanings, subjectivities and normality are constructed, framing the way in which topics can be discussed.

The major contribution of this framework resides in its capacity to highlight two inescapable tensions in discourse analysis. On the one hand it warns against the temptations of picturing a too-powerful, solipsistic discourse that cancels all other material and conceptual dimensions, in contrast to that of a mere description of linguistic details, where researchers become amanuenses who record a multifarious but scarcely relevant Babel of local idioms. On the other hand it highlights the trade-off between alternative foci in the analysis: a rigorous – but myopic – view of local contexts, versus a grandiose view where the research of significant aggregated patterns is conducted at the expense of a more fine-grained understanding.

According to Alvesson and Kärreman (2011) discourse studies tread dangerously between the Scylla and Charybdis of two opposite reductionist tendencies: a linguistic reductionism, laced with lack of clarity on what constitutes context, that can affect text-based (little 'd') discourse studies, versus a paradigmatic (big 'D') reductionism that traces everything back to the Foucauldian Word, a Discourse that is the beginning of any social creation. It is this latter, quasi-magical, belief in the generative capacity of language that is the target of these authors' fiercest attack. They advocate a decluttering of the concept of discourse, which has come to include too many different elements; a separation of little 'd' and big 'D' discourse studies; the contemplation of the interplay between textual and other non-discursive social elements (such as culture or institutions) and a relativization of the power of language, which can sometimes constitute reality but at other times simply connects or transfers meanings created elsewhere. These authors try to take a high epistemological ground, warning disingenuous researchers against the risk of acritically embracing the Foucauldian paradigm, ending up with tautological conceptions, in which, since discourse is postulated to be constitutive of reality, everything is discourse or is produced by discourse.

A highly critical stance towards paradigmatic discourse studies is not shared by everyone: Mumby (2011) has provided a strong argument showing that Alvesson and Kärreman's critique is founded on a misunderstood conception of the role of the linguistic turn. According to him, a discourse-based epistemology is based on transcending the subject-object dualism and on exploring "the linguistic character of all experience (and all knowledge claims!), and the ways that experiences and objects are constituted in dialectical relationship to one another"

(Mumby 2011, p. 1149). In other words, assuming a muscular view of discourse does not mean embracing a linguistic determinism where language creates reality. Rather, it means considering the pragmatic effects of a paradigmatic Discourse; for instance, investigating how discourse gives meaning to material objects, or how elements of phenomenological experience become discrete 'objects' in our collective view.

Defining the ontological nature of discourse does not simply concern deciding upon which elements should be included in a semiotic system, the "texts" that according to Parker (1992) constitute its tangible incarnation. Instead, it involves questioning the nature of those ingredients constituting what is taken to be the discourse. This important issue will be discussed in the next section; however, before doing so it is necessary to consider other accounts of the variety of discursive approaches, based on the recognition of differentiating features.

Phillips and Oswick (2012) offer two alternative taxonomies. Their starting point is the mainstream categorization of discursive approaches: either according to the 'level' of discursive analysis or according to the methodological approaches employed to investigate the phenomenon. The level refers to the amplitude of the context that is taken into account in the study. This is an articulation of the d–D discourses dichotomy discussed previously (Alvesson and Kärreman 2000), including four views of discourse: "micro-discourse", "meso-discourse", "macro-discourse", or "multi-level" approaches. A frequently employed alternative to this scaling of discourse refers to the different methods, deriving from different disciplinary traditions, that can be employed to study discourse, comprising conversation analysis (CA), narrative analysis, Foucauldian discourse analysis and critical discourse analysis (CDA). According to these authors, however, these two supposedly alternative ways of classifying organizational discourse analysis approaches "are inextricably linked insofar as the level of analysis largely dictates the methodology employed and *vice versa*" (Phillips and Oswick 2012, p. 456). In practice, they observe that micro-level discursive analysis is typically conducted using CA methods (e.g. analysing real-time interactions and examining the use of language in meetings to examine modes of organizing); meso-level studies usually employ narrative analysis (e.g. reconstructing the modalities and outcomes of organizational storytelling, investigating how this gives continuity and coherence to organizations); macro-discourses are normally studied using Foucauldian approaches (e.g. examining how discursive practices produce both objects, such as institutions and knowledge, as well as subjective identities and actions), while multi-level discourse analysis is the province of CDA (e.g. linking texts, their process of production, and the institutions and ideologies that frame them, reflecting on the power effects of these discourses). Phillips and Oswick lament that these alternative approaches are not typically seen as complementary views but as alternative paradigms, which creates a compartmentalization of the field, compounded by the existence of two separate sub-groups – scholars more interested in the 'discourse' part and those whose interest is in the 'organizational' aspect.

In order to overcome these dysfunctional methodological/disciplinary boundaries Phillips and Oswick advocate an approach using mixed-methods and addressing multi-level processes. More importantly, they suggest the opportunity to categorize organizational discourse studies along different lines, focusing on the crucial relationship between discourse and materiality. Four alternative positions are thus presented, ranging from a view that considers materiality/realism and discourse/constructionism as mutually exclusive, to an opposite view that defines these as mutually constitutive, passing from the two 'in-between' positions that see discourse and materiality as complementary (discrete but not competing) or connected (interpenetrating). In addition to drawing attention to the fundamental (and problematic) issue of the relationship between discourse and materiality, the value of this contribution resides in its capacity to show how different ways of segmenting the field discursively shape the identity and practices of researchers and the way in which knowledge is produced, thus providing a vivid example of how even the field of studies on organizational discourse is not free from discursive influences.

The need to investigate the relationship between discursive and non-discursive factors also features prominently in a further typology, proposed by Cederström and Spicer (2014). As with the previous schemes, their classification represents organizational discourse studies in terms of a fourfold table. They start by expanding Alvesson and Kärreman's (2011) dichotomy separating "Paradigm type discourse studies" (the Foucauldian variety, purporting that social reality is constituted by discourses) from "Text focused studies" (examining how organizational agents mobilize discourses), to include also "Realist discourse studies", which explicitly address the relationship between discursive and non-discursive elements. Paradigm type approaches are accused of under-estimating the role of agency, becoming trapped in a form of linguistic determinism. Text-based studies, they suggest, tend to have an overly 'muscular' conception of discourse, considering organizations as being nothing more than texts and conversations, while failing to explain the role of underlying generative structures (such as bureaucracy, capitalism, gender, etc.) that create the conditions in which discourses flourish. Even realist studies are limited by the ambiguity of some of their ontological claims: on the one hand, critical realists tend to reify discourse as a "phenomenon separated from material entities, artefacts and social structures" (Cederström and Spicer 2014, p. 184); on the other, they make the ambiguous claim that is possible to "go beyond discourse". In addition, all three streams share the same shortcoming: the failure to incorporate the affective dimension of discourse.

In order to overcome the limitations of these three traditional modes of organizational discourse analysis, Cederström and Spicer find inspiration in post-foundationalism, an epistemological doctrine based on the works of Žižek and Laclau, who posit that the 'Real' cannot be used as a foundation for discourse because of the contingent, contextual and negotiated nature of any system of meaning. Therefore, they propose a 'post-foundational' approach to discourse, based on three principles:

- Discourses are structured around "lacks", undefined and unsymbolizable elements (for instance the vague notion of the entrepreneur in entrepreneurship discourse).
- Discourses achieve coherence and unity in their disparateness through nodal points (empty names that bring together various loosely related discourse, such as the notion of knowledge).
- Discourses generate affective and emotional attachments. (Cederström and Spicer 2014)

While the two previous taxonomies move between being descriptive of existing approaches and prescriptive, in terms of the opportunity for new, 'better' heuristic orientations, a further categorization aims explicitly at stipulating a comprehensive picture of the process of discursive reality formation. Moving within an interpretive paradigm and expanding previous contributions (Heracleous 2004; Heracleous and Marshak 2004), Heracleous (2012) submits four propositions intended to clarify and integrate the different modalities through which discourse produces social reality:

1. The nature of discourse is described as *situated symbolic action*, thus highlighting, in addition to its linguistic basis, its performative character and its collocation in a specific context. These aspects have been investigated through the lens of speech-act theory, rhetoric and social constructionism.
2. Drawing from the theoretical perspective of social cognition, discourse and individual cognition are seen as mutually constituted.
3. Social reality is constructed through symbolic interaction (which clearly links to symbolic interactionism).

4. Discourse and power are linked, an approach based on social theory and CDA, which highlights how discursive reality constructs can be hegemonic and serve (implicitly or explicitly) the interest of specific stakeholders.

Contrary to the classifications previously considered, Heracleous' intent is not to contrast and differentiate alternative conceptualizations but rather bring them together in a coherent picture, illustrating the different ways in which discourses deploy their constructive capacities.

Beyond their respective merits and limitations, these alternative ways of mapping the 'discourse on organizational discourse' (summarized in Table 2.1) reveal several fundamental tensions and onto-epistemological problems that any researcher who wishes to employ a discursive lens will encounter. I will discuss these in the next section, with the intent of offering some concrete heuristic directions.

Table 2.1   Some influential classifications of organizational discourse analysis approaches

Model	Element of salience	Resulting type of discourses
Alvesson and Kärreman (2000)	Scope (local versus macro system) and 'muscularity' (relation between discourse and meaning)	1. Close-range/autonomy 2. Long-range/autonomy 3. Close-range/determination 4. Long-range/determination
Phillips and Oswick (2012)	Range of discourse *and* method of data analysis	1. Micro-discourses (conversation analysis) 2. Meso-discourses (narrative studies) 3. Macro-discourses (Foucauldian studies) 4. Multi-range (CDA)
	Relationship between discourse and materiality	1. Alternative/competing 2. Complementary 3. Connected 4. Mutually constitutive
Cederström and Spicer (2014)	Object of study and analytical focus	1. Textual-focused studies 2. Paradigm-based studies 3. Realist discourse analysis 4. Post-foundational approach
Heracleous (2012)	Propositions towards a theory of discursive reality construction	1. Discourse as symbolic action 2. Discourse and cognition as mutually constituted 3. Social reality is constructed through symbolic interaction 4. Discursive reality constructs are hegemonic

DISCOURSE AS A PROBLEMATIC 'BEING'

It would be simplistic (and ungenerous) to attribute the conceptual noise surrounding the idea of organizational discourse solely to the academic capacity for constant differentiation and criticism. Even attempts to arrange different views and methodological inclinations are complicated by the fact that discourse takes many forms, deploys multiple levels, in an ambiguous relationship with non-discursive elements. I am going to approach the thorny ontological issues surrounding organizational discourse by describing the irresolvable tensions that any statement on the 'essence' of discourse is destined to produce.

As discussed, there is a lack of consensus on the boundaries of discourse as well as what to include (or exclude) from organizational discourse. While everyone agrees that 'texts' should be included, there are divergent interpretations of what to include in this category: these "might include written or spoken language, cultural artifacts, and visual representations" (Hardy 2001, p. 26). Moreover texts alone do not constitute discourse. The intelligibility of text and the "orderliness of interactions depends upon taken-for-granted 'background knowledge'" (Fairclough 2010, p. 31): ideologies, structures of rationality and shared understanding are not only contained in physical texts but stored in the form of tacit knowledge. In addition, even performative acts play an essential role: "the structural properties of discourse are instantiated in daily communicative actions" (Heracleous and Barrett 2001, p. 758). The multifarious nature of the component of discourse (and in particular of 'paradigmatic' forms of discourse) is well captured by Gee:

> These distinctive ways of speaking/listening and/or reading/writing are coupled with distinctive ways of acting, interacting, valuing, feeling, dressing, thinking, and believing. In turn, all of these are coupled with ways of coordinating oneself with (getting in synch with) other people and with various objects, tools, and technologies. (Gee 2010, p. 177)

Why can't organizational discourse analysts specialize in the study of particular manifestations of discourse, without being assailed by doubts about their relationship with other loosely related elements? These distinctions do not appear to be unsurmountable problems: it could be simply a matter of establishing conventions separating one particular disciplinary research interest from the other, just as a chemist decides to focus his/her investigation on a particular class of chemical compound or a historian on a specific period in history, accepting a certain fuzziness in relation to the exact 'borders' of their field. The crux of the matter is the practical entanglement of discursive and non-discursive elements of long- and close-range discourses, of meaning and action, of observer and observed. I will examine these issues by considering three conceptual knots: the range of alternative ontological stances on the nature of discourse; the possibility to transcend discourse; and the separability of materiality and discourse.

Alternative Ontologies of Discourse

When discussing the 'essence' of discourse it is easy to reify discourse by treating it as an object that has specific attributes, limits and characteristics. In doing so we are unwittingly contradicting the construc- tionist principles on which discourse analysis is founded. Fairclough suggests that, rather than an 'object', discourse "is itself a complex set of relations including relations of communication (...) we cannot answer the question 'what is discourse' except in terms of both its 'internal' relations and its 'external' relations with such other 'objects'" (Fairclough 2010, p. 3) While discourse is often treated in sociological parlance as an entity, it is highly problematic to identify its substance or its borders. An analytic philosopher would probably trace the origins of these onto- epistemological difficulties to the lack of coherent definition and to the limits of the type of 'ordinary language' used to describe discourse. Shall we then follow Wittgenstein's caveat "whereof one cannot speak, thereof one must be silent" (Wittgenstein 1922, p. 90)?

Examining the literature it is possible to identify a whole range of ontological stances about discourse. These can be positioned in a continuum between a purely essentialist view and a totally constructivist view. At one end of the spectrum we find those who see discourse as a material collection of linguistic traces, "text and talk in social practices" (Potter 2004, p. 203). Here, discourse is text and texts are an objective, tangible reality. Still anchored to a substantive view of reality are the studies informed by critical realism. This approach combines realist ontology with a relativist epistemology, arguing that "reality could be analytically distinguished into structures, the outcome of their complex interplay, and human experience, perception, or interpretation of those outcomes" (Jack et al. 2012, p. 871). As a consequence, while the world is thought to exist independently of our knowledge an articulated view of reality is proposed, distinguishing between the 'real' (the domain of structures), the 'actual' (the domain of processes) and the 'empirical' (what is experienced by social actors) (Fairclough 2005). Within this framework discourse is concerned with the relationship and the tensions between texts, processes and structures (Fairclough 2005).

Another step away from the materiality of discourse but still distinct from a purely constructionist conception is the idea that materiality and discourse are non-separable but co-emergent (Iedema 2007a). A contingent, multi-modal view of discourse, which includes not just linguistic elements but also other modes of meaning making, such as architecture, technology, embodiment, etc., is entailed.

In the 'philosophy-physics' developed by Bohr to make sense of the weird realm of quantum mechanics, Barad finds support for challenging the representationally triadic structure of "words, knowers and things" (2003, p. 813). Things cease to have inherent properties or borders; measurements do not represent measurement-independent states of things: "phenomena are constitutive of reality. Reality is not composed of things-in-themselves or things behind-phenomena but 'things'-in-phenomena" (2003, p. 817). Consequently meaning is not a property but an ongoing performance and discourse is not (just) a human production. Even the distinction between epistemology and ontology collapses and she proposes instead the term "Onto-epistemology – the study of practices of knowing in being" (2003, p. 829).

Only characters that have now become almost mythical, such as Foucault, roam the far end of the spectrum, where things have no meaning outside discourse and consequently the presence of a material reality is not negated but made irrelevant. According to Foucault discourse "governs the way that a topic can be meaningfully talked about and reasoned about. It also influences how ideas are put into practice and used to regulate the conduct of others" (Hall 2001, p. 72). In line with his anti-essentialism, Foucault chose as his main objects of analysis not the statements that 'constitute' the discourse but rather the rules that govern their production and the way they structure the discourse (Foucault 1972, p. 38). He aspires to scrutinize and problematize the obvious and the familiar, by interrogating "the discourses of true and false [...] the correlative formation of domains and objects [...] the verifiable, falsifiable discourses that bear on them, and [...] the effects in the real to which they are linked" (Foucault 1980b, p. 237). Discourse here is more an epistemological tool than an ontological object, used to highlight the complex interplay among language, power, rationality and the many realities that these produce. All objects of our knowledge are defined and produced by discourses which "systematically form the object of which they speak" (Foucault 1979, p. 49).

In this paradigmatic view (Alvesson and Kärreman 2011) discourse is an idiosyncratic but pervasive way of representing and understanding the world, constituted by a set of statements that typify reality, enabling a "regime of truth" (Foucault 1980a, p. 131). These statements are not simply propositions or sentences that can be defined as true or false but they are a mesh of assertions, signs and practices, of norms and rules of inclusion and exclusion. The difference between linguistic utterances and social performances collapses in discourse since what matters is not the factual veracity of a statement but rather the fact that it is believed to be true and acted upon as such by society and institutions such that it has 'truth effects'. For instance, the 'truth' of statements about the nature of homosexuality is of little consequence. What really counts is whether homosexuals are accepted or rejected, committed to institutions or live openly, celebrated for who they are or persecuted. These 'practical statements' also demarcate social roles and ordering. According to Foucault discourse defines its subjects both by producing 'role models' (e.g. the madman, the homosexual, the criminal) and by creating positions for the subjects to interact through discursive practices (Hall 2001). As a consequence "power and discourse are mutually constitutive" (Hardy and Phillips 2004, p. 299), since discursive practices shape power relations and – in turn – discourses evolve as result of political struggles which produce new 'texts' (Hardy and Phillips 2004) or reconfigure circuits of power and domination (Clegg 1989). In Foucault's own words: "We are subjected to the production of truth through power and we cannot exercise power except through the production of truth" (Foucault 1980a, p. 93).

Foucault introduces two separate methods to perform this analysis. The first is an 'archaeological' approach, aimed at describing the *savoir*, the implicit knowledge base that gives meaning and coherence to the way of thinking, working and acting in a specific society. This knowledge, which is distinct from the formal bodies of learning found in literary, religious and scientific texts, *connaissances* (Levy 2013, p. 261), is not simply made of concepts but also includes the norms, institutions and practices that embody, empower and support social practices. For instance, the appearance of the discipline of psychiatry in the 19th century is, according to Foucault, made possible by "a whole set of relations between hospitalization, internment, the conditions and procedures of social exclusion, the rules of jurisprudence, the norms of industrial labour and bourgeois morality" (Foucault 1972, p. 179). *Savoir* is therefore not the consequence of "a rational historical trajectory" followed by a discipline (Durkheim 1915 [1976], p. 1773) but a construct emerging from an array of practices. As such it can be 'discovered' by analysing and collating a cross-section of the events, statements, artefacts that characterize a set of practices in an historical period, as archaeologists do when excavating a stratum of deposits.

The second 'approach' developed by Foucault, genealogical analysis, complements the archaeological method, showing that discourses are the outcome of contingent turns of history. Investigating the antecedents of a system of thought, one "must record the singularity of events outside of any monotonous finality [...] must be sensitive to their recurrence, not in order to trace the gradual curve of their evolution, but to isolate the different scenes where they engaged in different roles" (Ekman 1992a, p. 76). The effects of Foucauldian discourses seemingly resemble those of cultural domination or hegemony described by Gramsci (1975), those 'universal' and 'common sense' bourgeois values that are taken for granted by the majority. However, while Gramscian hegemony is the product of a dominant ideology, Foucauldian discourse does not serve any master or class interest: ideologies often deploy their effects more on the dominant class than on the dominated classes (Abercrombie, Hill and Turner 1980). Moreover, while ideologies distort truth as the counter-hegemonist views it, discourse produces its own truths. Influenced by Foucault's position, Laclau and Mouffe (1985) introduced a more radical form of constructivism into Marxist analysis that transcended the distinction between structure and superstructure and argued that all our perception of reality is mediated entirely by discourse, especially by virtue of its stable frames and closed interpretative horizons.

Similarities can also be drawn between a discursive and a cultural approach. Differences exist between discourse and culture, however, since culture has a subliminal character and, while it is reflected in symbols and language, it is not embedded in them as is discourse (Alvesson 2004, pp. 328–31). Again, discursive acts constitute meanings through language, while culture preserves and transmits them, also using non-verbal means. Finally, cultural studies are more 'humanistic' because they consider culture to be produced by subjects. Foucauldian discourse analysis reverses this picture, maintaining that the subjects are produced by the discourse.

Discourse is, therefore, the meta-sensemaking device (Weick 1988) implicitly in use in any specific historical and cultural context; it is taken for granted by its subjects, who end up assuming subject positions that the discourse makes available. Discourses are implicit in everyday use but can be made visible, escaping tautological truth, by comparing specific cases to alternative discourses, noticing differences and discontinuities. Foucault decided to focus, for instance, on the historical evolution of certain discourses (medicine, sexuality, madness, discipline, etc.) within the same cultural framework (France). However, it is possible to use space as an alternative to or addition to time, contrasting alternative industries, organizations or different geographical contexts.

Inescapabilty of Discourses

A further ontological tangle concerns the pervasiveness of discourse: discourse both enables and constrains knowledge through relationships of power, social arrangements, tacit and explicit norms, practices and ideas. If our thinking, acting, sensemaking are both rooted in and constituted by discourse it appears impossible to position oneself 'outside' discourse. We can compare and contrast discourses in a historical or cross-contextual perspective and by doing so we can even describe the specific characteristics of one discourse in relation to another. However, if we try to free our reasoning from its own discursive bolsters and blinkers we end up caught in an infinite regression, as when we put one mirror in front of another.

Such a paradox is not intrinsic to discourse but rather derives from the incompatibility between certain epistemological stances and particular representations of discourse. A positivist epistemology, one that treats social facts as existing independently from observers (Silverman 2010, p. 102), cannot be paired with a paradigmatic view of the discourse. While positivist approaches can be employed to examine 'fragile' discourses, where discourse is completely contained and resolved in its textual, linguistic component, if we consider a paradigmatic view of Discourse it is not possible to do so because positivist approaches are founded on the postulate that empirical knowledge can only be achieved through a separation between subject (observer) and object (observed phenomenon). Such knowledge is purely representational and based on the assumption that "human reality is constituted by discrete entities with distinct properties" (Sandberg and Tsoukas 2011, p. 340). This idea of ontological separateness is incompatible with the very idea of a constitutive Discourse, which forms the subjectivity of the observer that is supposed to examine it as an object of analysis.

The debate on the construction of scientific facts developed in the fields of sociology of scientific knowledge, and science and technology studies explicitly discuss this problem (see for instance Latour and Woolgar 1979; Knorr-Cetina 1981; Jasanoff et al. 1995; Bauchspies, Restivo and Croissant 2006). These studies describe how research practices are impinged by the instruments used; even in the hard sciences, propositions and empirical realities are tangled up in a socio-technical network in which research tools translate ('inscribe') physical phenomena, relating them to theoretical propositions (Latour and Woolgar 1979).

If we cannot approach discourse assuming the separateness of observing subject and observed object it is necessary to adopt a radically different epistemological standpoint. Such an alternative framework is offered by practice theory (Bourdieu 1977, 1990; Gherardi 2000; Schatzki 2001; Orlikowski 2010; Gherardi 2012). Central is the notion of *practical rationality*, a position that accepts that "we are never separated but always already entwined with others and things in specific socio-material practice worlds" (Sandberg and Tsoukas 2011, p. 343). The philosophical foundation of this concept is in the Heideggerian notion of *dasein*, or 'being-in-the world', the idea according to which our sense of being is the ongoing product of our practical engagement with the reality that surrounds us (Wheeler 2013).

A practical rationality stance allows us to reject the question "How do we escape discourse?", recognizing that it has no good answer – one simply cannot (Parker 1992, pp. 21–2). An "epistemology of practice" (Raelin 2007) thus rejects the subject–object separation and as such is particularly fitting to discourse analysis. The idea that discourses in-corporate not merely texts but also practices and actions predates the Foucauldian notion of discursive practice, and can be traced back to the idea of performativity, originally expressed by the philosopher J.L. Austin: "performatives are language as action, utterances that in saying something do it. They are utterances that in their enunciation change the world – they bring about a new social state" (Cameron and Kulick 2003, p. 126). This perspective enables us to overcome the view of discourse as a temporally fixed script guiding action, positing that the relationship between performance, context and texts is dialectic and constituted in mundane interactions (Ashcraft 2004). Heidegger himself highlights the relationship between phenomenological experience and discourse: "the attuned intelligibility of being in the world is expressed as discourse [...] What is talked about in discourse is always addressed in a particular view and within certain limits" (Heidegger 1927, p. 151). In this view, understanding is achieved through fulfilment in practice: the best way to comprehend what a hammer can do is by using it (Sandberg 2005, p. 51).

The problem with practical engagement is the lack of reflexivity: "actors are immersed in practice without being aware of their involve-ment in it" (Sandberg and Tsoukas 2011, p. 344). One way to become aware of the discursive-practical medium in which we are immersed is to produce a *breakdown*, a crisis which "interrupts the flow of habit and gives rise to changed conditions of consciousness and practice" (a definition by W.I. Thomas, cited in Schütz 1943, p. 502), an idea that is also central to Leont'ev's activity theory, according to which individual conscious actions, made of simpler, automatic operations, can only be understood against the framework of a coordinated activity. When we approach a new activity (e.g. learning to drive a car) we need to perform a series of actions in a deliberate, planned way; as we become proficient these actions become automated and are routinized into operations. Conversely, when a breakdown occurs and unconscious operations cannot produce the desired action fluidly in consequence, the operator will have to resort to conscious actions (Koschmann, Kuutti and Hickman 1998). Discourses can be understood as 'activities' and symbolic performances as actions or operations, so that it is only by introducing a breakdown in the taken-for-granted discursive context that we can reveal the attributes of a particular discourse which would otherwise be hidden in plain sight. Since reflexivity does not dissolve discourse the purpose of the analysis becomes to consign discourse to the past by transforming it and putting it in relation with other discourses (Parker 1992).

Investigating discourses through a practice theory lens implies, therefore, relating narratives, symbolic actions, non-human actants, institutions and everyday performances, describing how they come together in a meaningful (and full of meaning) whole. It also involves producing breakdowns, for instance by contrasting them with alternative discourses or observing the impact of 'abnormal' symbolic acts. Unfortunately, despite its potential, only rarely has this approach been used in studies of organizational discourse (one exception is Boczkowski and Orlikowski 2004). The reason for this lack of engagement with the practices of discourse could be linked to a third problematic issue: the ambiguous relationship between materiality and discourse.

Material Discourses

We have seen that discourse appears to be a very elastic concept; advocates of different approaches to the study of organizational discourse have accused each other of not including enough elements (or of including too many elements) in their conceptualization of discourse. Approaches that focus on the purely linguistic aspects of discourse are criticized for failing to incorporate non-linguistic components. On the other hand, when elements such as technology, material object, affects, ideologies and social structures are conflated into a single coherent system the utility of the notion of discourse is weakened, since discourse becomes synonymous with reality: if everything is discourse, then nothing is not.

It is therefore important to clarify the tangled relationship between symbolic elements (i.e. various forms of speech and 'texts') and non-discursive elements (for instance institutions, material objects, but also cognition, sensemaking, etc.). Since society and organizations are made possible by a shared understanding grounded on symbolic behaviour

(Weber 1922 [1978]; Schütz 1932, 1945; Berger and Luckmann 1967 [1990]; Silverman 1970; Chia 2000) it is highly problematic to separate discourse from material elements. In the absence of texts and conversations, of speech acts and symbolic practices, institutions, practices and organizations would cease to be seen as parts of a coherent whole: "A foreigner visiting Oxford or Cambridge for the first time is shown a number of colleges, libraries, playing fields, museums, scientific departments and administrative offices. He then asks 'But where is the University'?" (Ryle 1949 [2009], p. 6).

As material elements acquire meaning through symbolic practices, so all texts and speech acts are substantiated by their material underpinnings. To be instantiated, any sign needs to be 'set' in some medium, be it a sound, a piece of paper, a carved stone or an electronic pixels pattern. The coupling of materiality and semiotic elements can be tight, as in the case of writings on the wall, or loose, as in the case of the furniture in an office, but it is always present.

Material supports are certainly not permanent but they usually tend to have a longer life than the symbols they were meant to convey. We can only guess at the discursive elements embedded by Palaeolithic hunters in the rock painting in Lascaux cave. Even symbolic practices can have an extremely long life, but their meanings can shift, conveying and reproducing different discourses. An emblematic case is offered by the Uffington White Horse. This is a stylized figure about 100 metres long, carved on a hillside in Oxfordshire, England, that can be considered the world's longest surviving organized phenomenon. It is constituted by a deep trench filled with chalk, which has been archeologically assessed to be between 2500 and 3500 years old. Since vegetation tends to overgrow and rains wash away the chalk, the persistence of this figure has been made possible only by a constant work of scrubbing and cleaning of the site, which has been performed at least once every generation over the last three millennia. Clearly this practice has a symbolic character that has changed over time: it is likely that the original meaning was related to a tribal emblem or the cult of the deity Epona, while between the 17th and 19th centuries it was maintained thanks to a scouring festival which was a manifestation of local identity and pride (Green 2002). The current owner (The National Trust) and guardian (English Heritage) of the artefact are instead explicitly driven by discourse of preservation and restoration of national 'heritage' (Schwyzer 1999).

The reciprocal influence that symbolic practices and tangible elements exercise on each other appears to support the notion of co-emergence of materiality and discourse (Iedema 2007b), or at least of the existence of a dialectical relationship between the two (Fairclough 2010, p. 4). The problem with the notion of mutual constitution is that it could lead to *discoursism* (Conrad 2004), conflating the natural/material realm into the discursive domain. At the same time, maintaining a separation of discourse and materiality can lead to the opposite sin of marginalizing all practices that are not reducible to texts (Reed 2000).

Let's consider a passage from a textbook on discourse analysis:

> The view of discourse as the social construction of reality sees texts as communicative units which are embedded in social and cultural practices. The texts we write and speak both shape and are shaped by these practices. Discourse, then, is both shaped by the world as well as shaping the world. Discourse is shaped by language as well as shaping language. It is shaped by the people who use the language as well as shaping the language that people use. Discourse is shaped, as well, by the discourse that has preceded it and that which might follow it. Discourse is also shaped by the medium in which it occurs as well as it shapes the possibilities for that medium. The purpose of the text also influences the discourse. Discourse also shapes the range of possible purposes of texts. (Paltridge 2012, p. 7)

It is difficult to find any fault in these statements, yet they do not help much in tracing the boundaries of discourse and in reflecting on the dynamics of its 'embeddedness' in practices. What is the nature of this 'world' that is treated as a natural counterpart of discourse? Does it include practices, emotions, artefacts, natural phenomena? Through which processes does discourse 'shape' these elements? If discourses "take a variety of forms, including written documents, verbal reports, artwork, spoken words, pictures, symbols, buildings, and other artifacts" (Phillips, Lawrence and Hardy 2004, p. 636) can we still make a useful distinction between the material, pre-discursive structure and the discursive superstructure?

To approach these questions, approaches that view reality and discourse as complementarity or connected (Phillips and Oswick 2012) seem more useful than the more radical positions considering materiality and discourse either as mutually exclusive or as mutually produced. This is because they allow for examining the interplay of *logos* (the symbolic sphere) and materiality, without collapsing them in a singularity. For instance CDA offers a comprehensive methodology based on a separation of descriptive and critical objectives. While pursuing the former it focuses on micro-communicative events; then, when engaging in the latter, it puts them in relationship with the 'macro' level of naturalized ideological representations, the 'background knowledge' framing individual symbolic actions (Fairclough 2010, p. 31). What is still not clear in the CDA account is how processes of "semiosis, that is, meaning-making through the mediation of signs or symbols" (Lemke 2003, p. 131) happens, and, more specifically, how material artefacts become imbued with meaning (or contribute to produce new meanings). I will try to offer a schematic account of this relationship in the next section, with the intent of providing some epistemological clarification.

HOW TO POSITION DISCOURSE: AN EPISTEMOLOGICAL PROPOSAL

A serious shortcoming of constructionist conceptions is their tendency to incur an epistemic fallacy, confounding ontology (the reflection on the nature of being, of reality) and epistemology (studying what knowledge is and how it is possible). The problem is encapsulated in a simple assertion: "the fact that the knowledge of reality necessarily is discursive does not mean that the nature of reality is" (Alvesson and Kärreman 2011, p. 1139).

This is not a moot point, expression of the never-ending argument between realists and constructivists. While it is true that reflecting on the pragmatic consequences of organizational discourses is more important than splitting hairs on irresolvable epistemological conundrums (Parker 2000), a lack of clarity around these fundamental questions deprives discourse analysis of appeal and usefulness. More importantly it can cause scholars from different disciplinary backgrounds to unreflexively fall back on their idiosyncratic bodies of tacit knowledge, ending up at cross-purposes in relation to their object of study and methods.

There is indeed a conceptual gulf between the assertion that discourses are "practices that systematically form the objects of which they speak" (Foucault 1972, p. 49), and the apparently analogous designation defining them as "system of statements [that] do not simply describe the social world, but categorise it [bringing] phenomena into sight [and providing] frameworks for debating the value of one way of talking about reality over other ways" (Parker 1992, pp. 4–5). The first position assumes that discourses 'make the world', while the second implicitly accepts that discourse comes *after* the pre-discursive phenomena that it frames and interprets. To reconcile these differences we need first to reflect on the type of 'objects' that can be encountered in 'the world' and then to propose a model that can illustrate their interaction with discourse.

The first important distinction is based on the argument proposed by the philosopher John Searle: "Brute facts exist independently of any human institutions; institutional facts can exist only within human institutions. Brute facts require the institution of language in order that we can *state* the facts, but the brute facts *themselves* exist quite independently of language or of any other institution" (Searle 1995, p. 27).

To define institutions, Searle introduces a distinction between rules that are introduced to regulate activities that can occur independently of the rule, and constitutive rules which instead make possible by constructing social activities (e.g. the rules of chess). These latter rules come in systems and are those that create the possibility of institutional facts. They underpin how the complex intersubjective agreements that enable social constructions such as money, marriage, nation-states, and organizations can be maintained. These institutions are based on systems of rules that – albeit not universal – are not mere arbitrary conventions because the social reality they produce requires systemic coherence and therefore they cannot be whimsically altered without destroying the whole institution (Searle 1995).

Searle differentiates artificial brute facts (for instance a paperweight) from institutional fact (for instance money), because the former has characteristics that are independent from the context. The possible purposes and uses of a brute object do not depend on a collective agreement, and it does not have a constitutive function: individually I can choose to use a trophy or a hammer as a paperweight, while I cannot decide what to use as currency. There is a difference in the way in which discourse deploys its effects in the two cases: discursive effects are fully constitutive in the case of institutional facts, for instance making the difference between Monopoly money and a hard currency, while 'artificial' brute facts are influenced by discursive elements (one can easily picture a Nazi officer using a pistol as a paperweight, but it would be highly unlikely that a Scandinavian kindergarten teacher would do the same) but such influence does not produce obligatory outcomes. These constitutive effects of discourse are necessary but they do not follow prescribed, obligatory patterns. While social phenomena, differently from natural ones, require a constant reproduction by human agency in order to exist, with this reproduction mediated by symbolic practices, the example of the Uffington White Horse demonstrates that different discourses can produce the same organizing effects.

Since my purpose is not to analyse different modes of social construction but rather to account for the possible alternative ways in which discourse interacts with materiality in order to provide research directions, it is necessary to expand the distinction proposed by Searle. The problem is that the notion of brute fact considers only the ontology but not the ontogenesis of a fact. In other words it does not explain nor differentiate among different ways in which different brute facts come to existence. While all brute facts have material essence that is independent from symbolic practices, that is their actuality is not predicated on an ongoing social performance, the origin of *artificial* brute facts is rooted in social and symbolic practices and therefore discourse will exert some constitutive effects on them. Discourse cannot change the way in which my workspace is currently structured (even if it can influence my perception and affect in relation to it) but it certainly played a fundamental role in its design and creation.

To clarify the different ways in which discourse can interact with different types of 'reality' it is useful to present another simple taxonomy of materiality (Table 2.2). This table presents a formulation that is coherent with the fundamental tenets of critical realism, the idea that there is "a world [that] exists independently of our knowledge of it", made of "objects – whether natural or social – [which] necessarily have particular powers or ways of acting and particular susceptibilities" (Sayer 1992, p. 5). It helps articulate this reality by considering two different dimensions: whether an object has physical, material characteristics that are not determined by discursive influence or requires constant symbolic and social labour to be maintained, and whether these characteristics have emerged naturally or they are the outcome of purposeful action, of *design*.

Table 2.2   A typology of material facts

	Emergent phenomena ('natural facts')	Designed phenomena ('artefacts')
Physical objects	For example, a tsunami, a natural element, gravity, basic emotions *Discourse has only regulative effects (interpretation)*	For example, a building, a working tool, a uniform, a car *Discourse has regulative effects (but also constitutive, through design)*
Social objects	For example, language, the market, the traffic *Discourse has constitutive effects (but they are unplanned)*	For example, a ritual, an organizational routine *Discourse has constitutive effects (that are planned)*

Crossing the two dimensions conceptually separates four different types of material facts and reflects their relationship with discursive practices. The first category, 'emergent physical objects' groups natural brute facts. These phenomena include both physical and biological occurrences, and can have either a tangible, material substance (an earthquake, the weather, a rock, etc.) or an immaterial form, as in the case of emotional responses and affects. Discourse will not alter their intrinsic properties: we cannot 'talk our way' out of gravity, nor can we suppress pain by calling it another name. It has, however, regulative effects on interpretations. A storm will have the same duration, and will produce the same physical effects (e.g. the amount of rain falling from the sky). However, different discourses will activate different sensemaking processes and produce different pragmatic effects: think of the consequences of viewing it as a meteorological phenomenon, a divine punishment, or the type of atmospheric disturbance that enables us to make a legitimate insurance claim.

Also, social objects, i.e. phenomena that are constructed and maintained by means of social and symbolic practices, can be emergent. The status of these objects is sometimes ambiguous if seen through the lens of brute versus social fact. Think of a city. To exist, cities require the coherent performance of a large set of symbolic and social practices (that are constitutive of urban life), yet, with few exceptions, cities emerge in a spontaneous, unplanned manner (the notion of the foundation of the city is more often than not a rhetorical construction rather than a chronologically well-demarcated historical event). Therefore the majority of practices that are put in place to administer and govern a city are of a regulative nature; that is, they apply to a quasi-natural object the existence of which predates these sets of rules.

In the case of planned, designed social practices, for instance those which form the bundle of routines that are at the core of any modern organization, the constitutive role of symbolic practice is instead clear. Routines could not exist in the absence of coordinated, consistent symbolic behaviours, since they are not simply mindless repetition of actions but "involve a range of actions, behaviours, thinking, and feeling" (Feldman 2000, p. 622). Discourses express all their constructive and disciplinary potential on this type of object.

Finally, it is necessary to situate those designed artefacts (artificial brute facts) which typically represent the material embodiment of organizations: buildings, work tools, machines. While having a distinctively material manifestation, with the consequent bundle of physical properties that no discourse can alter, these objects incorporate a discursive influence in their design, which is not merely 'functional'. The impact of discourse on these objects is therefore more comprehensive than in the case of naturally emergent objects because they can often display a semiotic birthmark: their morphology is not only dictated by evolution, or by the laws of physics, but is often imbued with meaning.

A complex, phenomenologically entangled world is not amenable to neat classification. The separation between these conceptual niches is blurred. Artificial creations are mostly a recombination of pre-existing natural elements. On the other hand, even grand-scale natural events are the outcome of human activities, such as anthropometrically induced global warming, such that the separation between what is 'natural' and what is 'artificial' is often unclear: to what extent is an genetically modified organism (GMO) 'artificial'? What about a test-tube baby, or Dolly, the first genetically produced sheep?

Even within the category of 'physical natural facts' the relationship between discourse and physical reality can be problematic, especially in the case of emotions. Emotions are a difficult terrain where few venture to explore the cognitive side of organizational discourse (Grant et al. 2004, p. 23), leaving the issue of the interplay between 'affect' and 'discourse' almost unexplored (Iedema 2011). Emotions have long been recognized as being socially constructed. Durkheim (1915 [1976]) described the process of elicitation of shared emotional arousal, typical of rituals, as "collective effervescence". There is undoubtedly a normative component in emotions: paradigmatic Discourses always include rules about the appropriate way to display emotions, or dictate which emotions should be shown in particular contexts. Apparently spontaneous manifestations of empathy are in reality discursively regimented, for instance prescribing who are the legitimate recipients of compassionate feelings (Simpson, Clegg and Pitsis 2014). Also, organizations can require their members to perform emotional labour, stimulating or censoring correct emotions (Hochschild 1979; Ashkanasy 2003; Illouz 2007; Baumeler 2010).

At the same time there is ample evidence that basic emotions such as fear, anger, surprise, joy are universally expressed with the same facial configurations (Ekman 1992a, 1992b), which makes them independent from culture. Studies investigating the relationship between fear and courage show that there are both biological and cultural components at play: one individual can feel fear and decide to behave courageously, overcoming fear, while another can be genuinely fearless, because of an acquired habit (as in the case of an expert parachutist) or because of an innate disposition (Rachman 2004). The position of many sociologists on emotion is that, while it is possible to make analytical distinctions between emotion, cognition and bodily processes, "emotions cannot be divorced from the sociocultural meanings in which they are experienced and expressed" (McCarthy 1994, p. 269). The notion of romantic love is a historical construct associated with mediaeval times, when troubadours would serenade and woo ladies married for property with dreams of ardour and passion, creating the phenomenon of romantic love (Paris, 1883). For our purposes the possibility of analytic distinctions is crucial. There is a kernel of 'raw' bodily responses to threats and opportunities, attraction and repulsion, that is pre-discursive and that include certain affordances. We can fake joy or repress fear because of social pressures, but we cannot be truly happy, sad or afraid because of the dominant discourse.

Having clarified that the world of 'material facts' is very heterogeneous and that different objects can be differently impacted by (or be conveyors of) discursive practices, it is now possible to propose a diagram which schematically illustrates the relationship among different discursive and material elements, clarifying their complex relationship (Figure 2.2).

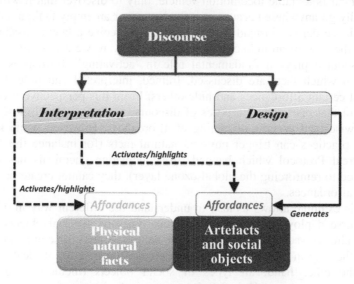

Figure 2.2　The interplay between materiality and discourse

This simplified diagram offers a representation of the complex inter-relationship between materiality and discourse. Rather than capturing all possible forms in which facts and discourse mutually influence each other, it is an ideal-typical abstraction: as such it suppresses some aspects of the empirical phenomenon while highlighting others (Weber 1922 [1978]). By no means does it define 'laws' of discourse: it merely serves as a heuristic instrument to guide organizational discourse analysis and to enable the emergence of useful questions.

What all material facts (including social phenomena) have in common is a set of attributes, with objectively measurable physical properties. We do not, however, use these 'objective' qualities to define things; for instance we do not 'recognize' a door because of a set of quantitative attributes, such as its volume, weight or density. What we perceive in objects are the multiple relations that we can establish with them, their *affordances* (Gibson 1979). These are latent possibilities of action that are provided by any material object that become actual only when an actor recognizes them. The theory of affordances is intrinsically connected with the notion of performativity: "people perceive the environment directly in terms of its potentials for action" (Gaver 1991, p. 79) but also has a strong component of realism. Affordances are present independently of perception, and we therefore can have false or hidden affordances (Gaver 1991). An example of false affordance is believing that a car is a viable locomotion vehicle, only to discover that it will not actually go anywhere because of a flat battery or an empty tank; a hidden affordance derives instead from a failure to perceive a latent possibility, as in the case of an unknown feature of a software we are using.

Discourse plays a fundamental role in 'activating' affordances. The way in which facts are discussed, framed, interpreted and judged will reveal certain affordances and hide others. From this perspective it could be said that one of the purposes of discourse analysis is to disclose this otherwise tacit process of editing of affordances. However, while symbolic practices can trigger physical natural facts (for instance the 1987 Montreal Protocol which banned ozone depleting chemicals has contributed to reinforcing the global ozone layer), they cannot create or alter their affordances.

This example allows us also to understand the different way in which discourse deploys its effect on different types of material objects. We have already seen that, in the case of natural objects, discourse affects only the way in which the fact is interpreted, made sense of, dealt with. On the other hand, all types of social objects (including material artefacts) possess a "dual capacity to serve as objects of action and as signs that enable action to proceed" (McCarthy 1994, p. 275). In other words they are *designed* both to serve a practical function and to act as semiotic carriers. Such an act of 'design' can be explicit and carried out by a specific agent (for instance an architect designing a building, or an executive restructuring an organization), emergent (a social practice that evolves over time) or both of these, but in any case it is shaped by symbolic practices. The influence of discourse over artefacts is therefore dual: on the one hand it operates through interpretation, as in the case of natural facts, by highlighting or hiding affordances. On the other hand, it acts through design, directly generating affordances (by shaping the attributes of the artefact) and emphasizing them (by virtue of its symbolic component). Artefacts and natural facts can also be in relation: certain natural facts will present affordances that permit the emergence of particular types of artefacts, for instance as the availability of a particular construction material, together with climatic conditions, will influence local building practices. But the reverse can be true: for instance the design of a religious ritual can facilitate the emergence of shared emotions or the form of a building can elicit awe or induce fear.

One might still ask: why bother with these metaphysical distinctions? After all, if we choose a stance inspired by phenomenological, practice theory it is neither possible nor useful to make any definitive ontological claims on the 'borders' of discourse or the boundary between what is socially constructed and what is given. If ontological claims are unnecessary we can de facto avoid the risk of epistemic fallacy. The problem is that the lack of distinction between material and discursive structures makes the comparison between alternative discursive worlds highly problematic. In a radical constructivist perspective "the relationship between discourses and that which they represent is entirely arbitrary" (Reed 2000, p. 525). Any comparison between discourses becomes impossible because made from the perspective of an equally arbitrary discursive viewpoint: it would become a spurious list similar to the one imagined by Borges:

> (In) a certain Chinese encyclopedia (...) is written that animals are divided into (a) those that belong to the emperor; (b) embalmed ones; (c) those that are trained; (d) suckling pigs; (e) mermaids; (f) fabulous ones; (g) stray dogs; (h) those that are included in this classification; (i) those that tremble as if they were mad; (j) innumerable ones; (k) those drawn with a very fine camel's-hair brush; (l) etcetera; (m) those that have just broken the flower vase; (n) those that at a distance resemble flies. (Borges 1937 [1952], p. 104)

It is ironic that Foucault himself cites this passage as a crucial inspiration to his work (Foucault 1970 [2002]). What he does not consider is that, in the absence of a common kernel of 'hard facts' to which one can anchor a comparison, any statements about *other* discourses are as meaningful as this 'schizophrenic' list. The problem with this taxonomy is not its lack of meaning but its overabundance of meanings, drawn from multiple alternative and inconsistent rationalities. The ideal typical model described above proposes a concrete solution to this problem: combining a critical realist stance with the concept of affordances enables to trace the processes, accounting for and putting in relationship both symbolic and non-symbolic practices, their outcomes and their antecedents.

Comparing alternative views on organizational discourse and clarifying epistemological issues is necessary but not sufficient to articulate the multiple ways in which discourse analysis has been employed and the manifold manifestations of its influences in organizational studies. In order to consider both the past achievements and the future potential of this vast literature I am going to employ, in the next chapters, a well-used discursive device, metaphors.

REFERENCES

Abercrombie, N., Hill, S. and Turner, B.S. 1980, *The Dominant Ideology Thesis*, Allen and Unwin, London.
Alvesson, M. 2004, 'Organizational Culture and Discourse', in D. Grant, C. Hardy, C. Oswick and L.L. Putnam (eds), *The SAGE Handbook of Organizational Discourse*, SAGE, London, pp. 317–35.
Alvesson, M. and Kärreman, D. 2000, 'Varieties of Discourse: On the Study of Organizations Through Discourse Analysis', *Human Relations*, vol. 53, pp. 1125–49.
Alvesson, M. and Kärreman, D. 2011, 'Decolonializing Discourse: Critical Reflections on Organizational Discourse Analysis', *Human Relations*, vol. 64, pp. 1121–46.
Alvesson, M. and Willmott, H. 2002, 'Identity Regulation as Organizational Control: Producing the Appropriate Individual', *Journal of Management Studies*, vol. 39, pp. 619–44.
Ashcraft, K.L. 2004, 'Gender, Discourse and Organization: Framing a Shifting Relationship', in D. Grant, C. Hardy, C. Oswick and L.L. Putnam (eds), *The SAGE Handbook of Organizational Discourse*, SAGE, London, pp. 276–98.
Ashkanasy, N.M. 2003, 'Emotions in Organizations: A Multi-level Perspective', *Research in Multi Level Issues*, vol. 2, pp. 9–54.
Barad, K. 2003, 'Posthumanist Performativity: Toward an Understanding of How Matter Comes to Matter', *Signs*, vol. 28, pp. 801–31.
Bauchspies, W.K., Restivo, S.P. and Croissant, J. 2006, *Science, Technology, and Society: A Sociological Approach*, Blackwell, Malden, MA.
Baumeler, C. 2010, 'Organizational Regimes of Emotional Conduct', in B. Sieben and A. Wettergren (eds), *Emotionalizing Organizations and Organizing Emotions*, Palgrave Macmillan, Basingstoke, pp. 272–92.
Berger, P.L. and Luckmann, T. 1967 [1990], *The Social Construction of Reality: A Treatise in the Sociology of Knowledge*, Anchor Books, New York.
Boczkowski, P.J. and Orlikowski, W.J. 2004, 'Organizational Discourse and New Media: A Practice Perspective', in D. Grant, C. Hardy, C. Oswick and L.L. Putnam (eds), *The SAGE Handbook of Organizational Discourse*, SAGE, London, pp. 359–77.
Borges, J.L. 1937 [1952], 'The Analytical Language of John Wilkins', *Other Inquisitions*, vol. 1952, pp. 101–5.
Bourdieu, P. 1977, *Outline of a Theory of Practice*, trans. R. Nice, Cambridge University Press, Cambridge.
Bourdieu, P. 1990, *The Logic of Practice*, B. Blackwell, Cambridge.

Cameron, D. and Kulick, D. 2003, *Language and Sexuality*, Cambridge University Press, Cambridge.

Cederström, C. and Spicer, A. 2014, 'Discourse of the Real Kind: A Post-foundational Approach to Organizational Discourse Analysis', *Organization*, vol. 21, no. 2, pp. 178–205.

Chia, R. 2000, 'Discourse Analysis Organizational Analysis', *Organization*, vol. 7, pp. 513–18.

Clegg, S.R. 1989, *Frameworks of Power*, SAGE Publications, London, UK.

Conrad, C. 2004, 'Organizational Discourse Analysis: Avoiding the Determinism – Voluntarism Trap', *Organization*, vol. 11, no. 3, pp. 427–39.

Durkheim, E. 1915 [1976], *The Elementary Forms of the Religious Life*, Allen and Unwin, London.

Ekman, P. 1992a, 'Are there Basic Emotions?', *Psychological Review*, vol. 99, pp. 550–53.

Ekman, P. 1992b, 'An Argument for Basic Emotions', *Cognition & Emotion*, vol. 6, no. 3-4, pp. 169–200.

Fairclough, N. 1992, *Discourse and Social Change*, Polity Press, Cambridge, MA.

Fairclough, N. 2005, 'Discourse Analysis in Organization Studies: The Case for Critical Realism', *Organization Studies*, vol. 26, p. 915.

Fairclough, N. 2010, *Critical Discourse Analysis*, Routledge, London.

Feldman, M.S. 2000, 'Organizational Routines as a Source of Continuous Change', *Organization Science*, vol. 11, pp. 611–29.

Foucault, M. 1970 [2002], *The Order of Things: An Archaeology of the Human Sciences*, Routledge, London.

Foucault, M. 1972, *The Archaeology of Knowledge*, vol. TB 1901, Harper & Row, New York.

Foucault, M. 1979, *Discipline and Punish: The Birth of the Prison*, Vintage Books, New York.

Foucault, M. 1980a, *Power/Knowledge: Selected Interviews and Other Writings, 1972–1977*, Harvester Wheatsheaf, New York.

Foucault, M. 1980b, 'Questions of Method', in J.D. Faubion (ed.), *Michel Foucault: Power*, vol. 3, The New Press, New York, pp. 223–38.

Gaver, W.W. 1991, 'Technology Affordances', *Proceedings of the SIGCHI Conference on Human Factors in Computing Systems*, ACM, pp. 79–84.

Gee, J.P. 2010, *How to do Discourse Analysis : A Toolkit*, 1st edn, Taylor and Francis, London and New York.

Gherardi, S. 2000, 'Practice-Based Theorizing on Learning and Knowing in Organizations', *Organization*, vol. 7, pp. 211–23.

Gherardi, S. 2012, *How to Conduct a Practice-based Study: Problems and Methods*, Edward Elgar Publishing, Cheltenham, UK and Northampton, MA, USA.

Gibson, J.J. 1979, *The Ecological Approach to Visual Perception*, Psychology Press, New York.

Gramsci, A. 1975, *Quaderni del carcere*, Einaudi, Torino, IT.

Grant, D., Hardy, C., Oswick, C. and Putnam, L.L. 2004, 'Organizational Discourse: Exploring the Field', in D. Grant, C. Hardy, C. Oswick and L.L.

Putnam (eds), *The SAGE Handbook of Organizational Discourse*, SAGE, London, pp. 1–35.

Green, M. 2002, *Animals in Celtic Life and Myth*, Routledge, Abingdon.

Hall, S. 2001, 'Foucault: Power, Knowledge and Discourse', in M. Wetherell, S. Yates and S. Taylor (eds), *Discourse Theory and Practice: A Reader*, SAGE Publications, London, UK, pp. 72–81.

Hardy, C. 2001, 'Researching Organizational Discourse', *International Studies of Management & Organization*, vol. 31, p. 25.

Hardy, C. and Phillips, N. 2004, 'Discourse and Power', in D. Grant, C. Hardy, C. Oswick and L.L. Putnam (eds), *The SAGE Handbook of Organizational Discourse*, SAGE, London, pp. 299–315.

Heidegger, M. 1927, *Being and Time*, trans. J. Stambaugh, State Universtity of New York Press, New York.

Heracleous, L. 2004, 'Interpretivist Approaches to Organizational Discourse', in D. Grant, C. Hardy, C. Oswick and L.L. Putnam (eds), *The SAGE Handbook of Organizational Discourse*, SAGE, London, pp. 175–91.

Heracleous, L. 2012, 'Four Proposals Towards an Interpretive Theory of the Process of Discursive Reality Construction', in J. Aritz and R.C. Walker (eds), *Discourse Perspectives on Organizational Communication*, Fairleigh Dickinson University Press, Lanham, MD, pp. 9–31.

Heracleous, L. and Barrett, M. 2001, 'Organizational Change as Discourse: Communicative Actions and Deep Structures in the Context of Information Technology Implementation', *Academy of Management Journal*, vol. 44, no. 4, pp. 755–78.

Heracleous, L. and Marshak, R.J. 2004, 'Conceptualizing Organizational Discourse as Situated Symbolic Action', *Human Relations*, vol. 57, no. 10, pp. 1285–312.

Hochschild, A.R. 1979, 'Emotion Work, Feeling Rules, and Social Structure', *The American Journal of Sociology*, vol. 85, pp. 551–75.

Iedema, R. 2007a, 'Discourse Analysis', in S.R. Clegg and J.S. Balley (eds), *International Encyclopedia of Organization Studies*, SAGE, London.

Iedema, R. 2007b, 'On the Multi-modality, Materially and Contingency of Organization Discourse', *Organization Studies*, vol. 28, no. 6, pp. 931–46.

Iedema, R. 2011, 'Discourse Studies in the 21st Century: A Response to Mats Alvesson and Dan Kärreman's "Decolonializing discourse", *Human Relations*, vol. 64, pp. 1163–76.

Illouz, E. 2007, *Cold Intimacies: The Making of Emotional Capitalism*, Polity Press, Malden, MA.

Jack, R.E., Garrod, O.G.B., Yu, H., Caldara, R. and Schyns, P.G. 2012, 'Facial Expressions of Emotion are not Culturally Universal', *Proceedings of the National Academy of Sciences*, vol. 109, pp. 7241–4.

Jasanoff, S., Markle, G., Petersen, J. and Pinch, T. (eds) 1995, *Handbook of Science and Technology Studies*, SAGE, Thousand Oaks, CA.

Keenoy, T., Oswick, C. and Grant, D. 1998, 'Introduction: Organizational Discourses: Of Diversity, Dichotomy and Multi-disciplinarity', in T. Keenoy, C. Oswick and D. Grant (eds), *Discourse + Organization*, SAGE, London, pp. 1–13.

Knorr-Cetina, K. 1981, *The Manufacture of Knowledge: An Essay on the Constructivist and Contextual Nature of Science*, Pergamon Press, Oxford.

Koschmann, T., Kuutti, K. and Hickman, L. 1998, 'The Concept of Breakdown in Heidegger, Leont'ev, and Dewey and its Implications for Education', *Mind, Culture, and Activity*, vol. 5, pp. 25–41.

Laclau, E. and Mouffe, C. 1985, *Hegemony and Socialist Strategy: Towards a Radical Democratic Politics*, Verso, London.

Lakoff, G. 1987, *Women, Fire, and Dangerous Things: What Categories Reveal about the Mind*, University of Chicago Press, Chicago, IL.

Latour, B. and Woolgar, S. 1979, *Laboratory Life: The Social Construction of Scientific Facts*, vol. 80, SAGE Publications, Beverly Hills, CA.

Lemke, J.L. 2003, 'Texts and Discourses in the Technologies of Social Organization', in G. Weiss and R. Wodak (eds), *Critical Discourse Analysis*, Palgrave Macmillan, Basingstoke, pp. 130–49.

Levy, S. 2013, *The Internship*. Distributed by 20th Century Fox.

McCarthy, E.D. 1994, 'The Social Construction of Emotions: New Directions from Culture Theory', in W.M. Wenthworth and J. Ryan (eds), *Social Perspective on Emotion. A Research Annual Volume 2*, Emerald, Bingley, pp. 267–79.

Mumby, D.K. 2011, 'What's Cooking in Organizational Discourse Studies? A Response to Alvesson and Kärreman', *Human Relations*, vol. 64, pp. 1147–61.

Orlikowski, W.J. 2010, 'Practice in Research: Phenomenon, Perspective and Philosophy', in D. Golsorkhi, L. Rouleau, D. Seidl and E. Vaara (eds), *The Cambridge Handbook on Strategy as Practice*, Cambridge University Press, Cambridge, pp. 23–33.

Paltridge, B. 2012, *Discourse Analysis: An Introduction*, Bloomsbury Publishing, London.

Paris, G. 1883, 'Études sur les romans de la Table Ronde-Lancelot du Lac-II Le Conte de la Charrette', *Romania*, vol. 12, pp. 459–534.

Parker, I. 1992, *Discourse Dynamics: Critical Analysis for Social and Individual Psychology*, Routledge, New York.

Parker, M. 2000, '"The Less Important Sideshow": The Limits of Epistemology in Organizational Analysis', *Organization*, vol. 7, no. 3, pp. 519–23.

Phillips, N. and Oswick, C. 2012, 'Organizational Discourse: Domains, Debates, and Directions', *The Academy of Management Annals*, vol. 6, no. 1, pp. 435–81.

Phillips, N., Lawrence, T.B. and Hardy, C. 2004, 'Discourse and Institutions', *Academy of Management Review*, vol. 29, no. 4, pp. 635–52.

Potter, J. 2004, 'Discourse Analysis as a Way of Analysing Naturally Occurring Talk', in D. Silverman (ed.), *Qualitative Research: Theory, Method and Practice*, 2nd edn, SAGE, London.

Rachman, S.J. 2004, 'Fear and Courage: A Psychological Perspective', *Social Research*, vol. 71, no. 1, pp. 149–76.

Raelin, J.A. 2007, 'Toward an Epistemology of Practice', *Academy of Management Learning & Education*, vol. 6, p. 495.

Reed, M. 2000, 'The Limits of Discourse Analysis in Organizational Analysis', *Organization*, vol. 7, no. 3, pp. 524–30.

Ryle, G. 1949 [2009], *The Concept of Mind*, Routledge, London.

Sandberg, J. 2005, 'How do we Justify Knowledge Produced within Interpretive Approaches?', *Organizational Research Methods*, vol. 8, pp. 41–68.

Sandberg, J. and Tsoukas, H. 2011, 'Grasping the Logic of Practice: Theorizing through Practical Rationality', *Academy of Management Review*, vol. 36, p. 338.

Sayer, A. 1992, *Method in Social Science. 2nd Edition*, Routledge, London.

Schatzki, T.R. 2001, 'Introduction: Practice Theory', in E.V. Savigny, T.R. Schatzki and K. Knorr-Cetina (eds), *The Practice Turn in Contemporary Theory*, Routledge, London, pp. 10–23.

Schütz, A. 1932, *The Phenomenology of the Social World*, Northwestern University Press, Evanston, IL.

Schütz, A. 1943, 'The Stranger: An Essay in Social Psychology', *American Journal of Sociology*, vol. 49, p. 499.

Schütz, A. 1945, 'On Multiple Realities', *Philosophy and Phenomenological Research*, vol. 5, pp. 533–76.

Schwyzer, P. 1999, 'The Scouring of the White Horse: Archaeology, Identity, and "Heritage"', *Representations*, vol. 65, pp. 42–62.

Searle, J.R. 1995, *The Construction of Social Reality*, Simon and Schuster, New York.

Silverman, D. 1970, *The Theory of Organisations: A Sociological Framework*, Heinemann Educational, London.

Silverman, D. 2010, *Doing Qualitative Research: A Practical Handbook*, SAGE, London.

Simpson, A.V., Clegg, S.R. and Pitsis, T. 2014, 'Normal Compassion: A Framework for Compassionate Decision Making', *Journal of Business Ethics*, vol. 119, pp. 473–91.

van Dijk, T.A. 1997, *Discourse as Social Interaction*, vol. 2, SAGE, London.

Weber, M. 1922 [1978], *Economy and Society: An Outline of Interpretive Sociology*, University of California Press, Berkeley, CA.

Weick, K.E. 1988, 'Enacted Sensemaking in Crisis Situations', *Journal of Management Studies*, vol. 25, pp. 305–17.

Wetherell, M. and Potter, J. 1987, *Discourse and Social Psychology: Beyond Attitudes and Behaviour*, SAGE Publications, Newbury Park, CA.

Wheeler, M. 2013, 'Martin Heidegger', *The Stanford Encyclopedia of Philosophy*, Spring 2013 edn, accessed 10 March 2013 at http://stanford.io/ 11Xn4R8

Wittgenstein, L. 1922, *Tractatus Logico-Philosophicus*. Kegan Paul, London.

Zerubavel, E. 1993, *The Fine Line*, University of Chicago Press, Chicago, IL.

3. The power of metaphors

We believe that we know something about the things themselves when we speak of trees, colors, snow, and flowers; and yet we possess nothing but metaphors for things[.]

(Nietzsche 1873 [1990], pp. 890–91)

WHAT ARE METAPHORS?

As discussed in Chapter 1, the functional purpose of language is to convey meaning, and this is typically achieved by the use of abstract codified symbols representing concepts and objects. Nevertheless, this 'digital' mode of communication is not exclusive, since it is frequently accompanied (if not replaced) by an 'analogic' mode of information transmission, which uses body language or other performative acts, and evokes a concept by creating a reference to similarities and relationships. The resulting communication is less precise and presents specific problems: for example, it is extremely difficult to express negation without recurring to a digital (i.e. symbolic) code: for instance, "while it is simple to convey the analogic message 'I shall attack you', it is extremely difficult to signal 'I will *not* attack you'" (Watzlawick, Jackson and Bavelas 1967, p. 81). On the other hand, analogic communication is available even in the absence of a shared language and therefore can be used in a broader variety of contexts (Bateson and Ruesch 1951; Watzlawick et al. 1967).

Natural languages are different from designed codes (such as software source code or musical notation) because they contain both analogic and digital elements. As a consequence the words we use in everyday language include both a denotative component, their strict 'dictionary meaning', and a connotative one, the bundle of emotional and imaginative associations surrounding them, which is highly specific and contextual. For instance the word 'mother' simply denotes a female who gave birth to a child; however, the same word can evoke a multitude of different meanings depending on the socio-cultural context and the idiosyncratic individual experiences of motherhood. Mixing these elements enables the production of new meanings, based on the association of different concepts, with metaphors representing the most intentional expression of this mixing of the literal and the figurative. As their very name indicates (*metaphor* derives from the Greek *meta* [through] and *pherein* [to carry]), metaphors involve a transfer of meaning between two terms or concepts, producing a tension fuelled by their dissimilarity (Ortony 1975). The process is well summarized by Tsoukas in these terms: "a metaphor involves the transfer of information from a familiar domain (called the 'base' or 'source' domain) to a new and relatively unfamiliar domain (called the 'target' domain)" (1993, p. 336). This 'hybridization' of meanings can be either unidirectional, involving imagining the target domain in terms of the source domain *or* vice versa, or bidirectional, when the target domain is imagined in terms of the source domain *and* vice versa (Schoeneborn, Vásquez and Cornelissen 2016).

Since "the primary function of a metaphor is to provide a partial understanding of one type of experience in terms of another kind of experience" (Lakoff and Johnson 1980, p. 154), the perceived likeness of the concepts that are juxtaposed is what makes a metaphor useful. They can be employed either to explicate or to investigate an unfamiliar or confounding concept with the help of a more familiar or unambiguous one; therefore, it can be said that metaphors "operate within the 'cognitive comfort zone' of similarity" (Oswick, Keenoy and Grant 2002, p. 294). The similarity which any metaphor conjures does not rest, however, on inherent semantic likeness of the paired expressions, since "similarities do exist, but [...] must be considered similarity of interactional, rather than inherent properties" (Lakoff and Johnson 1980, p. 215; emphasis in the original). This means that intertextuality (Kristeva 1980) applies to metaphors because they are typically based on other conventional metaphors. In practice, metaphorical language does not reflect 'naturally' occurring linkages between different ideas but "forces us to make *semantic leaps*" (Cornelissen 2006, p. 1584). It is therefore our symbolic action which produces the meaning that we then 'rediscover' in the metaphor.

Intertwinement between experience, cognition and knowledge led Nietzsche to view metaphors as a vehicle for the transformation of subjective perceptions in supposedly universal concepts, thus revealing the constructed and language-dependent nature of knowledge: "truths are illusions which we have forgotten are illusions – they are metaphors that have become worn out and have been drained of sensuous force" (Nietzsche 1873 [1990], p. 891). Essentially Nietzsche recognized that "our conceptual system [...] is fundamentally metaphorical in nature"

(Lakoff and Johnson 1980, p. 3). Embracing this view, one must acknowledge that even the concept of 'discourse' is nothing but a metaphor, an analogic image connecting many disparate experiences of speech, text, rhetoric, power, manipulation, symbolism, etc.

An interesting feature of metaphors, well recognized since antiquity, is the fact that they can express synaesthetic capacities, short-circuiting different sensorial spheres: "all metaphors, at least those that have been chosen with discrimination, appeal directly to the senses, especially to the sense of sight, which is the keenest" (Cicero 55 BCE [2001], p. 271). Unfortunately, this embodied character of metaphors has been lost to many who discussed the use of metaphors in organizations, who seem more intent on reflecting on the cognitive and communicative effects of the merging of different conceptual (rather than emotional) domains. One example of this 'intellectualization' of metaphor is offered by a recent statement by Morgan: "for metaphor to have specific meaning the metaphorical image needs to be tied down and articulated through a metonymical process focused on the naming of detailed elements" (2016, p. 1030). The focus on analytic functions, such as labelling, ordering and categorizing ignores the emotional, sensorial and aesthetic impacts of metaphors, despite their demonstrably significant impact on our cognitive processes (Damasio 2006; Kahneman 2011). One remarkable exception is offered by Hogler et al., who highlight the value of metaphors as vehicles of aesthetic knowledge, which produce "an affective state that simultaneously invokes cognition and produces a crucial sensory response" (2008, p. 406).

BEYOND METAPHORS: WHERE TO STOP?

It has already been noted that metaphors are generated by the perception of similarity between two otherwise unrelated concepts. In cognitive processes, however, similarities operate in conjunction with differences, since it is the latter that enable us to identify an event or an object as discrete entities: "what we perceive easily is difference and change – and difference is a relationship" (Bateson and Ruesch 1951). So, rather than the degree of similarity, it is the relationship we construct around two elements that gives substance to analogic reasoning. In fact, a pairing of two concepts that are similar is not even perceived as a metaphor but as a tautological statement or a definition ('a corporation is an organization'). Analogously, when concepts are too distant, the connection is lost and the analogy becomes practically meaningless (as in the statement 'our recruiting system is magnesium').

Relationships can take several forms; indeed, there are several types of analogies used in language, based on different relationships between source and target. Rhetoric recognizes four master 'tropes', or figures of speech: in addition to metaphors we encounter metonymy, synecdoche and irony. All are based on the juxtaposition of two concepts but are the expression of different types of relationships: resemblance, part-whole or whole-part substitution, and contradiction, respectively (Oswick, Putnam and Keenoy 2004).

Thus, in *metonymy*, a part of an object is used to replace the whole, for instance when workers are defined as 'blue collars', from one element of their attire. *Synecdoche* follows the same substitution logic but in reverse, using the whole to represent a part. This is the case of the manager telling a subordinate 'the company is unhappy with your performance', thus taking upon him-/herself the identity of an entire organization in order to reinforce the legitimacy of the reprimand (Oswick et al. 2002). In the case of *irony* (and *paradox)* figurative speech is based on contrast, rather than similitude. This happens for instance when an oxymoron (e.g. 'an oppressing freedom') is used. These dissimilarities can be very effective tools to expand our visual field, generating new meanings and challenging received wisdoms (Oswick et al. 2002). In this regard they are useful in producing a breakdown in normality by distancing, estrangement and defamiliarization (Ybema and Kamsteeg 2009). Irony can facilitate the emersion of tacit and taken-for-granted discursive components by ridiculing, lampooning or contradicting commonplace ways of acting and speaking.

Different tropes can reveal different aspects about our object of enquiry. Saying that 'discourse is text' (a metonymy) is useful shorthand but neglects some aspects while putting others on the forefront (Tsoukas 1993; Oswick et al. 2002). Using a metaphor, for instance saying that discourse is a map (see Chapter 4), opens more heuristic possibilities because the juxtaposition of ideas from different domains enables the emergence of new meaning and new insight into an object of discussion (Cornelissen 2005). The use of these two tropes is not mutually exclusive: for instance metaphors and metonymy are strongly interrelated and their interplay can generate different types of meaning relationships between the source and the target domains, offering different heuristic possibilities (Schoencborn et al. 2016). By looking at discourses as ways of organizing (Chapter 5) I will fully employ this metonymy–metaphor dynamic. Finally, arguing that discourse is given substance not by a clear referent but by a central lack, by the impossibility to describe, symbolize or to ground its core concepts (Cederström and Spicer 2014), we are utilizing a paradox that not only generates an incremental form of learning but opens completely new understandings of the idea (something to be explored further in Chapter 6).

Using tropes based on dissimilarities poses dangers. Since any juxtaposition of words is theoretically possible, we might end up with a sophistic use of the analogy, using it as a device with which to parade rhetorical skills. Commentators interpreting complex organizational phenomena might be tempted to fabricate implausible associations with the mere intent of astounding their audience, flaunting their ability to provide a justification for creative pairings of meaning. One could, for instance, suggest that 'a corporation is like an asparagus' and then proceed to justify that statement by arguing that this simile highlights how it includes both high-value assets (the tip) and apparently worthless parts (the stem) which are instead essential for its existence; or that it can thrive in difficult environments provided that is adequately tended; maybe even that stakeholders interacting with it can extract value but will also be cursed by undesired side effects! Such a forced use of the powers of language is often practised by 'management gurus' who employ contrasts and eccentric analogies to grab attention and to persuade readers of the validity of their less than robust organizational theories and managerial recipes (Greatbatch and Clark 2005). In other words, it is possible to harness the power of tropes not for the purpose of empowering heuristic sensibility but merely to *bullshit* the audience. 'Bullshitting' does not simply mean to lie but rather it represents a use of language unconcerned with the truth that is deployed instrumentally to promote the purposes and interests of the bullshitter (Frankfurt 2005).

The possibility of a misuse of analogic representations does not entail that one should stick exclusively to the safe ground of commonly used metaphors. Neither does it suggest that it is opportune to establish formal boundaries to constitute a 'correct' comparison on the basis of a quantifiable level of semantic overlapping between the two conceptual domains being associated. It is rather a matter of keeping the use of metaphors grounded or 'performatively relevant'. With this formula I refer to two connected aspects. In the first place, since the similitudes on which they are founded are not pre-existent but are constructed by the very use of metaphors, they are "primarily a matter of thought and action and only derivatively a matter of language" (Lakoff and Johnson 1980, p. 153). Second, this social metaphorical behaviour is better investigated not as a separate object of knowledge but by engaging in an investigation based on a pragmatic rationality (Sandberg and Tsoukas 2011), which accepts the impossibility of transcending the examined phenomenology. Doing such investigation involves embracing a form of knowledge that is intrinsically involved and critical rather than detached and disinterested.

To paraphrase (Flyvbjerg (2004, p. 405) we should enquire "where are we going [with this metaphor]? Who gains and who loses, and by which mechanisms of power [by virtue of its use]? Is this [generation of meaning] desirable? What, if anything, should we do about it?"

Such an approach to the use of metaphors as research tools is explicitly based on the Aristotelian concept of *phronesis*, or 'practical wisdom', an intellectual virtue that transcends both analytic knowledge (*episteme*) and technical know-how (*techne*), and that implies using the understanding we gain from our enquiry to inform future choices (Flyvbjerg 2001; Flyvbjerg, Landman and Schram 2012). This implies recognizing that metaphors as more than mere rhetorical embellishment or effective means to clarify ideas to a non-specialist audience. It means acknowledging that they have concrete cognitive and performative effects, deriving from the fact that different metaphors will reveal (or hide) different possibilities of cognition and action, both by shaping cognition and by inducing particular dispositions and affects. Calling the person in charge of a change management initiative a 'director' will produce completely different consequences from considering the person a 'nurturer' (Palmer and Dunford 1996; Palmer, Akin and Dunford 2008). Similarly, thinking of discourse as a discipline constructing subjectivity will set us on a totally different course from conceiving of it as the sum of traces left by symbolic interaction.

Considering the pragmatic outcomes of different metaphors enables us also to overcome the epistemological nihilism that could stem from acknowledging the relativity of truth. Even if "the hardening and congealing of a metaphor guarantees absolutely nothing concerning its necessity" (Nietzsche 1873 [1990], p. 893), their use can deploy concrete effects. With all their biases, the intersubjective agreements that are achieved by virtue of the analogical power of metaphors have, as any social constructions do, tangible consequences: "if men define situations as real, they are real in their consequences" (Thomas and Thomas 1928, p. 572, cited in Merton 1995, p. 380). To consider these different effects we need to understand the different social functions that metaphors can perform. The observation of the entangled relationship between cognition and metaphors makes it problematic to analyse the 'mechanics' of metaphorical production: "the question, 'How do metaphors work?' is somewhat similar to the question, 'How does one thing remind us of another thing?' There is no single answer to either question" (Searle 1979, p. x). Since it is futile to determine whether the 'linguistic' egg comes a priori of the observed 'chicken', it is more productive to focus on the performative effects of metaphors. In this regard it is very useful to consider, following Davidson (1978), that metaphors, similarly to jokes, have a *point*, which someone gets and others miss. Understanding what is the point that a metaphor makes means highlighting their function as interpretive and political instruments.

THE FUNCTIONS OF METAPHORS: A DESCRIPTIVE MODEL

Metaphors are indeed put to many different uses, becoming "pervasive in everyday life" (Lakoff and Johnson 1980, p. 3). To analyse all the multiple ways in which they are employed one can use a simple diagram to position alternative accounts of how the power of metaphors can be expressed. Two dimensions outline the diagram: the axis descriptive-generative and the axis denotative-connotative.

The first dimension refers to the two alternative ways of conceiving metaphors: either as rhetorical devices, the purpose of which is to enable communication, by illustrating and describing; or as cognitive tools, constitutive of meaning and social reality. The first view is coherent with Ortony (1975), with his description of the instrumental role of metaphors in overcoming a structural inadequacy of language and logic. These are systems based on discrete symbols and therefore they are ineffective in describing experiences that are continuous flows. Metaphors help fill the gap between analogic and digital by transferring some chosen character-istics from one domain ('the vehicle') to another one ('the topic'), assisting the recipients' sensemaking processes by offering an analogy with a better-known experience, conveying inexpressible feelings and ideas and helping to visualize experiences (Ortony 1975). As such they facilitate and enrich communication, by embellishing, clarifying and concentrating information (Pablo and Hardy 2009); as such, they are instruments to represent, describe and transmit complex experiences and ideas.

The alternative view considers the 'generative' potential of metaphors, that is, their capacity to create meaning (Schön 1993). The way in which metaphors construct our cognition is well represented by our constant use of 'ontological metaphors' in everyday language. These are the implicit analogies that we use to define our experiences and which prompt us to think in terms of objects and substances, thus enabling us to treat complex phenomena as discrete entities (Lakoff and Johnson 1980, pp. 25–9). Metaphorical understanding often trumps scientific knowledge or philosophical sophistication: in their everyday dealings physicists treat time as a quantifiable element even if they are well aware of Einstein's lessons; similarly, it is possible that even a post-modern sociologist may be likely to use an essentialist vocabulary when referring to power ('I don't have the power to do so'), despite a firm conviction in the relational nature of the concept. Metaphors might bias perception but they can also reveal new meanings, since they possess a "heuristic quality in opening up new and multiple ways of seeing, conceptualizing, and understanding organizational phenomena" (Cornelissen 2005, p. 753). Such effects apply to the academic organizational discourse, in which metaphors "operate as creative catalysts in organizational theory building" (Boxenbaum and Rouleau 2011, p. 276).

The differentiation between descriptive and generative metaphors has been presented in terms of the *impact* of the metaphor (Pablo and Hardy 2009). On the one hand there are purely cosmetic analogies, such as those that Black (1993, cited in Pablo and Hardy 2009) defines as 'weak' or 'replaceable'. These "superficial metaphors" are used both "to 'dress up' speech and text in order to make it more palatable and in some case more memorable [... or] to aid the process of making the complex appear simple" (Grant and Oswick 1996, p. 216): as such, they are merely a communication tool. On the other hand it is possible to identify 'high impact' metaphors, which directly shape people's understanding of phenomena and which cannot be easily replaced. According to Grant and Oswick (1996, p. 217) these "meaningful metaphors are discovered rather than created", in the sense that they emerge from particular discourses rather than being applied or 'imposed' by one commentator.

The concept of *root* metaphors implies depictions that express a fundamental, underlying worldview and act as symbolic frameworks (Smith and Eisenberg 1987; Ashcraft, Kuhn and Cooren 2009). The paradox of the deep embedding of metaphors in cognition is that metaphors can become so deeply ingrained in our way of making sense of things that they become "dead metaphors" (Lakoff and Johnson 1980, pp. 211–13; Chia 1996). These have "become sedimented through habitual use" (Hogler et al. 2008, p. 408): examples include the use of the word 'digest' for an abridged book, or using the expression 'a chair leg'. When we encounter an utterance such as 'we must improve our (organizational) machine', it is therefore important to understand whether this usage conveys a particular paradigmatic view of an organization or whether the two terms are merely used as synonyms.

The second dimension, the denotation-connotation axis, is intended to capture a distinction that is underplayed in most of the above-mentioned literature. It is implicitly assumed that much of the meaning that is carried forward from the source to the target domain is denotative. However, metaphors, as a rhetorical device, can also be intended to persuade or to arouse specific emotions in the audience, their primary function being "the conversion of the subject from one state to another" (Hopfl and Maddrell 1996, p. 211). They operate through the "predication of a sign-image upon an inchoate subject" for which they provide identity (Fernandez 1974, p. 120), leading to the notion that the 'movement' achieved by the metaphor is not just a movement of conceptual content but also a movement in terms of emotional stirring (Hopfl and Maddrell 1996). Such usage draws attention to the expressive and implicitly conative functions of language; that is, its capacity to convey emotions and to incite the receiver to action (Jakobson 1960). The use of metaphors as a rhetorical instrument of political persuasion is well documented (Charteris-Black 2005): in organizational studies Czarniawska (2004) has shown how metaphors are used to dramatize and sensationalize events, with controversial outcomes; in the entrepreneurial literature Lundmark and Westelius (2014) highlighted the use of dissimilar images for entrepreneurship (as elixir or as mutagen) which are loaded with distinctive connotations, thus serving different purposes and interests.

Differentiating between the connotative and denotative components of the meaning that is transferred from one domain to the other does not imply that there will be either denotative *or* connotative transfer, since both components are usually associated. It rather indicates that a particular association, either by design or as a consequence of an emergent usage, deploys its effects predominantly by arousing affects or stimulating an aesthetic experience or by articulating ideas and connecting attributes. A useful exemplification is offered by the catalogue of body/medical metaphors used in popular management discourse to describe the internal conditions of pre-downsized firms that Dunford and Palmer (1996, p. 100) record: companies are defined as "overweight", "fat", "bloated" or even "constipated". While the explanatory potential of these tropes is clearly limited and open to the use of ironic counter-metaphors (if the organization is constipated then change management consultants are a laxative?) the type of imagery they evoke is clearly meant to demonstrate the necessity of the 'cure', to project a healthier and fitter future for the organization, to implicitly delegitimize resistance to the downsizing and, finally, to reduce the station of the employees being downsized to that of excess fat, if not ordure. By contrast, the type of metaphors of change management which the same authors identify in other works (Palmer and Dunford 1996; Palmer et al. 2008) represent the change manager as a coach, a navigator, or a director; these certainly have emotional implications but mostly as a device to project different philosophies of management and organizational transformation, succinctly conveying alternative possibilities of actions, constraints and opportunities.

Once crossed, the two axes inscribe four possible functions of metaphors (Figure 3.1). The *decorative* purpose indicates that the trope is used to describe and facilitate communication, making "novel connections with a distinctive flourish" (Pablo and Hardy 2009, p. 823). In this sense they are a stylistic device that also can be used for pedagogic purposes, aiding memorization of complex unfamiliar concepts thanks to their visual properties (Ortony 1975). If instead the emphasis is more on the content being transmitted, the value of the metaphor is *informative*, being used as a tool to succinctly transmit complex information. By facilitating communication, metaphors are unavoidably enriching its content, activating a circular process of meaning making based on indexicality and reflexivity (Garfinkel 1967). Metaphors have an indexical function since they ground an abstract idea by using a concrete example, acting ostensively to indicate a tangible entity with which to illustrate a concept. For instance the use of metaphors such as 'theatre', 'game' or 'battle' enables managers to reconcile practical experiences and theory in their talk and links complex organizational phenomena with well-known experiences (Latusek and Vlaar 2015). Metaphors also have a reflexive use, making a specific phenomenon meaningful by classifying it as an instance of a general category or pattern, thus showing that this unique experience is simply a reflection of a recurrent idea. When organizations are represented in terms of biological organisms or as pieces of machinery (Burns and Stalker 1966; Morgan 2006) they are also presented as specific cases of a broader class of phenomena or forms of existence.

On the other side of the diagram we find the more explicitly generative consequences of metaphors. These can occur in two different forms: when a trope is predominantly based on the transfer of denotative information it becomes a *constructive* element, either in the form of a purposely generated heuristic instrument or interpretive tool, or a spontaneously emergent root metaphor. When instead the accent is on the connotative components, we have situations in which the metaphor is used as a persuasive rhetoric instrument, to make emotional appeals (Sillince 1999) or to make an identity and legitimacy claim (Sillince and Brown 2009). Metaphors can also make use of connotative transfer to produce aesthetic understanding (Strati 2010), achieving knowledge that is sensible (i.e. perceived through the senses) rather than ratiocinative (Strati 2007). Such aesthetic apprehension of meaning is integral to organizational life and permits the inclusion of tacit aspects of knowledge that defy any attempts at codification and standardization.

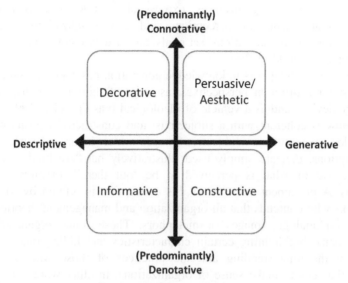

Figure 3.1   Functions of metaphors

Figure 3.1 is not intended as a mapping device to situate different metaphors but as a way to represent and relate the multiple pragmatic uses of metaphorical language. Any given metaphor can deploy its effect in more than one quadrant. For instance the metaphor of organizations as machines is, at the same time, constructive, informative, persuasive and decorative. The capacity to operate at different levels, both helping to describe and to produce meaning, to count attributes and to arouse emotional responses, can account for the success and robustness of different metaphors in use. As such it will be used to 'design' the particular metaphors that I am going to employ in the following chapters to expand upon our understanding of organizational discourse, to communicate it effectively and, hopefully, to encourage its use. However, before doing this it will be useful to consider the use of metaphor in management and organization studies.

METAPHORS IN MANAGEMENT AND ORGANIZATION STUDIES

The plasticity and multiple uses of metaphors and analogies have not been lost on organizational scholars: "In organizational studies, metaphors contribute to theory construction, help to structure beliefs and guide behavior in organizations, express abstract ideas, convey vivid images that orient our perceptions and conceptualizations, transfer information, legitimate actions, set goals, and structure coherent systems" (Hogler et al. 2008, p. 396).

The role of metaphors in knowledge generation has been interpreted in at least three different perspectives: as ways of thinking, as disposable literary devices and as a vehicle of ideological bias (Tsoukas 1993). The first view is coherent with a subjectivist and constructivist position and considers metaphors as subjective images which incorporate particular assumptions, that are simply used illustratively but "are fundamentally constitutive of what is perceived to be 'out there'" (Tsoukas 1993, p. 325). A prominent example of this conception is offered by Morgan (2006),[1] who contends that all organization and management theories are based on analogic images or metaphors. These frame organizational phenomena, highlighting certain characteristics and hiding others, thus shaping the understanding and the practices of those who use that particular lens to make sense of organizations: in other words their use "implies a way of thinking and a way of seeing" (Morgan 2006, p. 12). It is therefore preferable to consider several alternative metaphors of organizations in order to gain a well-rounded comprehension of their complex reality. Another influential manifestation of this use of metaphor as a generator of variety and meaning is the concept of theory generation as "disciplined imagination" (Weick 1989; Cornelissen 2006), which considers the centrality of the role of metaphors as a vehicle for the production of new theoretical representations.

On the opposite end of the spectrum, realist and positivist approaches to social reality argue the necessity to shun (or at least to limit) the use of figurative language in the account of social phenomena because, it is thought, metaphors are imprecise, lack objectivity and are potentially confusing. They elicit idiosyncratic emotional responses confounding data and representations; even borrowing concepts from other scientific fields is risky because the lack of disciplinary expertise can result in "pushing the metaphor too far" (Tsoukas 1993).

The third perspective recognizes the potential value of metaphors but warns about the ideological distortions that they can conceal: "the use of metaphors resides at the centre of the politics of management theory and practice" (Alvesson and Willmott 2012, p. 87). It is therefore important to reflect critically on the political consequences of the application of a particular metaphor (Tsoukas 1993).

---

[1]   The title of my book is an explicit homage to this landmark contribution.

All these different uses of metaphors as research tools have limitations: the 'way of thinking' proponents typically fail to explain how different images develop and how some gain more currency than others. For its part, the 'objectivist' view, rejecting the use of metaphors, underestimates the rhetorical potential of metaphors and ignores that hypothesis generation requires some pre-existing image of the phenomenon to be investigated. Finally, some critical views appear founded on the doubtful claim that it is possible to produce a truly independent or absolutely 'non-oppressive' descriptive framework (Tsoukas 1993).

Cornelissen (2006) offers a completely different take on the issue of the function of metaphors in organizational theory. By examining the aforementioned idea of disciplined imagination (Weick 1989), he strives to determine the factors that make a metaphor 'apt' to be used as a source of theoretical imagination. Considering the constraints under which the blending of meaning from different conceptual domains characterize metaphors, he identifies eight 'optimality principles' in the literature that can assist researchers "consciously assess whether a metaphor connects a target concept with a source that is concrete, relational and distant and that includes a representation with different relations and elements which can be unpacked and integrated with it" (Cornelissen 2006, p. 1591). These principles include:

1. *Integration principle* (representations in the metaphorical blend can be manipulated as a single unit);
2. *Topology principle* (relations in the metaphorical blend should match the relations of their counterparts in other semantic domains);
3. *Web principle* (representation in the metaphorical blend should maintain a relationship to the input target and source concepts);
4. *Unpacking principle* (given a metaphorical blend, the interpreter should be able to infer the structure in relation to other subjects and applications);
5. *Good reason principle* (that creates pressure to attribute significance to elements in the metaphorical blend);
6. *Metonymic tightening principle* (when metonymically related elements are projected into the metaphorical blend, there is pressure to compress the 'distance' between them);
7. *Distance principle* (the target and source concepts need to come from semantically distant semantic domains);
8. *Concreteness principle* (the source concept compared to the target is sufficiently concrete to be understood and manipulated). (Adapted from Cornelissen 2006, p. 1588)

This list of principles can be interpreted as a checklist to predict and explain the success of a metaphor. The idea that some metaphors can be more 'apt' than others because of their compliance with a set of optimality principles is intriguing but it appears to clash with a constructivist view of language. To assume that metaphors have a set of discrete attributes that can be precisely measured and assessed against some benchmark means treating them as neutral objects, and also to neglect completely their connotative aspects (indeed, Cornelisson does not mention the emotional impact of metaphors in the list). This aspect reveals a fundamental allegiance of the optimality model to the Cartesian and positivistic notion of knowledge and theory as context-free, observer-independent and disembodied.

Moreover, empirical observation appears to disconfirm the explanatory value of the optimality principles. Two metaphors that Weick generated and employed, organizational improvisation as jazz (Weick 1998) and organizational behaviour as a collective mind (Weick and Roberts 1993), and that 'tick the boxes' of metaphorical aptness, have been very influential in the academic literature but have had minimal impact on the practice of management. Contrast this with the success of a metaphor such as 'the blue ocean strategy' (Kim and Mauborgne 2005a, 2005b). Kim and Mauborgne formulate the idea that companies should aim to create an uncontested market space (which is like a blue ocean) rather than competing with other sharks for prey in mature markets, creating bloodstained waters that attract more competitors. Irrespective of the actual validity of this theory, the idea of blue ocean strategy has become part of standard managerial talk. Even in the context of academic discourse its impact has not been negligible, with one of Kim and Mauborgne's papers (2005a) receiving more than 2000 citations to date (less than the 'collective mind' paper, but many more than the 'jazz' one). The issue here is not to weight the importance of one contribution against the other but rather to reflect on the factors that have an effect on the propagation of a metaphor as well as to highlight how the successful 'blue ocean' metaphor does not appear to satisfy any of Cornelissen's optimality principles, with the sole exception of the distance principle.

To account for the pragmatic, performative effects of metaphors fully, as well as the intertwinement of emotions, context and rationality that characterizes their existence, I propose that the heuristic potential of metaphors can be better harnessed using an *abductive* epistemological framework, rather than one that is deductive or inductive. A deductive view of metaphors implies a syllogism in which the metaphor is the major premise and a specific phenomenon is the minor premise. Thus the metaphor acts as schemata, a theory-in-use that influences organizational behaviour and change (Marshak 1996). Deduction provides the typical way in which metaphor-based analysis is employed in organization studies (Palmer and Dunford 1996). If we consider the constructive role of metaphor it is impossible to transcend its use, which impairs the possibilities of a critical analysis: critical scholars could be seen as merely promoting their favourite metaphors (e.g. 'organization as oppression' versus 'organization as a wealth producing machine'). The incommensurability between these alternative interpretations makes any dialectic resolution highly problematic, producing a shouting match between deaf people.

An inductive approach, such as that proposed by Weick (1989) and expanded by Cornelissen (2006) is predicated on the assumption that it is possible to formulate a general theory of metaphor, an enterprise that is fraught with difficulties and controversies, as an attempt at a general theory of language. Moreover the effects of a metaphor cannot be fully predicted because of their intertextual character: they will activate different meaning-making processes in different receivers, depending on the web of further metaphorical connections. If they display coherence (Marshak 1996) it is not because of some design principles but because an intersubjective agreement has been reached through their usage and effects.

The notion of abductive reasoning (Rowe 1987) can offer an alternative. In abduction, solutions are found intuitively by formulating plausible connections between causes and effects and then by testing them in action, using this experience to further refine them. It is an iterative process, one that requires "selective inattention", involving backtracking and switching between different heuristics (Rowe 1987, pp. 102–9). Abductive logic, the logic of what might be (Dunne and Martin 2006), is therefore based on tinkering and experimenting rather than on the application of predetermined principles (Schön 1983). Consequently, the knowledge that is developed is context bound (an abductive solution is not universally valid but only within the context in which it has been developed). The simple model presented above describing the possible functions of metaphors (Figure 3.1) is meant to be employed in this framework. It is neither a prescriptive nor a descriptive model of what a metaphor to be applied in social practice and theory should be but rather a set of design principles that can be used to test how well a metaphor can perform in a particular context, in terms of its capacity to inform, decorate, persuade and construct new meaning. Such design is consistent with the idea of starting research by producing 'mystery' by means of a breakdown (Alvesson and Kärreman 2007) and with the model of "top down inductive reasoning" proposed by Shepherd and Sutcliffe (2011).

An abductive view of metaphor considers the production, use and assessment of metaphors in the context of social practices, thus eschewing the Cartesian separation between body and mind (Gherardi 2012, p. 207). Doing so avoids overemphasizing the importance of rationality in organizational settings, as is the tendency with Morgan's eight metaphors; moreover, it allows us to consider metaphors that place components of absurdity and disorder in the foreground (McCabe 2016). Since abduction also relies on the generation of new possibilities to be tested and employed in the further 'learning by tinkering' process it is also useful in considering alternative ways to generate new metaphors. Örtenblad, Putnam and Trehan (2016) suggest that at least three generative mechanisms are available to scholars: from empirical observation, though conceptual development based on the comparison of tropes that are already in use (for instance developing meta-metaphors), or by extending the relationship between the source and the target domains (for instance building on the view of organizations as political systems to develop other 'political' metaphors). However, as noted before, metaphors have features in common with jokes: like jokes their origins are often mysterious and, at any rate, usually less important than their effects. In this regard an abductive framework offers the opportunity of treating metaphors as tools to probe the possibilities of knowledge offered by the application of a discourse perspective to the study of organizations.

INTRODUCING SOME IMAGES OF ORGANIZATIONAL DISCOURSE

By making a summary review of the characteristics, uses and consequences of metaphors in the context of organizational scholarship and practice, the choice of some specific metaphors that I will employ in the following chapters to expand and articulate the discussion on organizational discourse has been introduced and explained. These specific metaphors are not intended as root metaphors that can be empirically traced in the extant literature on discourse, even if in several cases previous examples of such use can be found. As designed metaphors, they have the purpose of both illustrating and enabling the emergence of new knowledge and meaning. No single metaphor can have the pretence of being exhaustive: on the contrary each metaphor highlights particular aspects and implications of organizational discourse, seen both as a category of phenomena and as a heuristic device.

Discourse as a Map

As a metaphor, discourse considered as a map focuses on the role of differences and contrapositions and how they can be used to describe and compare discourses, identifying areas of tension that can become generative of transformation or that mark the borders between alternative discourses. The map is not the territory but in practice it produces our understanding of geography, and the act of mapping shapes our territorial thinking and behaviour. Its conventional symbols (for instance the tracing of a national border) invoke and activate concrete performances and feelings. Analogously discourse is not reality but its forms define our experience and understanding of experience.

Discourse as Organizing

Discourse and organizing appear to be intrinsically connected: any organization produces discourses but organizing is also enabled by existing discourses. Discourse is indeed an organizing device, and there are many parallels between how discourse and organizations deploy their effects. The organizing metaphor also highlights how discourses define fields of action where individual actors and groups compete for supremacy, strategically making use of the dominant discourse. It also highlights how the normative aspects of the discourse do not create an 'even pitch' where players can compete fairly but how some positions are privileged over others. At the same time, the set of rules, constraints and 'normal modes of action' that each discourse imposes on actors leave space for individual tactics which, in turn, allow the reproduction of the discourse as happens in any sporting activity: it is only thanks to the players' actions that a game comes to life. Using this idea helps us reflect on the different meanings of organizing and consequently how language and discourse can be employed in different ways to create and maintain organization.

Discourse as Attire (or Mask)

The final mask metaphor is employed to stress the capacity of discourse to produce subjectivities and identities but also to draw attention to the paradoxical 'emptiness' of discourse. Each discourse pigeonholes the variety of human expression, with their emotionally and intellectually subtle differences and unevenness of desires, into standardized roles. Similar to the masks used in Greek tragedy, in the Noh theatre or in *Commedia dell'arte* they set limits on the possibilities of individual expression and they lock characters in set pieces, limiting and enabling their collective performances. The metaphor also helps us in reflecting on the discourse of organizational studies, discussing the role of fashions and fads, and on the vices and virtues of emptiness.

As discussed in this chapter these metaphors are to be considered as heuristic devices which I will use to probe and critically reflect on the implications and applications of looking at organizations through a discursive lens. I will also employ them as rhetorical devices, to present in a meaningful and coherent manner different theories and perspectives that are either directly inspired or indirectly influenced by a 'linguistic' informed apprehension of organizational phenomena.

REFERENCES

Alvesson, M. and Kärreman, D. 2007, 'Constructing Mystery: Empirical Matters in Theory Development', *The Academy of Management Review*, vol. 32, pp. 1265–81.
Alvesson, M. and Willmott, H. 2012, *Making Sense of Management: A Critical Introduction*, SAGE, London.
Ashcraft, K.L., Kuhn, T.R. and Cooren, F. 2009, 'Constitutional Amendments: "Materializing" Organizational Communication', *The Academy of Management Annals*, vol. 3, no. 1, pp. 1–64.
Bateson, G. and Ruesch, J. 1951, *Communication, the Social Matrix of Psychiatry*, Norton, New York.
Black, M. 1979, 'More about Metaphor', in A. Ortony (ed.), *Metaphor and Thought*, Cambridge University Press, Cambridge, UK.
Boxenbaum, E. and Rouleau, L. 2011, 'New Knowledge Products as Bricolage: Metaphors and Scripts in Organizational Theory', *Academy of Management Review*, vol. 36, no. 2, pp. 272–96.
Burns, T. and Stalker, G.M. 1966, *The Management of Innovation*, vol. SSP 6, Tavistock, London.
Cederström, C. and Spicer, A. 2014, 'Discourse of the Real Kind: A Postfoundational Approach to Organizational Discourse Analysis', *Organization*, vol. 21, no. 2, pp. 178–205.
Charteris-Black, J. 2005, *Politicians and Rhetoric: The Persuasive Power of Metaphor*, Palgrave Macmillan, Basingstoke, UK.
Chia, R. 1996, 'Metaphors and Metaphorization in Organizational Analysis: Thinking Beyond the Thinkable', in D. Grant and C. Oswick (eds), *Metaphor and Organizations*, SAGE, London, pp. 127–46.

Cicero, M.T. 55 BCE [2001], *Cicero on the Ideal Orator*, trans. J.M. May and J. Wisse, Oxford University Press, New York.

Cornelissen, J.P. 2005, 'Beyond Compare: Metaphor in Organization Theory', *The Academy of Management Review*, vol. 30, pp. 751–64.

Cornelissen, J.P. 2006, 'Making Sense of Theory Construction: Metaphor and Disciplined Imagination', *Organization Studies*, vol. 27, no. 11, pp. 1579–97.

Czarniawska, B. 2004, 'Metaphors as Enemies of Organizing, or the Advantages of a Flat Discourse', *International Journal of the Sociology of Language*, vol. 2004, pp. 45–65.

Damasio, A. 2006, *Descartes Error*, 2nd edn, Vintage, London.

Davidson, D. 1978, 'What Metaphors Mean', *Critical Inquiry*, vol. 5, no. 1, pp. 31–47.

Dunford, R. and Palmer, I. 1996, 'Metaphors in Popular Management Discourse: The Case of Corporate Restructuring', in D. Grant and C. Oswick (eds), *Metaphor and Organizations*, SAGE, London, pp. 95–109.

Dunne, D. and Martin, R. 2006, 'Design Thinking and How it Will Change Management Education: An Interview and Discussion', *Academy of Management Learning & Education*, vol. 5, p. 512.

Fernandez, J.W. 1974, 'The Mission of Metaphor in Expressive Culture', *Current Anthropology*, vol. 15, no. 2, pp. 119–45.

Flyvbjerg, B. 2001, *Making Social Science Matter: Why Social Inquiry Fails and How it Can Succeed Again*, Cambridge University Press, Cambridge, UK.

Flyvbjerg, B. 2004, 'A Perestroikan Straw Man Answers Back: David Laitin and Phronetic Political Science', *Politics & Society*, vol. 32, pp. 389–416.

Flyvbjerg, B., Landman, T. and Schram, S. 2012, *Real Social Science: Applied Phronesis*, Cambridge University Press, Cambridge, UK.

Frankfurt, H.G. 2005, *On Bullshit*, Princeton University Press, Princeton, NJ.

Garfinkel, H. 1967, *Studies in Ethnomethodology*, Prentice Hall, Englewood Cliffs, NJ.

Gherardi, S. 2012, *How to Conduct a Practice-based Study: Problems and Methods*, Edward Elgar Publishing, Cheltenham, UK and Northampton, MA, USA.

Grant, D. and Oswick, C. 1996, 'The Organization of Metaphors and the Metaphors of Organization: Where are we and Where do we Go from Here', in D. Grant and C. Oswick (eds), *Metaphor and Organizations*, SAGE, London, pp. 213–26.

Greatbatch, D. and Clark, T. 2005, *Management Speak: Why we Listen to What Management Gurus Tell Us*, Psychology Press, New York.

Hogler, R., Gross, M.A., Hartman, J.L. and Cunliffe, A.L. 2008, 'Meaning in Organizational Communication: Why Metaphor is the Cake, not the Icing', *Management Communication Quarterly*, vol. 21, no. 3, pp. 393–412.

Hopfl, H. and Maddrell, J. 1996, 'Can you Resist a Dream? Evangelical Metaphors and the Appropriation of Emotion', in D. Grant and C. Oswick (eds), *Metaphor and Organizations*, SAGE, London, pp. 200–12.

Jakobson, R. 1960, 'Closing Statement: Linguistics and Poetics', in T.A. Sebeok (ed.), *Style in Language*, John Wiley & Sons, New York, pp. 350–77.

Kahneman, D. 2011, *Thinking, Fast and Slow*, Farrar, Straus and Giroux, New York.

Kim, W.C. and Mauborgne, R. 2005a, 'Blue Ocean Strategy: From Theory to Practice', *California Management Review*, vol. 47, no. 3, pp. 105–21.

Kim, W.C. and Mauborgne, R. 2005b, *Blue Ocean Strategy: How to Create Uncontested Market Space and Make the Competition Irrelevant*, Harvard University Press, Boston, MA.

Kristeva, J. 1980, *Desire in Language: A Semiotic Approach to Literature and Art*, Basil Blackwell, Oxford.

Lakoff, G. and Johnson, M. 1980, *Metaphors we Live By*, University of Chicago Press, Chicago, IL.

Latusek, D. and Vlaar, P.W. 2015, 'Exploring Managerial Talk through Metaphor: An Opportunity to Bridge Rigour and Relevance?', *Management Learning*, vol. 46, no. 2, pp. 211–32.

Lundmark, E. and Westelius, A. 2014, 'Entrepreneurship as Elixir and Mutagen', *Entrepreneurship Theory and Practice*, vol. 38, no. 3, pp. 575–600.

Marshak, R.J. 1996, 'Metaphors, Metaphoric Field and Organizational Change', in D. Grant and C. Oswick (eds), *Metaphor and Organizations*, SAGE, London, pp. 147–65.

McCabe, D. 2016, '"Curiouser and curiouser!": Organizations as Wonderland – A Metaphorical Alternative to the Rational Model', *Human Relations*, vol. 69, no. 4, pp. 945–73.

Merton, R.K. 1995, 'The Thomas Theorem and the Matthew Effect', *Social Forces*, vol. 74, pp. 379–422.

Morgan, G. 2006, *Images of Organization*, SAGE Publications, Thousand Oaks, CA.

Morgan, G. 2016, 'Commentary: Beyond Morgan's Eight Metaphors', *Human Relations*, vol. 69, no. 4, pp. 1029–42.

Nietzsche, F. 1873 [1990], 'On Truth and Lies in a Nonmoral Sense', in P. Bizzell and B. Herzberg (eds), *The Rhetorical Tradition: Fredrich Nietzsche. Readings from Classical Times to the Present*, Bedford Books, Boston, MA, pp. 888–96.

Örtenblad, A., Putnam, L.L. and Trehan, K. 2016, 'Beyond Morgan's Eight Metaphors: Adding to and Developing Organization Theory', *Human Relations*, vol. 69, no. 4, pp. 875–89.

Ortony, A. 1975, 'Why Metaphors are Necessary and not just Nice', *Educational Theory*, vol. 25, no. 1, pp. 45–53.

Oswick, C., Keenoy, T. and Grant, D. 2002, 'Note: Metaphor and Analogical Reasoning in Organization Theory: Beyond Orthodoxy', *Academy of Management Review*, vol. 27, no. 2, pp. 294–303.

Oswick, C., Putnam, L. and Keenoy, T. 2004, 'Tropes, Discourse and Organizing', in D. Grant, C. Hardy, C. Oswick and L.L. Putnam (eds), *The SAGE Handbook of Organizational Discourse*, SAGE, London, pp. 105–27.

Pablo, Z. and Hardy, C. 2009, 'Merging, Masquerading and Morphing: Metaphors and the World Wide Web', *Organization Studies*, vol. 30, no. 8, pp. 821–43.

Palmer, I. and Dunford, R. 1996, 'Conflicting Uses of Metaphors: Reconceptualizing their Use in the Field of Organizational Change', *Academy of Management Review*, vol. 21, no. 3, pp. 691–717.

Palmer, I., Akin, G. and Dunford, R. 2008, *Managing Organizational Change: A Multiple Perspectives Approach*, McGraw-Hill Higher Education, Boston, MA.

Rowe, P.G. 1987, *Design Thinking*, The MIT Press, Cambridge, MA.

Sandberg, J. and Tsoukas, H. 2011, 'Grasping the Logic of Practice: Theorizing through Practical Rationality', *Academy of Management Review*, vol. 36, p. 338.

Schoeneborn, D., Vásquez, C. and Cornelissen, J. 2016, 'Imagining Organization through Metaphor and Metonymy: Unpacking the Process-Entity Paradox', *Human Relations*, vol. 69, no. 4, pp. 915–44.

Schön, D.A. 1983, *The Reflective Practitioner: How Professionals Think in Action*, Basic Books, New York.

Schön, D. 1993, 'Generative Metaphor: A Perspective on Problem-setting in Social Policy', in A. Ortony (ed.), *Metaphor and Thought*, Cambridge University Press, Cambridge, pp. 137–63.

Searle, J.R. 1979, *Expression and Meaning: Studies in the Theory of Speech Acts*, Cambridge University Press, Cambridge, UK.

Shepherd, D.A. and Sutcliffe, K.M. 2011, 'Inductive Top-down Theorizing: A Source of New Theories of Organization', *Academy of Management Review*, vol. 36, no. 2, pp. 361–80.

Sillince, J.A.A. 1999, 'The Role of Political Language Forms and Language Coherence in the Organizational Change Process', *Organization Studies*, vol. 20, pp. 485–518.

Sillince, J.A.A. and Brown, A.D. 2009, 'Multiple Organizational Identities and Legitimacy: The Rhetoric of Police Websites', *Human Relations*, vol. 62, no. 12, pp. 1829–56.

Smith, R.C. and Eisenberg, E.M. 1987, 'Conflict at Disneyland: A Root-metaphor Analysis', *Communications Monographs*, vol. 54, no. 4, pp. 367–80.

Strati, A. 2007, 'Sensible Knowledge and Practice-based Learning', *Management Learning*, vol. 38, pp. 61–77.

Strati, A. 2010, 'Aesthetic Understanding of Work and Organizational Life: Approaches and Research Developments', *Sociology Compass*, vol. 4, pp. 880–93.

Thomas, W.I. and Thomas, D.S. 1928, *The Child in America: Behavior Problems and Programs*, Knopf, New York.

Tsoukas, H. 1993, 'Analogical Reasoning and Knowledge Generation in Organization Theory', *Organization Studies*, vol. 14, no. 3, pp. 323–46.

Watzlawick, P., Jackson, D.D. and Bavelas, J.B. 1967, *Pragmatics of Human Communication: A Study of Interactional Patterns, Pathologies, and Paradoxes*, Norton, New York.

Weick, K.E. 1989, 'Theory Construction as Disciplined Imagination', *The Academy of Management Review*, vol. 14, pp. 516–31.

Weick, K.E. 1998, 'Introductory essay—Improvisation as a Mindset for Organizational Analysis', *Organization Science*, vol. 9, no. 5, pp. 543–55.

Weick, K.E. and Roberts, K.H. 1993, 'Collective Mind in Organizations: Heedful Interrelating on Flight Decks', *Administrative Science Quarterly*, vol. 38, no. 3, pp. 357–81.

Ybema, S. and Kamsteeg, F. 2009, 'Making the Familiar Strange: A Case for Disengaged Organizational Ethnography', in S. Ybema, D. Yanow, H. Wels and F. Kamsteeg (eds), *Organizational Ethnography. Studying the Complexities of Everyday Life*, SAGE, London, pp. 101–19.

4. Discourse as a map

Metaphorical images aid us in capturing the complexity, ambiguities and tensions that are inherent to the concept of discourse. I will employ these analogies to reflect on the implications of discourse, and to explore some of the conceptual tensions and pragmatic consequences of employing a discursive lens to interpret organizational phenomena.

The first of such metaphors is the *map*. My argument is that the processes and the outcomes of discourse production and reproduction have much in common with the representation of a territory on a map, implying that, on the one hand, discourse (as an entity) is comparable to a map and, on the other hand, that a parallel is drawn between discursive practices and discourse formation (as a process) and the practices of map-making. Since, as described in Chapter 3, at the core of any metaphorical transposition we can find a similitude, I will start by considering the semantic overlapping between the concept of the map and the concept of discourse. The dictionary definition of a map is:

> A drawing or other representation of the earth's surface or a part of it made on a flat surface, showing the distribution of physical or geographical features (and often also including socio-economic, political, agricultural, meteoro-logical, etc., information), with each point in the representation corresponding to an actual geographical position according to a fixed scale or projection. (*Oxford Dictionary of English* 2011)

Some similitudes jump to the eye: maps are symbolic representations and map-making is a form of symbolic practice aimed at representing the physical reality of a geographical space. Moreover, maps possess a 'scale', similar to discourses. Finally, by means of the inclusion of social, political and economic information, maps produce the subjects that they are supposed to describe: the idea of 'national borders' as sites with defined coordinates is only conceivable thanks to the existence of modern cartography (Branch 2011).

At the same time it is possible to identify divergences. When referring to a map, we typically think of a physical object; even when we consider the abstract notion of map (as in the concept of a 'mental map' of something), there is a strong element of embodiment linked to the fact that a map is always visual, a graphic arrangement representing distribution of items in space. Conversely, as discussed in Chapter 2, the ontological status of discourses is highly problematic: while according to some they are 'embodied' in texts, discourses are much more than their linguistic traces. Another dissimilitude concerns the origin of maps: these are always the product of a purposive design, while discourses are emergent phenomena.

In this chapter I offer some reflections both on these similarities and on these tensions, in order to harness the generative power of the mapping metaphor (Schön 1993). The purpose is to exploit the potential of this analogy as a heuristic device, to develop ideas and identify methodological pointers, first by finding correspondences between the two concepts, then blending them and finally producing an emergent meaning (Cornelissen 2005). I will start by discussing and expanding the above-mentioned similarities, reflecting on what they reveal and generate in terms of the meaning of discourse.

THE SIMILARITIES BETWEEN MAPS AND DISCOURSES

There are three major similitudes that justify the connection between maps and discourses: maps (as discourses) are at the same time representational and generative, deploying power/knowledge effects that create their own subjects; both maps and discourses come in different scales; maps and discourses are (re)produced by means of symbolic practices and artefacts.

As Foucauldian discourses produce their subjects, equally maps do not simply describe but *construct* nations and regions (Foucault 1980). Discourses and maps' representational practice are not a reproduction of reality but a selection of the differences that matter. This idea, based on Korzybski's (1933) remark that "the map is not the territory", has been articulated by Bateson:[1]

> Differences are the things that get onto a map. But what is a difference? [...]
> I suggest to you, now, that the word "idea" in its most elementary sense, is

---

[1]   A related idea, highlighting how meaning is produced only within contexts, is also proposed by Jacques Derrida with his concept of *différance,* which plays on the double meaning in French of 'to differ' and 'to defer', and shows how our knowledge is always produced by dynamic patterns of references, a form of intertextuality (Derrida 1982).

synonymous with "difference." [...] There is an infinite number of differences around and within the piece of chalk. [...] Of this infinitude, we select a very limited number, which become information. In fact, what we mean by information—the elementary unit of information—is a difference which makes a difference. [...]

But what is the territory? Operationally, somebody went out with a retina or a measuring stick and made representations which were then put upon paper. What is on the paper map is a representation of what was in the retinal representation of the man who made the map; and as you push the question back, what you find is an infinite regress, an infinite series of maps. The territory never gets in at all. The territory is *Ding an sich* and you can't do anything with it. Always the process of representation will filter it out so that the mental world is only maps of maps of maps, ad infinitum. All "phenomena" are literally appearances. (Bateson 1972, pp. 320–22)

What Bateson is showing is that maps are not a faithful representation of a territory but an edited record of impressions based on other representations (e.g. sets of geographical coordinates and other selected information on the examined territory), which in turn represent but one particular way of making sense of a perceived space. They play a central role in the social production of space, the process through which the 'raw material' fabricated by nature is turned into an organized, regimented realm (Lefebvre 1991).

Maps and discourses create a shared *Grand Illusion* that allows us to give coherent meanings to an ever-transforming and infinitely textured world: by doing so they emphasize or hide features of the territory, allowing certain readings of it. They do so by representing and highlighting (thus legitimizing) or ignoring (thus negating) the existence of a region, of an ethnic group, or of a feature of the terrain, such as a mountain or a water stream. On other occasions, map-makers explicitly choose to ignore certain dimensions completely to serve the purpose of the map: for instance topological maps, as with the famous London Tube map, focus only on the relations between places, ignoring distances or elevation: "How many maps, in the descriptive or geographical sense, might be needed to deal exhaustively with a given space, to code and decode all its meanings and contents? It is doubtful whether a finite number can ever be given in answer to this sort of question" (Lefebvre 1991, p. 85).

Something similar often happens in discourses, when complex realities are simplified and pigeonholed, sometimes with sinister effects. An example of this is the way in which the dominant discourse of psychiatry categorizes and labels complex human conditions in a discrete set of 'mental disorders', with dramatic consequences for the lives of patients.

In discourse analysis, acknowledging what is absent, and observing the ways in which discourse reduces the complexity of experience by ignoring 'inconsequent' details or by neglecting distinctions, can be as important as identifying what is present. A practical way to recognize what is absent in a discourse is to focus on differences among discourses as a means to disclose the implicit assumptions that bolster explicit discursive statements. The comparison and contrast of alternate discourses generates the possibility of a critical standpoint, since the production of alterity breaks down the hegemonic sense of normality and obviousness that is the outcome of any discourse when considered in isolation.

These considerations bring the realization that, despite claiming to offer a 'correct' representation of the world, both cartography and discourse are ineluctably political instruments. The map is a "spatial panopticon" (Harley 1989, p. 13) used to normalize and discipline subjects, influencing their perception of the world. Power can shape cartographic knowledge in more or less explicit ways. These can include situations in which political interest openly censors or alters maps, as used to happen in the Soviet Union, where cities and even physical features of the land were erased for political and military purposes (Harley 1989, p. 5). In a less explicit, but still highly 'muscular' fashion, political maps give a social meaning to a territory, highlighting artificial borders, overrepresenting human-made features such as roads or infrastructures, marking administrative divisions and cancelling undesirable ethnic or tribal realities. Nevertheless, even the supposedly objective and neutral 'physical maps' are loci of power/knowledge production: the rule of ethnocentricity, for instance, has almost universally brought cartographers to use either their homeland or their 'holy city' as the centre of the map. All together these elements might have contributed to reversing the causal relationships between map-making and governmentality. We tend to think of government agencies as pivotal actors in the effort to map the world, considering the knowledge produced by maps as an instrument of power and domination (Wood and Fels 1992). Yet the opposite might also be true: the development of cartographic science might have been instrumental to the formation of nations. By creating a new way of thinking about dominions and territory, as areas characterized by clearly defined boundaries and centralized control, rather than loose zones of influence, maps enabled the emergence of modern national states (Branch 2011), thus offering an example of the recursive relationship between knowledge and power.

Analogously, in order to describe the rules employed by a discourse it is necessary to investigate the interplay between knowledge and power, trying to understand how power constitutes discourse. Not only investigating visible power struggles but also especially stable power relations is necessary to understand how these produce rationality and rationalizations, knowledge and ignorance, truth and falsity (Flyvbjerg 1998, pp. 319–25).

The second parallel between discourse and map is connected to the issue of *scale*. It is common knowledge that maps can use different scales, either focusing on a local territory, or representing a broader worldview. Analogously, discourses can be local, i.e. the expression of quite well limited communities, and also global, characterizing multiple societies and producing a specific *zeitgeist* (a 'spirit of the times'), as is the case with the discourses of managerialism, neoliberalism, technical rationality, etc. (Alvesson and Kärreman 2000). A first implication of the notion of scale concerns the instrumental value of different scales of representation: the trade-off between detail and scope makes them useful for different purposes. Consulting a topographic map enables us to navigate a local area, while using a planisphere permits us to contemplate geopolitical and economic issues. In a similar way, micro-discourse analysis can help a researcher to understand the internal debates and plot the political geography of an organization, while macro-Discourse analysis can be useful to identify both the ideas that can be mobilized by local actors and the sensemaking devices that they will use. To understand the relationship between discourses and practices it is useful to employ both a local and general 'cartography', and investigate the relationship between the two, that is how local discourses tap into macro-Discourses and how the former contributes to shaping the latter.

Another, more complex, implication of scale, raises questions on the ontological nature of maps and discourses. As mentioned before, despite their claims, maps cannot faithfully mirror natural features of territory because, in order to do so, they should be drawn on a 1:1 scale, overlapping perfectly with the object of their representation. The vibrant imagination of Jorge Louis Borges allows us to contemplate this idea:

> In that Empire, the Art of Cartography attained such Perfection that the map of a single Province occupied the entirety of a City, and the map of the Empire, the entirety of a Province. In time, those Unconscionable Maps no longer satisfied, and the Cartographers Guilds struck a Map of the Empire whose size was that of the Empire, and which coincided point for point with it. The following Generations, who were not so fond of the Study of Cartography as their Forebears had been, saw that that vast Map was Useless, and not without some Pitilessness was it, that they delivered it up to the Inclemencies of Sun and Winters. In the Deserts of the West, still today, there

are Tattered Ruins of that Map, inhabited by Animals and Beggars; in all the Land there is no other Relic of the Disciplines of Geography. (Borges 1946 [1999])

The creation of such a map would have numerous paradoxical consequences, considered in detail and humorously described by Eco (1992, pp. 83–7), and can metaphorically provide a cautionary tale against the temptation of "collapsing materiality into discursivity" (Putnam and Cooren 2004, p. 326). While it is acceptable to regard materiality and discourse as co-emergent (Iedema 2007) it is necessary to be wary of the temptation of reducing materiality to discourse. Even if we accept the perspective according to which our subjectivities (and therefore our sensemaking processes) are entirely shaped and determined by discourse it is still necessary to distinguish (as discussed in Chapter 2) between raw experience and interpretation. For instance, basic emotions are pre-discursive, as demonstrated by the fact that they appear universal and not culturally bound (Ekman 1992a, 1992b). Moreover, discourses produce material artefacts that often outlive them, and these traces of the past might end up constraining and shaping behaviours. For instance, buildings such as schools and offices are purposefully designed to separate and group different organizational members, enforcing upon them a certain model of "organizational civility" (Muetzelfeldt 2006). Standards of civility, which include correct or acceptable ways to interact with others, are the expression of a particular discourse. However, the "re-placing of place" (Muetzelfeldt 2006, p. 126) might be contested, or might be too onerous, and as a consequence the efforts of a university lecturer who is keen to employ interactive learning methodologies can be frustrated by the traditional form of a lecture theatre that was designed according to a different pedagogy.

Other material conditions, such as the lack of resources, or the presence of physical dangers, constitute elements that maintain an actual capacity to affect and constrain decisions and actions. Discursive forces might interpret, highlight or gloss over such elements but cannot alter their material essence, which is not exclusively made of 'signs'. The 'territory' that the discourse maps always comprises fragments of discourse, but these are just as the 'Deserts of the West' imagined by Borges, still containing the Tattered Ruins of the Map of Empire.

The third similarity between map and discourse concerns their production. Mapping the world entails a socio-technical network, which enmeshes a set of propositions – the codified signs that we use to symbolize the features of the territory – and empirical realities, mediated by inscriptions (Latour and Woolgar 1979). These inscriptions (topo-logical coordinates) are produced using cartographic instruments, such as theodolites, sextants, satellite positioning systems, etc., which act as translation devices (Latour 2005). The back and forth translation between map and territory involves rational practices, which are founded on conventions. These produce apparently objective but in effect socially constructed representations of the world. More importantly, these effects are often the expression of specific political intents: "The cartographic processes by which power is enforced, reproduced, reinforced, and stereotyped consist of both deliberate and 'practical' acts of surveillance and less conscious cognitive adjustments by map-makers and map-users to dominant values and beliefs" (Harley 2009, p. 142).

Equally, discourses are based on a language that pretends to give a coherent and truthful account of what is correct, just or desirable. They 'seek' legitimacy in reason and sentiment; they develop or enrol tech-niques and technologies to extend their reach and to be reproduced. In order to understand discourses and their genealogy, it is useful to see them not just as sets of fixed statements found in texts but rather as actor-networks, produced and reproduced by an entanglement of declar-ations, conversations, technologies, practices and performances.

TRANSFORMATIONS: THE ROLE OF DESIGN IN MAP AND DISCOURSE

The power of metaphors does not exclusively reside in similarities: even the divergence of meaning between two apparently cognate concepts can help us to reflect on the nature of the target concept. An important difference between maps and discourses is that the former are explicitly designed, while the latter are emergent from social interaction and communication. In reality, this is not a real discrepancy but rather a tension between the two concepts. In both cases, explicitly designed components intermix with emergent, unintentional aspects, whereas maps mostly are designed and discourses mostly are emergent.

Not all features of maps are purposefully devised in order to produce an appropriate "conceived space" (Lefebvre 1991). For instance a number of map-making practices have included unconscious biases, such as ethnocentrism (e.g. placing the map-maker nation at the centre of the map), "silencing" (e.g. omitting the dwellings of undesirable inhabitants), or the use of an iconography reproducing the hierarchical status quo (Harley 2009). At the same time, it is evident that maps are not 'emergent' products: they comply with specific standards, principles and models, and it is their conformity to such principles that makes them intelligible. They are explicitly prepared with clear instrumental object- ives (to support property claims, to guide the traveller, to prepare defence or conquest, etc.), with their features (e.g. their scale and detail) chosen according to their intended purposes.

Discourses, on the other hand, can be the outcome of an explicit rhetorical strategy. Organizational discourse can be seen as a rhetorical process meant to project a desired corporate identity and to influence public views and beliefs in a manner functional to the organizational elites' interests (Cheney et al. 2004). The use of rhetoric in management has been widely discussed in the recent literature (see Hartelius and Browning (2008) for a review of the debate). Rhetoric is defined as the use of language in order to persuade and to establish identification (Sillince 2005). It is the emphasis on identity production that differenti- ates the classic Aristotelian idea of rhetoric from the contemporary uses. 'New rhetoric' is more concerned with values, the construction of self and identification, as a means of identifying the self in relation to a particular issue, and of using that self-identification persuasively (Jarzab- kowski, Sillince and Shaw 2010).

When used to formulate strategic intents, rhetoric creates consistency by removing uncertainty about future actions, or by eliminating options that are incompatible, creating purpose by setting directions, regulating internal debate by relativizing and managing opinions and interpretation, and emphasizing context by defining and protecting organizational boundaries (Mantere and Sillince 2007). Also, while rhetoric usually involves the use of language it also has a symbolic meaning beyond the literal (Sillince 2006). By leveraging its symbolic meaning rhetoric also provides a means of managing organizational ambiguity (in goals, means, directions) and of using it as a resource (Jarzabkowski et al. 2010).

Viewing discourse as the outcome of persuasive communication appears at odds with the Foucauldian lesson[2] which understands power not as a mere form of imposition but as productive of reality: "it produces domains of objects and rituals of truth. The individual and the knowledge that may be gained of him belong to this production" (Foucault 1979, p. 194). The usefulness of Foucault's position is that it

---

[2]   Here I am focusing on the Foucauldian interpretation because it is the most radically anti-humanistic form of discourse, based on the strongest form of constructivism and leaving less space to agency (see Chapter 2). Conversely, there it is not problematic to reconcile 'realistic' views of discourse (as a particular way of communicating and representing the reality) with the notions of design and rhetoric.

disposes with the notion of an essential self, the problematic notion according to which we can identify a universal human nature, characterized by specific needs, desires and interests, an authentic consciousness that is threatened by structural forces such as religion, capital, ideologies, etc. (Newton 1998). This means accepting that individuality is a precarious result of social practices and of the different discourses they have been confronted with during their life experience (Knights and McCabe 2003). Foucault describes the social machinery that generates these identities as a *"dispositif"*, an apparatus, which is:

> [F]irstly, a thoroughly heterogeneous ensemble consisting of discourses, institutions, architectural forms, regulatory decisions, laws, administrative measures, scientific statements, philosophical, moral and philanthropic propositions – in short, the said as much as the unsaid. Such are the elements of the apparatus. The apparatus itself is the system of relations that can be established between these elements. Secondly, what I am trying to identify in this apparatus is precisely the nature of the connection that can exist between these heterogeneous elements. (Foucault 1980, p. 194)

Foucault aligns with Weber's idea of "structures of dominancy" that ground alternative forms of legitimate authority, based on alternative modes of rationality (Weber 1922 [1978]). If discourse is not 'shrouding' but is generating reality by creating subjectivity and meaning, it is difficult to conceive of agencies who can manipulate discourse to their own ends, since in such a framework the motivations, desires, strategies of these schemers are a product of discourse; however, this creates a problem that is made evident by the use of the map metaphor. If map-makers can know the world only by means of their understanding of the apparatus of cartography, then how can we explain transformation in map-making? Should we not still be using portolans instead of Google maps to find our way?

Despite the usefulness of the Foucauldian call for decentring from (and of) the subject, his view on discourse has been criticized for underplaying the role of agency, in particular with reference to change (Newton 1998; Reed 2000; Caldwell 2007). What can explain transformation in discourse? How do new discourses emerge to replace old ones? What is the role for resistance and agentic power in transforming discourses? Not answering these questions limits the application of Foucauldian discourse analysis to organizational studies: what is the practical use of an analytic lens that cannot account for, or help in shaping, change? We are left with "an infinite space of discursive possibilities, filled with nothing but discourses about discourses, possible agential selves with no agency, change without any fixed starting point or outcome" (Caldwell 2007,

p. 786). It also led to neglecting the power of material conditions, and caustically Alvesson and Kärreman compare academics who believe in the magical power of words to *Harry Potter* fans, "living in a world where text and talk matter more than for bus drivers, carpenters and factory managers" (2011, p. 1141).

One way to reconcile the transformative role of individual agency with the structural constraints posed by discourses can derive from another plausible metaphorical transposition, linking discourse with a particular type of map: genetic code. Genes are a portion of an organic molecule, DNA, which encodes instructions that enable cells to produce specific proteins. Operating together, as a genome, they provide the blueprint for the reproduction of an organism. Obviously, DNA molecules do not possess intents or desires. Nevertheless, their survival is guaranteed only if the organism they encode is successful at reproducing itself, together with its genome. The process is random and shaped by evolutionary forces but, in hindsight, it is possible to attribute a clear logic to it: only genes which are 'selfish', i.e. which produce an organism that can adequately serve their intrinsic reproduction interests, will be able to survive natural selection (Dawkins 2006).

If we extend our metaphor, considering discourse as a gene (which is ultimately a biological map), and the knowing subjects produced by it as organisms, then a human agent using rhetoric can be seen as a vehicle for the reproduction of discourse. To paraphrase Samuel Butler's aphorism "a hen is merely the egg's way of making another egg" (Gould 2010, p. 89). One might say, for instance, that the proponents of trickle-down economics are the way for the discourse of neoliberism to reproduce itself. Thinking in terms of similitude with genes allows us to overcome the risk of a reification and agentification of discursive structures: they are not purposely tasking individuals to act in ways that guarantee their reproduction, since they have neither self-consciousness nor desires. It is simply the case that, while discourses which provide sufficient incentives to their human carriers to replicate and propagate them through symbolic behaviour will survive, weaker discourses which carriers are not intent at reproducing, will go extinct. This is an example of "intentionality without subject" (Hoy 1989, cited in Bardon, Clegg and Josserand 2012, p. 355).

In other words, if the type of subjects they create are sufficiently empowered and are able to divulgate, spread and perform them, discourses will embed themselves in institutions and become prevalent, even hegemonic. This means that, while subjectivities emerge from a regulatory apparatus, this "should not be interpreted as a Machiavellian plot conspired by cunning managers to further exploit employees but simply as [...] the precarious result of various decentralized exercises of power in interaction" (Bardon, Clegg and Josserand 2012, p. 355).

Coherently with this framework, mutations and hybridizing can explain change and transformation, whereas "new discourses emerge through 'reweaving' relations between existing discourses" (Fairclough 2005, p. 932). Individual agents can effect changes through a process of bricolage (Iedema et al. 2004). An even more comprehensive model that can be used to explain the process linking individual agencies with the structures of meaning and patterns of social action that underlie and overarch them is offered by Stewart Clegg's Circuits of Power model (Clegg 1989). This model underpins a multidimensional approach to power, understood as a spatial-temporal arrangement of relations including both episodic and systemic forms. This approach has great analytical potential because it allows for understanding of the movement and transformation of power and social relations. For Clegg, power flows through three circuits representing the terrains of social experience: the first is the episodic agency level, which reflects a causual model of power, as a means to alter others' behaviour according to specific ends. The second level, dispositional power or social integration, refers to the local 'rules of the game' played by agents. The third, facilitative power or system integration, represents both the discursive, disciplinary power described by Foucault and the Weberian structures of dominancy (Gordon 2007). What Clegg's model does is to put in relation these different layers of power, explaining how the outcomes of episodic power reproduce, reinforce or transform the architecture of power relationships, flowing through, while also forging, a dispositional circuit made up of rule-fixing relations of meaning and membership (Clegg 1989).

In the dispositional power circuit, resistance to power wanes thanks to a redefinition of meaning; here the use of direct, discretional commands based on the control of uncertainty (Crozier and Friedberg 1980) is replaced by a rationalization of power relationships, which become routinized in the form of impersonal norms and procedures, or included in a hegemonic organizational culture. At the same time, organizations are embedded in an overarching 'facilitative circuit' of power where ruling becomes a "sensemaking process", politically producing meaning (Clegg 1989, p. 200), fixing it in discourses, rationality and technologies, all of which have a disciplinary content. At this level, different elites try to outflank each other or are outflanked because of changes produced by non-human actants and events. While episodic power relations, which are explicit and coercive, unavoidably cause resistance and political struggle, in dispositional circuits based on disciplinary systems conflict becomes tacit and consensus is produced, while in the facilitative circuit the outcome of political transformations is a new regime of truth, a process of meaning making and rationalization that reifies beliefs into accepted realities (Haugaard 2009).

By accounting for concrete ways in which individual power acts can bring about transformation in facilitative power circuits (hence even in Grand Discourses) Clegg's model salvages the role of agency. The identity of these change agents is without doubt predicated on pre-existing discursive structures but the pragmatic effect of their intentional actions remains, regardless of whether they are motivated by a moral desire to 'make a difference' or by an aesthetic craving to 'act otherwise' (Caldwell 2007). This can happen through recursive attribution of meaning that connects contingent events into coded events and reconstructs them, and might not lead to the desired effects. For instance, the policy of *glasnost* (transparency) and *perestroika* (restructuring) promoted by Mikhail Gorbachev in an attempt to reform the declining socio-economical order of the Soviet Union in the 1980s caused, in an already fragmenting institutional field marred by corruption and increasing nationalism, a collapse in the system (Deroy and Clegg 2015). Looking at the interaction between different circuits of power it is therefore possible to reconcile individual actions with discursive change, without implicating the problematic idea of pre-discursive intentions. Discursive revolutions are usually not the outcome of the designs of the revolutionaries but emerge from various acts, some of which paradoxically are aimed at conserving the status quo.

MULTIPLE SCALES OF REPRESENTATION

A second tension fuelled by the dissimilarity of maps and discourses has to deal with an issue of correspondence that has been mentioned previously: the notion of scale. If discourses are not intentionally designed then how can they have a 'scale'? Empirically, we can find local discourses; for instance, the specific ways of talking and making sense of events that characterize a specific organization or organizational unit. The 'borders' of such discourses are not well determined however; they blur into a multiplicity of other discourses. It is our descriptive and interpretive acts which bring discourse to life, granting the object 'discourse' a defined form. A question arises: is discourse a particular type of phenomena or is it an epistemological device to order a particular set of phenomena? The answer to this question depends on the onto-epistemological stance one decides to embrace. A constructionist viewpoint collapses the difference between the two (reality is produced by the means we use to gain knowledge of it), while in a positivist perspective it is crucial to single out clearly the object of our enquiry in order to guarantee the falsifiability of our hypothesis. The latter approach is clearly incompatible with a Foucauldian type of discourse but can be applied if discourse is interpreted in a 'realist' perspective: in this case, whereas discourse is distinct from meaning and is considered in a specific context (Alvesson and Kärreman 2000), a delimitation of its limits becomes feasible and opportune. Therefore, for instance, it is possible to investigate the discourse emerging from a specific community of practice, or produced by the members of a single organizational unit, and then compare it with the discourses of other localities.

The issue therefore regards the nature of the 'territory' (social reality) that the 'map' (discourse) is representing. As discussed previously, both realist and constructivist approaches acknowledge the existence of an extra-discursive layer of existence, made of natural phenomena and emotions. The fundamental difference resides in the pre-discursive co-herence manifested by such elements: according to a realist account, discourse represents or, at best, is an additional element contributing to a set of structures that exist independently of discourses. The constructivist positions argue instead that these elements are an inchoate accumulation of phenomena that are only given coherence and meaning by discourses. The metaphor of the map can be employed to clarify this distinction, describing how the elements of the map metaphor can find different correspondences in realist and constructivist approaches to discourse analysis (Table 4.1).

Table 4.1   Using the map metaphor to describe the relation between discourse and reality

Map metaphor	Realist accounts	Constructivist accounts
Territory	Social reality	Discourse (generating reality)
Map	Discourse	Discourse analysis
Cartography (discourse)	Discourse analysis	Discourse on discourse analysis

The parallel between map and discourse is easier to make when one considers the realist perspective: since discourse 'plugs in' to a pre-existing social and natural reality, such a reality is analogue to a territory that the discourse is describing and regulating, acting similarly to a map. It is then possible to consider a higher level of abstraction. In the case of the source concept this refers to the cartographical rules, templates and practices employed in the production of maps; in the case of the target concept, it denotes instead the methodological apparatus that enables the analysis of discourse, i.e. the theorization on organizational discourse analysis.

If we move from a constructivist perspective (thus focusing on paradigmatic, big 'D' Discourses) the metaphorical transposition is more complicated, because of a semantic asymmetry between the notion of 'territory' in map and discourse. From a map-making perspective the existence of physical geographical elements cannot be denied. Such 'natural features' are activated and made more or less relevant by the application of symbolic devices, according to the intentions of the cartographer. Nevertheless, representation cannot completely trump material effects: the gradient of an elevation on the Earth's surface is a fact that is not affected by naming it a 'hill' or a 'mountain'. On the other hand, constructivist views consider organization and discourse as in-extricability intermingled: "language constructs organizational reality, rather than simply reflects it" (Hardy, Lawrence and Grant 2005, p. 60). On this assumption, material elements (whose existence is not necessarily neglected) present themselves as an inchoate flow of experience that is only given recognizable structure and meaning through discursive prac-tices. Consequently, discourse is an essential component of the organ-izational 'territory', and organizing is talk, symbolic practice. From this viewpoint, discourse analysts are the map-makers: the Foucauldian archaeologist-genealogist is the one who charts alternative life worlds, making them 'visible'. In this case, the higher abstract ground of 'cartography' can be seen as representing the ongoing debate on methodological and heuristic approaches to the study of discourse, the 'discourses on discourse analysis'.

The semantic tension that emerges between the concept of map and that of paradigmatic Discourse (i.e. discourse seen in a radical con-structivist perspective) demonstrates the problematic effects of collapsing meaning into discourse or assuming that discourses can shape reality irrespective of other material factors, for instance personalities, emotional responses, environmental conditions, etc. (Alvesson and Kärreman 2011). The fact that language has constitutive properties does not necessarily imply that meaning is produced exclusively by means of language. The role of cultural norms and institutions in sensemaking processes is well documented (Weick 1969 [1979], 1988, 1993, 1995). While culture incorporates linguistic and symbolic elements it should be distinguished from discourse, since the former includes non-verbal elements and deep-assumptions that can predate the currently prevailing discourses

(Alvesson 2004). Doing otherwise implies that the notion of discourse is "stretched to incorporate almost everything" (Alvesson and Kärreman 2011, p. 1135). It is therefore more useful to embrace a more nuanced view, accepting that discourses can have multiple effects, influencing reality at various levels and with different degrees of intensity. Language and discourse is sometimes employed only with communicative purposes, acting as "ephemeral talk"; in other cases it can shape attention, set agendas, offer a context and connection to behaviours, and even provide a template for action; finally it can produce reality, providing all the necessary "constitutive agency" (Alvesson and Kärreman 2011, pp. 1140–41). However, these effects are not necessarily always deployed.

Our cartographic metaphor can offer a practical illustration of the concept: different maps can have different purposes and may produce different effects. Some maps are merely decorative items. More often, however, maps have instructional purposes, and they are used for pathfinding, or to illustrate concepts, or for highlighting risks and opportunities. Sometimes maps also have a constitutive effect, enabling positive and negative identification with reference with the otherwise fluid and blurry notion of 'homeland', and therefore becoming instrumental in the construction and maintenance of social identity (Tajfel 1974, 1978).

Therefore, different maps (similarly to discourse) can have different performative effects, but not every map will have the same effects. Sometimes these effects are strong and direct: purposefully altering the borders of an electoral district ('gerrymandering') will have direct effects on a political consultation. In other cases, the impact is far less deterministic: redrawing national borders to include a new section of the territory will not change the language, customs or values of its denizens. The analogy applies to discourse perfectly: we are not just puppets manoeuvred by discursive forces (Newton 1998). Newton (1994) offers an illustration of the implicit resistance that existing beliefs and attitudes can offer to discursive dictates. In his study of the assessment centres established by the British Army during WWII, he describes how the personnel, who favoured forms of subjective appraisal, deliberately subverted the rationality principles informing the personnel psychology discourse. This is not only a matter of resistance to change, which could be interpreted as a conflict between an old and new discourse; rather, the relationship between cognition and discourse is complex and cannot be reduced to simple causation.

Again, the story of a famous map can illustrate this point. One way in which a map can generate performative effects is by revealing connections between otherwise unrelated information; this is the case of the first epidemiological map, drawn by an English physician, John Snow. In 1854, numerous cholera cases affected the poverty-stricken London area of Soho. Mainstream medicine of the time attributed infectious diseases to miasmas, 'foul air', and therefore prophylactic measures were usually ineffective. Thanks to a map that he used to plot the location of infected households, Snow was able to establish a causal link between infection and water pollution. The geographical representation highlighted how all the people who were getting sick were residing in the area adjacent to the Broad Street water pump: he deduced that they were drawing water for domestic usage from the pump. The simple expedient of blocking that particular pump made it possible to stop the epidemic as well as providing strong empirical support for the emerging germ theory of disease (Johnson 2006). The story, as presented in this linear narrative, suggests that the map produced by itself a new course in medicine; in reality, the relationship is more complex, since the map was produced by Snow to verify and support his theories: maps (as discourses) do not operate in isolation but interact with other political, material and cultural elements.

In conclusion, conceiving discourse as a map has revealed a number of limitations and opportunities in the different theorizations of discourse. It is possible to summarize some of these key ideas in terms of practical 'heuristic guidelines' which can be recommended when using discourse as a theoretical lens with which to study organizations:

1. Discourses are to be analysed in their interaction with socio-material actor-networks, not (exclusively) as stand-alone linguistic apparatuses; this way it is possible to better account for the interplay between materiality and discourse, avoiding reducing everything to 'texts'. Any organization includes and is made possible by language but cannot be reduced to language, both because the map is not the territory and because 'organizational territory' is made by more than pure words.

2. Discourses elide and highlight, as maps do. Looking at remarkable omissions in a discourse can be as enlightening as counting occurrences. The 'dog that did not bark' for instance is the absence in a local discourse of rhetoric or of symbolic behaviour that is otherwise widespread in similar organizational settings.

3. Connected to the previous point is the idea that the interplay between local and global scale is constant, and the influence of small 'd' discourses and capital 'D' Discourses must be taken into account; local discourses are not just small-scale projections of global Discourses and should be compared and contrasted with

other discourses in order to understand how and why this influence does or does not have effects.

4. Power and knowledge are imbricated and shape each other, and power is not just oppressive but productive; however, this process does not happen exclusively through the agency of language and symbolic practices. Processes of knowledge management and of sensemaking should be considered in a political perspective; in this regard, the use of a phronetic perspective (Cairns and Śliwa 2008; Flyvbjerg 2001, 2006; Flyvbjerg, Landman and Schram 2012; Clegg, Flyvbjerg and Haugaard 2014) appears to be particularly useful. Phronetic discourse analysis is in this sense a necessary extension of the idea of critical discourse analysis (Fairclough and Wodak 1997), to incorporate a critique of Foucauldian 'logo-centrism'. To clarify and explicate this argument, and to better understand how power is productive of knowledge not *just* by means of discourse but *also* through discourse, we need to expand our metaphorical exploration, including a new metaphor, that of *discourse as organization*.

REFERENCES

Alvesson, M. 2004, 'Organizational Culture and Discourse', in D. Grant, C. Hardy, C. Oswick and L.L. Putnam (eds), *The SAGE Handbook of Organizational Discourse*, SAGE, London, pp. 317–35.

Alvesson, M. and Kärreman, D. 2000, 'Varieties of Discourse: On the Study of Organizations through Discourse Analysis', *Human Relations*, vol. 53, pp. 1125–49.

Alvesson, M. and Kärreman, D. 2011, 'Decolonializing Discourse: Critical Reflections on Organizational Discourse Analysis', *Human Relations*, vol. 64, pp. 1121–46.

Bardon, T., Clegg, S.R. and Josserand, E. 2012, 'Exploring Identity Construction from a Critical Management Perspective: A Research Agenda', *M@n@gement*, vol. 15, p. 351.

Bateson, G. 1972, *Steps to an Ecology of Mind: Collected Essays in Anthropology, Psychiatry, Evolution, and Epistemology*, Intertext, Aylesbury.

Borges, J.L. 1946 [1999], 'On Exactitude in Science', in J.L. Borges (ed.), *Collected Fictions*, Penguin, New York.

Branch, J.N. 2011, 'Mapping the Sovereign State: Cartographic Technology, Political Authority, and Systemic Change', ProQuest, UMI Dissertations Publishing.

Cairns, G. and Śliwa, M. 2008, 'The Implications of Aristotle's Phronēsis for Organizational Inquiry', in D. Barry and H. Hansen (eds), *The SAGE Handbook of New Approaches in Management and Organization*, SAGE, Thousand Oaks, CA, pp. 318–28.

Caldwell, R. 2007, 'Agency and Change: Re-evaluating Foucault's Legacy', *Organization*, vol. 14, no. 6, pp. 769–91.
Cheney, G., Christensen, L.T., Conrad, C. and Lair, D.J. 2004, 'Corporate Rhetoric as Organizational Discourse', in D. Grant, C. Hardy, C. Oswick and L.L. Putnam (eds), *The SAGE Handbook of Organizational Discourse*, SAGE, London, pp. 79–103.
Clegg, S.R. 1989, *Frameworks of Power*, SAGE Publications, London.
Clegg, S.R., Flyvbjerg, B. and Haugaard, M. 2014, 'Reflections on Phronetic Social Science: A Dialogue Between Stewart Clegg, Bent Flyvbjerg and Mark Haugaard', *Journal of Political Power*, vol. 7, no. 2, pp. 275–306.
Cornelissen, J.P. 2005, 'Beyond Compare: Metaphor in Organization Theory', *The Academy of Management Review*, vol. 30, pp. 751–64.
Crozier, M. and Friedberg, E. 1980, *Actors and Systems: The Politics of Collective Action*, University of Chicago Press, Chicago, IL.
Dawkins, R. 2006, *The Selfish Gene*, Oxford University Press, Oxford, UK.
Deroy, X. and Clegg, S.R. 2015, 'Back in the USSR: Introducing Recursive Contingency Into Institutional Theory', *Organization Studies*, vol. 36, no. 1, pp. 73–90.
Derrida, J. 1982, 'Différance', *Margins of Philosophy*, University of Chicago, Chicago, IL, pp. 1–28.
Eco, U. 1992, *Il secondo diario minimo*, Bompiani, Milano.
Ekman, P. 1992a, 'Are there Basic Emotions?', *Psychological Review*, vol. 99, pp. 550–53.
Ekman, P. 1992b, 'An Argument for Basic Emotions', *Cognition & Emotion*, vol. 6, no. 3–4, pp. 169–200.
Fairclough, N. 2005, 'Peripheral Vision Discourse Analysis in Organization Studies: The Case for Critical Realism', *Organization Studies*, vol. 26, no. 6, pp. 915–39.
Fairclough, N. and Wodak, R. 1997, 'Critical Discourse Analysis', in T.A. van Dijk (ed.), *Discourse Studies. A Multidisciplinary Introduction*, vol. 2, SAGE, London, pp. 258–84.
Flyvbjerg, B. 1998, *Rationality and Power: Democracy in Practice*, University of Chicago Press, Chicago, IL.
Flyvbjerg, B. 2001, *Making Social Science Matter: Why Social Inquiry Fails and How it Can Succeed Again*, Cambridge University Press, Cambridge, UK.
Flyvbjerg, B. 2006, 'Making Organization Research Matter: Power, Values and Phronesis', in S.R. Clegg, C. Hardy, T. Lawrence and W.R. Nord (eds), *The SAGE Handbook of Organization Studies*, SAGE, London, pp. 370–87.
Flyvbjerg, B., Landman, T. and Schram, S. 2012, *Real Social Science: Applied Phronesis*, Cambridge University Press, Cambridge, UK.
Foucault, M. 1979, *Discipline and Punish: The Birth of the Prison*, Vintage Books, New York.
Foucault, M. 1980, *Power/Knowledge: Selected Interviews and Other Writings, 1972–1977*, Harvester Wheatsheaf, New York.
Gordon, R. 2007, *Power, Knowledge and Domination*, Universitetsforlaget, Copenhagen.
Gould, S.J. 2010, *The Panda's Thumb: More Reflections in Natural History*, WW Norton & Company, New York.

Hardy, C., Lawrence, T.B. and Grant, D. 2005, 'Discourse and Collaboration: The Role of Conversations and Collective Identity', *Academy of Management Review*, vol. 30, no. 1, pp. 58–77.

Harley, J.B. 1989, 'Deconstructing the Map', *Cartographica: The International Journal for Geographic Information and Geovisualization*, vol. 26, pp. 1–20.

Harley, J.B. 2009, 'Maps, Knowledge, and Power', in G. Henderson and M. Waterstone (eds), *Geographic Thought. A Praxis Perspective*, Routledge, Abingdon, pp. 129–48.

Hartelius, E.J. and Browning, L.D. 2008, 'The Application of Rhetorical Theory in Managerial Research: A Literature Review', *Management Communication Quarterly*, vol. 22, pp. 13–39.

Haugaard, M. 2009, 'Power and Hegemony', in S.R. Clegg and M. Haugaard (eds), *The SAGE Handbook of Power*, SAGE, London, pp. 239–55.

Hoy, D.C. 1989, *Michel Foucault: Lectures Critiques*, De Boeck Université, Bruxelles.

Iedema, R. 2007, 'On the Multi-modality, Materiality and Contingency of Organization Discourse', *Organization Studies*, vol. 28, no. 6, pp. 931–46.

Iedema, R., Degeling, P., Braithwaite, J. and White, L. 2004, '"It's an Interesting Conversation I'm Hearing": The Doctor as Manager', *Organization Studies*, vol. 25, no. 1, pp. 15–33.

Jarzabkowski, P., Sillince, J.A.A. and Shaw, D. 2010, 'Strategic Ambiguity as a Rhetorical Resource for Enabling Multiple Interests', *Human Relations*, vol. 63, pp. 219–48.

Johnson, S. 2006, *The Ghost Map: The Story of London's Most Terrifying Epidemic – And How it Changed Science, Cities, and the Modern World*, Penguin, London.

Knights, D. and McCabe, D. 2003, 'Governing through Teamwork: Reconstituting Subjectivity in a Call Centre', *Journal of Management Studies*, vol. 40, no. 7, pp. 1587–619.

Korzybski, A. 1933, *Science and Sanity: An Introduction to Non-Aristotelian Systems and General Semantics*, The Institute of General Semantics, Lakeville, CT.

Latour, B. 2005, *Reassembling the Social: An Introduction to Actor-Network Theory*, Clarendon, Oxford, UK.

Latour, B. and Woolgar, S. 1979, *Laboratory Life: The Social Construction of Scientific Facts*, vol. 80, SAGE Publications, Beverly Hills, CA.

Lefebvre, H. 1991, *The Production of Space*, Blackwell, Cambridge, MA.

Mantere, S. and Sillince, J.A.A. 2007, 'Strategic Intent as a Rhetorical Device', *Scandinavian Journal of Management*, vol. 23, pp. 406–23.

Muetzelfeldt, M. 2006, 'Organizational Space, Place and Civility', in S.R. Clegg and M. Kornberger (eds), *Space, Organizations and Management Theory*, Liber, Oslo, pp. 113–28.

Newton, T.J. 1994, 'Discourse and Agency: The Example of Personnel Psychology and "Assessment Centres"', *Organization Studies*, vol. 15, no. 6, pp. 879–902.

Newton, T. 1998, 'Theorizing Subjectivity in Organizations: The Failure of Foucauldian Studies?', *Organization Studies*, vol. 19, pp. 415–47.

Oxford Dictionary of English 2011, 3rd edn, Oxford University Press, Oxford, UK.

Putnam, L.L. and Cooren, F. 2004, 'Alternative Perspectives on the Role of Text and Agency in Constituting Organizations', *Organization*, vol. 11, no. 3, pp. 323–33.

Reed, M. 2000, 'The Limits of Discourse Analysis in Organizational Analysis', *Organization*, vol. 7, no. 3, pp. 524–30.

Schön, D. 1993, 'Generative Metaphor: A Perspective on Problem-setting in Social Policy', in A. Ortony (ed.), *Metaphor and Thought*, Cambridge University Press, Cambridge, UK, pp. 137–63.

Sillince, J.A.A. 2005, 'A Contingency Theory of Rhetorical Congruence', *The Academy of Management Review*, vol. 30, pp. 608–21.

Sillince, J.A.A. 2006, 'Resources and Organizational Identities: The Role of Rhetoric in the Creation of Competitive Advantage', *Management Communication Quarterly*, vol. 20, pp. 186–212.

Tajfel, H. 1974, 'Social Identity and Intergroup Behaviour', *Social Science Information*, vol. 13, pp. 65–93.

Tajfel, H. 1978, *Differentiation Between Social Groups: Studies in the Social Psychology of Intergroup Relations*, vol. 14, Academic Press, New York.

Weber, M. 1922 [1978], *Economy and Society: An Outline of Interpretive Sociology*, University of California Press, Berkeley, CA.

Weick, K.E. 1969 [1979], *The Social Psychology of Organizing*, 2nd edn, Addison-Wesley, Reading, MA.

Weick, K.E. 1988, 'Enacted Sensemaking in Crisis Situations', *Journal of Management Studies*, vol. 25, pp. 305–17.

Weick, K.E. 1993, 'The Collapse of Sensemaking in Organizations: The Mann Gulch Disaster', *Administrative Science Quarterly*, vol. 38, pp. 628–52.

Weick, K.E. 1995, *Sensemaking in Organizations*, SAGE Publications, Thousand Oaks, CA.

Wood, D. and Fels, J. 1992, *The Power of Maps*, Guilford Press, New York.

5. Discourse as organizing

A BAD METAPHOR?

The use of 'organization' as a metaphor for discourse is at the same time straightforward and difficult. The idea of language and discourse as organizing devices is well accepted, making this analogy so obvious that it can be considered almost a 'dead' metaphor. Many authors have made this point and these are just some examples: "the idea of a discourse about organizations is an oxymoron. Discourse itself is a form of organization" (Chia 2000, p. 517); "organizations exist only in so far as their members create them through discourse" (Mumby and Clair 1997, p. 181); "most of the activity in organizations (i.e. organizing and managing) is primarily discursive" (Grant et al. 2004, p. 26); "organizations can be understood as collaborative and contending discourses" (Boje, Oswick and Ford 2004, p. 571).

What is problematic in this metaphor is that organizations are not clearly defined entities. They appear in many different forms, ranging from large formalized structures (e.g. multinational corporations or national governments) to small ephemeral associations (e.g. start-ups, interest groups). They can be constituted by individuals or by other organizations, as in the case of meta-organizations (Ahrne and Brunsson 2005). Despite being ubiquitous, it is not easy to discriminate organizations from their surrounding environment, which is made up of other organizations (Pfeffer and Salancik 1978), and is not pre-given but enacted, created by the actions of the organization (Weick 1969 [1979]). Despite having many tangible manifestations (buildings, infrastructures, etc.) their reproduction depends on patterned actions and routines. "'Organizations' are conceptually-stabilized abstractions: 'islands' of fabricated coherence in a sea of chaos and change" (Chia 2002, p. 866).

As discussed in Chapter 3, multiple metaphors have been proposed to capture this complexity, making it amenable to conceptual manipulations and explications. Organizations have been metaphorically equated to machines, organisms, brains, cultures, political systems, prisons (Morgan 2006), or even to Wonderlands where absurdity cohabits with rational ordering (McCabe 2016). Employing such an indistinct, multifaceted source concept as a figurative anchor is not ideal, since it defies one of the principal advantages of the use of metaphors, the opportunity of using a "more concrete concept to understand and relate to [...] abstract or complex idea" (Cornelissen 2005, p. 753). Further confusion derives from the fact that organizations are not just produced by discourse but they are also one of the main 'producers' of discourses. Since "where there is organizational activity, there is normally talk" (Alvesson and Kärreman 2011, p. 1122), many diverse discourses are constantly emerging from organizational contexts (Boje et al. 2004).

Numerous studies have explored and conceptualized the connections between organization and discourse, and Fairhurst and Putnam (2004) offer a comprehensive literature review, identifying three different interpretations of their relationship. A first perspective ('object') considers organizations as distinct, pre-existing and influencing discourse; a second position ('becoming') describes organizations as in a constant state of becoming, highlighting the formative role of discourse; finally, according to a third viewpoint ('grounded') organizations are substantiated in actions that include social practices and symbolic acts. According to the 'object' orientation, organizations possess specific attributes, distinct from the actions of their members, and discourse is reflective, rather than formative, shaped by organizational outcomes. The 'becoming' perspective investigates the formative role played by discourses, seen both as language in use and as pre-existing power/knowledge systems, in producing organization and disorganization. Also the 'grounded' view examines how organizations are constantly reproduced, but focusing both on human and non-human agencies, regarding organization as a transitory network emerging from the association between objects and individual accounting processes. All three perspectives can provide useful insights and they are complementary rather than alternative, since they imply each other. It is therefore useful to interplay the perspectives, accepting their duality and the opportunity of learning from their dialectic tensions (Fairhurst and Putnam 2004).

The patterned symbolic practices that constitute organizational discourse do not simply emerge from communication efforts aimed at coordinating actions or at promoting specific values and interests. Organizations are also knowledge management devices, a repository of capability integrating the specialized knowledge of multiple individuals (Kogut and Zander 1992; Grant 1996). As a consequence, discourses also have a knowledge ordering purpose: they are sensemaking devices purposefully producing intersubjective agreements and circulating information and intelligence according to preordained patterns: organizational discourses express a specific 'logic', intended as an ostensibly effective modality to manage knowledge. However, such logic is not absolute: there is no optimal way to integrate the tacit know-how of organizational members, or to determine how much effort should be invested in codifying such knowledge.

The need and opportunity for such investment will be for instance minimal in an organization which opts for a distributed mode of control, characterized by a loose coupling between formulation and execution of strategies (Pina e Cunha, Rego and Clegg 2011). Such an approach offers more flexibility and adaptability but far less control and predictability of outcomes than a hierarchical system; the choice of adopting either logic is not simply predicated on contingencies, as contingency theories predict (Donaldson 2001), such as objective characteristics of the external environment in which an organization is operating. The classic idea according to which a turbulent task environment demands an organic structure, based on adaptation and horizontal teamworking, while a stable context calls for a hierarchical and standardized (mechanistic) structure (Burns and Stalker 1966) is founded on the discursive assumption that, in both cases, a well-defined bureaucratic corporate structure is required to perform a complex task.

Different organizing discourses can successfully operate in the same context, adopting structural choices that express different values and purposes, enacting different environmental constraints and opportunities. Take for instance the divergent organizational models chosen by Al Qaida and by ISIS. The former is a flexible, geographically diffuse and non-hierarchical network of autonomous cells, while the latter is a top-down bureaucratic structure which requires a territory to be fully legitimized as a promise of an independent fundamentalist state, the 'Islamic caliphate' (Wood 2015). Analogously, both the Linux collaborative community and Microsoft operate in the same industry and deliver a comparable set of products. Nevertheless they are founded on diametrically opposed canons, in one case the principle of massive open collaboration based on a creative commons agreement, in the other a traditional corporation based on the strict protection of intellectual property and on a bureaucratic organizational structure (Pina e Cunha et al. 2011). Such diversity does not derive (uniquely) from the different rationalities that can be involved in organizing processes. Even a single ideal-typical form of rationality (for instance the 'vanilla variety' of corporate reason, technical rationality) when expressed in action can assume non-linear forms.

Contrary to espoused managerial common-sense preaching the need to foster innovation through knowledge integration, learning orientation and the nurturing of talent (Peters and Waterman 1982; Senge 1994), the way in which most organizations guarantee action alignment is not by fostering knowledge integration but by producing 'functional stupidity', that is, by reducing opportunities for individual action, reflection and doubt, thus providing that order and sense of certainty that allows organizations to function smoothly (Alvesson and Spicer 2012). In practice, in order to maximize their rationality, potential bureaucratic organizations compel their members to suspend their judgement, deferring decisions to other individuals who are less informed and involved. It is even possible to extend this argument further, arguing that something becomes organized only as a consequence of a semantic act of meaning making, since "the meaning of the concept [organization] is not separable from the signifying operation" (Clegg et al. 2005, pp. 151–2). In other words, 'organization' is uniquely in the eye of the discursive beholder and so are its positive connotations of coherent ordering.

In sum, organizations function by integrating knowledge and behaviours, but the way in which this amalgamation works is not univocal and can assume multiple forms, being influenced by different discourses. While organization and discourse are clearly implicated in each other they cannot be resolved in a metonymical equation, whereas organization is discourse and discourse is organization. This would be misleading because, as discussed at length in Chapter 4, organizations are not just made by talk and text but also because discourse is not exclusively 'organizing'. "If communication creates and maintains organization, it is also the nexus where systems are contested and dismantled" (Ashcraft, Kuhn and Cooren 2009, p. 7).

Communication can be an organizing as well as a disorganizing factor (Bisel 2009). Weick (1990), investigating the causes of a tragic air accident, shows that incomprehension and misunderstanding can arise not only by 'human errors' but as a result of the very systems (hierarchy and routines) that are supposed to coordinate activities, which can collapse disastrously in particular crisis situations. From a different perspective, Czarniawska (2004a) has compared the media representation of accidents impacting public transportation systems in Italy and Sweden, showing how metaphors, employed to overdramatize events, can become a discursive vehicle for disorganization. It is evident that "ordering and dis-ordering are interdependent, supplementary and parasitic" (Clegg et al. 2005, p. 153), so even disruptive consequences of discursive acts can be generative of alternative orders that advantage different interest groups.

The relationship between the linguistic and material components of organization is well represented by Ashcraft et al. (2009, p. 34), as they describe "communication as the ongoing, situated, and embodied process whereby human and non-human agencies interpenetrate ideation and materiality toward meanings that are tangible and axial to organizational existence and organizing phenomena". Two important notions are expressed in this statement: first, communication is not just the abstract product of human agents but is the outcome of the relationship between individuals and non-human actants; second, the meanings produced by communication are axial to organization. While they are generated by organizing practices and have an impact on them, they do not equate to them.

These considerations suggest that, instead of clarifying and opening new heuristic opportunities, a mere tropological juxtaposition of organization and discourse only confounds the two concepts. At the same time the interrelations between the two constructs are so substantial that a semantic overlapping between organization and discourse cannot be ignored. It is therefore important to explicate this relationship in a manner that eschews both linguistic reductionism (equating organization to discourse) and organizational reification (seeing discourse as a mere product of organization).

DISCOURSE AS ORGANIZING

One way to address this problem is to associate discourse with *organizing*, rather than with organization. This is based on the acknowledgement that only 'live' discourse can fully deploy their effects. A live discourse is one which is actively reproduced in everyday or ritual performances of actors and actants: examples in social life include the summer 'marching season', when Protestant fraternities and Ulster loyalists organize hundreds of parades in the streets in Northern Ireland (Bryan 2000), but also the celebration of Anzac Day in Australia, the Diwali Hindu festival in India, the Hajj pilgrimage to Mecca, etc. Conversely, in the case of a 'dead discourse' we might still find archaeological traces embedded in material objects that were created according to its logic, be these texts, symbolic structures or ways of talking. Aztec and Egyptian pyramids constitute obvious examples but one can also find archaeological relics in unexpected places. As noted in Chapter 4, one can still encounter material remnants of discourses long after they have been effectively displaced by new discourses, and these vestiges of the past can still produce effects. For instance, companies such as Zappos or Valve (Silverman 2012; Useem 2015) which are embracing the anti-managerial and anti-hierarchical gospel of "holacracy" (Robertson 2015) still widely employ the term *employees* to describe their personnel. Such terminology, evolved as part of the discourse of modernist organizations (Jacques 1995), clearly maintains a strong instrumental meaning, implicitly portraying individuals as tools employed by the company's owners to serve their aims. This is a stark contrast with the notion of empowerment preached by cutting-edge employers who, incidentally, do not appear keen on using the term 'workers' to define their workforce, possibly because of the Marxist/unionist connotation that such a term has. For instance such a term is *never* used, apart from a few mentions in the construct 'co-workers', in the entire website that Zappos maintains to "share its culture with the world" (www.zapposinsights.com). This example shows how the 'live' organizational discourses deal with the traces of past discourses, actively deciding to edit them in coherence with the system of meanings that they intend to highlight.

The coherent set of performed symbolic practices that can be recognized as a manifestation of a living discourse make use of the relics produced by older discourses, activating specific affordances of the material objects (words, texts, objects that they left behind). To use another metaphor connected with the idea of emerging organization, 'big D' Discourses can be represented as a rainforest (or as a coral reef) in which multiple local 'small d' discourses interact and intersect (as individual organisms do), competing, collaborating or ignoring each other, but together contributing to sustain a complex interrelated ecosystem. Picturing discourse as organizing is therefore not an implicit endorsement of the primacy of a 'becoming' or 'grounded' perspective over an 'object' one (Fairhurst and Putnam 2004). It means rather privileging the active, productive role of the living component over the passive function of actants that can only offer some resistance to certain forms of activation, as in the example (described in Chapter 4) of the older-style lecture theatre.

Focusing on organizing implies assuming process views of organizing, that is, looking at the *becoming* of organizations, rather than assuming their *being* (Nayak and Chia 2011). In other words, it means ceasing to pay attention to the *ostensive* character of the observed entities, understood as objects, considering their performative character as emergent constructs of social interactions and interpretations (Czarniawska 2014, p. 6). In this 'phenomenological' perspective subjectivity is "understood as inextricably involved in the process of constituting objectivity" (Moran 2000, cited in Holt and Sandberg 2011, p. 238), with the consequence that organizational structures have a dual character: they are the ongoing outcome of the performances of actors who, in turn, are influenced and constrained by the same structures (Giddens 1984).

This relationship can be expressed at a micro-level, where organizing is achieved through local discursive acts that differentiate and integrate:

> organizing emerges through linguistic forms that signal relational differences (such as, requests versus commands), align group members into categories (high versus low status), legitimate actions (affirm versus reject), enact powerful versus powerless speech forms (for instance, interruptions, hesitations, nonfluencies, forms of address), or signal domination (specifically, monopolizing turn taking and controlling topic shifts). (Fairhurst and Putnam 2004, p. 13)

Discourse can also operate as an organizing device at a macro, paradigmatic, level, acting as a sensemaking device. Organizing and discourse perform similar functions: as "organization is a censoring/centring device that works to create a figure/ground effect so that attention, focus and purposefulness are directed towards productive outcomes" (Chia 2002, p. 866), so discourse "is that which constrains and enables what can be said" (Barad 2003, p. 819).

This parallel between micro (local) and macro (paradigmatic) effects of discourse and organizing form can be further extended, to show that organizations, similarly to discourses, can be conceived at different scales of abstraction. On the one hand there are small 'o' organizations, concrete empirical objects possessing individual identities: corporations, small businesses, public agencies, etc. On the other hand there are big 'O' Organizations, ideal-typical constructs that either offer a template for individual concrete organizational entities, or that constitute generalized abstractions used by researchers to account for regularities, patterns of behaviours and common features characterizing many different empirical specimens. In the former category we can place, for instance, the different forms in which a collaborative entity can be 'incorporated', assuming a legal identity. In the latter are theoretical constructions such as the notion of *institutions* (DiMaggio and Powell 1983; Powell and DiMaggio 1991; Lawrence, Suddaby and Leca 2011; Greenwood et al. 2012), or that of *practices* (Bourdieu 1977; Gherardi 2000, 2012; Raelin 2007; Corradi, Gherardi and Verzelloni 2010).

Individual speech acts, conversations and texts will affect the organizing process in specific local contexts (organizations); these discursive performances interact with material, non-symbolic elements such as natural resources, individual personalities and emotions, cognitive schemes, physical objects, etc., communicating and persuading about concrete ways of arranging these elements in purposive and productive patterns, thus becoming the mortar that helps keep these "conceptually-stabilized abstractions" together (Chia 2002, p. 866).

Organizing activities do not happen in a void but use pre-existing conceptual building blocks and models that derive from an overarching field of paradigmatic Organizations/Discourses. Actors devise concrete organizations following templates dictated by institutional logics; the evidence of this is found in the uncanny similarity of many organizations, which is explained as the result of mimetic isomorphism, the drive to adopt similar structural forms in the belief that they are beneficial because socially (and discursively) legitimated (DiMaggio and Powell 1983). Similarly, concrete structures are the outcome of political decisions that are constrained by a broader circuit of 'system integration', a combination of discursive and material components which prescribes techniques of production and discipline (Clegg 1989; Oliveira and Clegg 2015). Finally, agentic behaviours and organizational routines are neither the outcome of the unthinking application of rigid rules, nor the fortuitous result of idiosyncratic inventiveness (Orr 1990; Feldman 2000; Orlikowski 2007), but the local expression of broader practices which incorporate institutional norms, material tools, implicit and codified knowledge and individual improvisation. Therefore, local organizations can be understood as constantly practised fields of practices (Gherardi 2006, p. 227), or bundles of practices that are performed in the present while being anchored to memories of the past (Schatzki 2005, 2006). Similarly, in local organizational contexts, stable identities and subjectivities are produced by the interaction of different domains of discourse rather than by the obligatory imposition of a single hyper-muscular discourse (Taylor 2011).

An organizational agent's "subjectivity" should be seen as "a medium and outcome of processes of resistance" (Brown, Clarke and Hailey 2009, p. 345), produced by actors as they reflexively and discursively narrate themselves (Kuhn 2006, p. 1360). In these self-narrations individuals actively mix fiction and history, anticipated events and past experiences, to produce a coherent account that gives them a sense of self-continuity (Ezzy 1998) around the identity being posited. Identity itself is "instituted through a stylized repetition of acts" (Butler 1988, p. 519) that allow individuals to "gain and confirm a [...] sense of their own normality" (Willmott 1994, p. 106). Consequently, individual subjectivities are not cast by discourse but emerge from the interplay of a sheaf of discourses. Depending on their cognitive, emotional and material resources agents can, to an extent, choose to position their self in this discursive plexus, enacting identity work by emphasizing or understating the relevance of specific discourses in defining their identity. Different discourses offer alternate "ideal selves" (Markus and Nurius 1986; Markus and Ruvolo 1989), and organizational members play an identity game not just by attempting to fill the gap between actual, ideal and 'ought to' identity (Higgins 1987) but also by selecting desirable combinations of identities. For their part, organizations take part in this identity game by emphasizing and rewarding certain identity performances while absconding or penalizing others, and also by selecting candidates who appear to impersonate the correct set of identities. The entire process implies negotiation strategies rather than the acquisition of a predefined subjectivity (Swann, Johnson and Bosson 2009).

The negotiated process of construction of subjectivity is based not only on linguistic and symbolic performances but also includes material acts and involves both human and non-human agencies, an *actor-network*. It is useful at this point to make a short detour to explicate this concept, delineating the theoretical framework known as 'sociology of translation' or actor-network theory (ANT) (Callon 1986; Czarniawska 2004b; Latour 2005; Law 2009). Actor-networks should not be considered as ontological entities but rather as epistemological devices (analogously to discourse). The purpose of ANT is to capture the elusive and ever-changing reality of social associations: "what the social sciences usually call 'society' is an ongoing achievement. ANT is an attempt to provide analytical tools for explaining the very process by which society is constantly reconfigured" (Callon 2002). *Network* is "meant [as] a series of transformations, translations, transductions [and not as] a transport without deformation" (Latour 1999, p. 16). Rejecting essentialism, the purpose of ANT researchers is to expose the processes through which any network grows in influence and/or contracts — (Fox 2005). *Associations* are the objects of enquiry, such that the "social, for ANT, is the name of a type of momentary association" (Latour 2005, p. 65). This forming and dissolving net is not a linear chain of events but a multidimensional, scarcely predictable spread, like a crack on a glass or the diffusion of an epidemic.

Even *actors* are not ontologically stable, since social groups and organizations are never durable: "if you stop making and remaking groups, you stop having groups" (Latour 2005, p. 35), and it is consequently necessary to focus on *performativity*, on actions: "if an actor makes no difference, it's not an actor" (Latour 2005, p. 130). This approach permits us to analyse those stable socio-technical assemblages that are taken for granted and "black-boxed in the form of an artefact" (Callon 2002, p. 64). For instance, by turning the ignition key in a car we might think we have total agency but in reality we are just a link in a complex socio-technical web of relationships involving other human actors (car builders, car sellers, fuel station attendants, etc.) and non-human entities (engine, tyres, petrol, etc.): "the driver not only starts up

the engine, but also triggers a perfectly coordinated collective action"
(Callon 2002, p. 63).

The role of non-sentient objects is crucial to mediate relationships.
Again taking the example of the car, an accident cannot be explained nor
discussed by human actors without calling upon a number of non-human
agencies, including traffic lights, road lines, mechanical malfunctioning,
etc. This is especially true in a contemporary society where technological
devices are omnipresent, and capable of performing highly complex
tasks. Stories of accidents caused by people who were following their
GPS navigator's instructions are common: puppeteers are not the only
ones who "say queer things like 'their marionettes suggest them to do
things'" (Latour 2005, p. 60). Looking at the role of scallops (Callon
1986), sea currents (Law 1987), and personal transport vehicles (Latour
1996), ANT studies restore the key role that artefacts have in the
development of human affairs (Czarniawska 2008). ANT is committed
to the principle of symmetry, which holds that both human and non-
human elements of any network must be treated analytically in the same
way, and they often manifest themselves as hybrid agents (Castor and
Cooren 2006): this is especially evident for knowledge workers, who
operate in an increasingly cybernized fashion, a human-machine blend
(Czarniawska 2011).

Human actors and non-human actants interact through constantly
changing networks of associations and reciprocal influence. In this
system of relationships certain actors become obligatory passage points
(Callon 1986) by effecting a translation. This is the process through
which one actor manages to 'black-box' other agents, becoming their
spokesperson or even metonymically appropriating their identities. For
instance, a galley black-boxes elements such as pitch, wood, canvas,
labourers, sailors, portolans, compasses, dry docks, merchants, etc. (Law
1987). This process implicates both discourse and power/knowledge:
black-boxing is both a process of semantic simplification, through which
the constituent parts of a network cease to be perceived as individual
entities, and a process of political integration and domination, through
which one becomes the voice of many, collapsing diversities and
differences of interest.

The conceptual arsenal of ANT appears highly relevant for our
discussion of the relationship between organization, materiality and
discourse. It provides a useful vocabulary and methodology to describe
organizing as the outcome of both discursive and material activities. The
resulting 'organization' can be conceived as an impermanent lattice in
which a symbolic action-net intersects material action-nets, interlacing as
warp and weft in a fabric.

The fabric analogy is imperfect, both because the 'threads' are not stable entities but transient assemblages (actor-networks), and because it is not always possible to separate the effects and the implications of discursive and material elements. Elements with a strong symbolic valence, such as attire or office layout, also have a tangible manifestation. Conversely, other events (for instance a dismissal) are discursively relevant and impact subjectivities but their most dramatic consequences concern a concrete alteration in possibilities of action and access to resources.

When collecting research data it is useful to distinguish between what is symbolic material (narratives, accounts, texts) and what are substantial, factual elements. It is possible to object that even facts are the product of a social construction, since "methodologies and research questions are inevitably theoretically informed" (Silverman 2010, p. 103). Scientific propositions and empirical realities are tangled up in a socio-technical network where research tools translate ('inscribe') physical phenomena relating them to theoretical propositions (Latour and Woolgar 1979; Knorr-Cetina 1981; Jasanoff et al. 1995; Bauchspies, Restivo and Croissant 2006). Nevertheless there is still a difference between the two. When researchers are collecting and analysing data on material events (e.g. looking at data on working hours or directly observing how people use workspaces) a single interpretative act is performed by the research-ers as they inscribe raw experience (observations) in a given heuristic framework. If researchers are instead gathering narrative accounts through interviews, or analysing corporate reports, raw data are already imbued with symbolic meanings or are filtered through linguistic perfor-mances. Two separate acts of discursive interpretation occur: one per-formed by the informant, and the other performed by the researcher. Using these sources of information requires therefore an additional analytic work, with the intent of deconstructing the translation process through which assemblages have been black-boxed, to reconstruct the categories and implicit theories employed by the informants to produce their accounts or to reflect critically on the discursive conditions that have determined their interpretation.

In this regard it is important to remember that the 'discursive trans-lations' operated by human agents are compounded by the active role of actants which – unwittingly but effectively – establish specific obligatory passage points. Mindless objects prompt behaviours, direct actions, influence cognition and decisions with organizational members fre-quently acted on by semiotic and material actants, and in particular by texts: "the paper that circulates within an administration is a full-fledged actor in that it literally transforms the people to whom it is addressed" (Cooren 2000, p. 176).

When texts assume the form of stories their influence is enhanced, since storytelling is "the preferred sensemaking currency of human relationships" (Boje 1991, p. 106). Stories provide simplified descriptions of reality, provided that they resonate with some experiences of the audience, or with story templates with which they are familiar (Wilkins 1983; Kitzinger 2000). Stories do what Gabriel (2000) defines as "story-work", based on weaving together fact and imagination with the purpose of conveying the idea of a deeper meaning in the narrated events. Stories can be conceptualized as actants that black-box, by 'editing' events and agencies, offering a potentially univocal translation of meaning. "The raw material of everyday organizational life consists of disconnected fragments, physical and verbal actions that do not make sense when reported with simple chronology [...] *Narrating involves organizing* [...] Simultaneously, *organizing makes narration possible* because it orders people, things and events in time and place" (Czarniawska and Gagliardi 2003, p. vii; emphasis in the original).

While storytelling is highly practised in organizations, not all texts assume the form of a narrative, since many other textual sensemaking and communication devices are used, "including theories, reports, statistics and numbers, opinions, platitudes, images, clichés, acronyms, logos and so forth" (Gabriel 2004, p. 75). Yet all these forms of generative communication are discursive and they perform actions formulating commands, enabling actions, supporting performances and sanctioning results (Cooren 2000).

In sum, considering the organizing metaphor reiterates and expands a point that was already made in the previous chapter: studying organization through a discursive lens is better achieved not by bracketing or ignoring what happens 'outside the text', but by considering how signs and materiality are imbricated. Employing a set of heuristic tools such as those provided by ANT, can for instance reveal how texts are actants that at times black-box and at others are black-boxed. ANT can therefore be employed as a complementary approach to, for example, a Foucauldian type of discourse analysis. This approach would provide a more comprehensive account of power relations than the one made possible by ANT alone. Sociology of translation does not overlook power, since it is interested in understanding how relations materialize as actors enrol and mobilize other actors in the network: "for ANT power is an explanandum, not the explanans" (Alcadipani and Hassard 2010, p. 423), an emergent property of the network.

The ANT view of power neglects the existence of enduring forms of power and domination, forgetting that some actors might enter the association from a position of advantage because they are better placed in already existent networks. Hence, the opportunity to triangulate this methodology with theoretical lenses more suited to understanding durable forms of domination, such as Foucauldian discourse analysis or *phronetic* approaches (Flyvbjerg 1998, 2001; Flyvbjerg, Landman and Schram 2012b), is suggested. In the last section I will consider in particular the contribution of phronesis as a means to reveal how pre-existing forms of power/knowledge, embedded in discourses, condition the associative possibilities of actor-networks.

POWER/KNOWLEDGE AND ORGANIZING

Considering the power/knowledge relationship in the context of organization studies implies acknowledging that the way in which knowledge is performatively generated in a context of discursive forces defines the very nature of an organization. *Phronesis* offers a theoretical framework and a methodology to investigate these phenomena. In order to clarify what phronetic social science is, it is useful to cite Flyvbjerg:

> In Aristotle's words, *phronesis* is an intellectual virtue that is "reasoned, and capable of action with regard to things that are good or bad for man." *Phronesis* concerns values and goes beyond analytical, scientific knowledge (*episteme*) and technical knowledge or know-how (*techne*) and it involves judgments and decisions made in the manner of a virtuoso social actor. [...]
>
> *Episteme* concerns universals and the production of knowledge that is invariable in time and space and achieved with the aid of analytical rationality. *Episteme* corresponds to the modern scientific ideal as expressed in natural science. [...]
>
> *Techne* can be translated into English as 'art' in the sense of 'craft'; a craftsperson is also an artisan. [...] *Techne* is thus craft and art, and as an activity it is concrete, variable, and context dependent. The objective of *techne* is application of technical knowledge and skills according to a pragmatic instrumental rationality. [...]
>
> Whereas *episteme* concerns theoretical know why and *techne* denotes technical know-how, *phronesis* emphasizes practical knowledge and practical ethics. Phronesis is often translated as 'prudence' or 'practical common sense.' [...] *Phronesis* is a sense or a tacit skill for doing the ethically practical rather than a kind of science. (Flyvbjerg 2004a, pp. 399–401; emphasis in the original)

The phronetic approach is "problem-driven, not methodology driven [and aiming] to arrive at social and political sciences that effectively deal with deliberation, judgment and praxis ..." (Flyvbjerg 2001, p. 196). It is a form of enquiry based on the key tenet that "social science cannot avoid context" (Flyvbjerg 2004a, p. 397). In sum, a phronetic approach "privileges context as a means to illustrate normative values and power dimensions in social issues" (Jarvis 2009, p. 63). This is not meant to be an alternative to other methods (for instance of positivistic enquiry) but rather a complementary approach to knowledge (Flyvbjerg 2004a) that, while renouncing grand theories, allows one to tackle practically and morally relevant social issues.

While *phronesis* is specifically concerned with the context-specific nature of knowledge (and morals) it also aims at developing general knowledge by providing a critical input in the ongoing theoretical dialogue (Cairns and Śliwa 2008). While sceptical of a view where the choice of correct action follows the application of an a priori theory, a phronetic approach is not a-theoretical but links action and theory in a bottom-up, contextual and action-oriented manner (Flyvbjerg, Landman and Schram 2012a). The type of key research question that is asked by a phronetic researcher best exemplifies the implications of the use of such an approach. Instead of posing hypotheses concerning causal relationships or advancing mere intellectual curiosities they have a strong political and ethical undertone:

1. Where are we going?
2. Who gains and who loses, and by which mechanisms of power?
3. Is this development desirable?
4. What, if anything, should we do about it? (Flyvbjerg 2004a, p. 405)

These questions, albeit stimulating and eye-opening, can be made sharper if the phronetic lens is reflexively trained on its own heuristic methods, revealing that even the shrewdest phronetic researcher is not immune to power/knowledge effects. As a consequence, it is useful to complement the previous list with some reflexive questions:

1. Am I conscious of the *illusio* of both the academic and the everyday research field?
2. What are my underlying pre-assumptions on the specific topic of my research?
3. How are my pre-assumptions going to affect the design of my research?
4. What are the consequences of the knowledge that I am going to produce? What is the political rationale of my work? (Lancione 2013, p. 154)

A phronetic approach is perfectly suited to investigating organizational discourse, especially when used to reinforce a critical discourse analysis perspective. Phronetic discourse analysis can be defined as "a form of critical inquiry that regards texts as particular instantiations of those public values and norms that, at a particular moment in time, happen to be dominant in our culture" (Chouliaraki 2008, p. 688). In this regard, its finalities appear very close to critical discourse analysis (CDA) but the two approaches diverge in the emphasis they put on texts or practices. According to CDA discourse is not limited to 'texts', defined as a product of communication processes but includes "the whole process of social interaction of which a text is just a part" (Fairclough 1989, p. 24). CDA analysis is inscribed in a broader context that includes social conditions of production and interpretation of texts, which includes structures of power and domination. Nevertheless, text remains the focus of the analysis and it is the primary empirical source to explicate underlying power relations.

A phronetic approach instead puts practices before discourse: "what people actually do [...] is seen as more fundamental than either discourse, text, or theory – what people say" (Flyvbjerg 2004b, p. 296). Practices are then examined in their contextual relations:

> If it is established, for example, that a certain planning practice is seen as rational according to its self-understanding – that is, by those practicing it, but not when viewed in the context of other horizons of meaning – the researcher then asks what role this ambiguous rationality plays in a further context, historically, socially, and politically, and what the consequences might be. (Flyvbjerg 2004b, p. 296)

A phronetic approach to discourse can reveal the tension underlying the way in which extant power relations produce knowledge, showing how the relationship between different discourses (big 'D' or small 'd') can produce, in a specific locale, particular performances which, in turn, reproduce discourse through translation activities. For instance, all large contemporary organizations appear to be cut out of the same cloth, being formally designed in accordance with a model of efficient allocation of means to calculated ends. The dominant rationality is expressed in a very 'muscular' Discourse, based on a belief in an objective, value-free, technical-instrumental rationality. Nonetheless, alternative discourses are still alive and powerful and the boundaries between discordant discursive fields are highly porous: practices bring actors and actants to operate across different discourses, creating tensions that are resolved in concrete power relations.

A concrete organizational case makes these power relations more evident. The struggles of the Vatican to reform its financial practices in the wake of scandals, allegations of money laundering, corruption and poor management practices offer an exemplary case. Various attempts have been made, starting under Pope Benedict XIII, to put order in the system in order to avoid the enormous reputational and financial risks involved, with the main reform efforts involving two highly criticized institutions: the Vatican Bank (formerly known as the 'Institute for the Works of Religion') and the Administration of the Patrimony of the Apostolic See (APSA) (McDaniel 2015, p. 152). There has actually being a flurry of change management initiatives aimed at the introduction of 'legal-rational' principles (such as standardized accounting practices, formalized norms and procedures, or technical expertise-based appointments) that have involved the central structure of the Vatican since the 1980s (Faggioli 2015). To this day they do not appear to have altered a situation marred by favouritism, opacity, waste and corruption. Even if these legal-rational practices constitute the standard modus operandi of any modern bureaucracy, any concrete bid to implement them has been thwarted by the passive-aggressive resistance of the establishment, embodied by the Roman Curia, the local members of the clergy administering the Vatican. While this type of struggle between 'rationalization' intents and local interest is quite common, what makes the case of the Vatican interesting is both the way in which the leadership of the organization, embodied by the pontiff, has dealt with this resistance as well as the type of discursive resources employed to resist change.

Any 'modern' organization would have tackled the issue by performing or commissioning an independent technical survey and analysis of the situation. This move would then be typically followed by the execution of decisions legitimized by a 'rationalization' need, including restructuring or downsizing the organization, removing any offending party and appointing new administrators, together with a mandated introduction of new sets of rules.

Instead, the approach of the reigning popes has been much more circuitous: unlike modern CEOs, they have often tip-toed around the challenge to their authority posed by a strong coalition of executives (the cardinals) bent on maintaining the status quo. John Paul II completely avoided any attempts at reforming the structure of the central government, creating instead a charismatic model of governance based on his entourage (Faggioli 2015), and by doing so both preserved and indirectly legitimated a culture of 'irrational' management. Benedict XVI's approach was even more peculiar, underplaying the role of the curia as "an object lacking theological substance" (Faggioli 2015, p. 566). In addition to this discursive move he also tried to circumvent the problem by appointing an 'outsider' cardinal as Secretary of State, bypassing a curia that in his view "need not rule nor be reformed" (Faggioli 2015, p. 567). This strategy proved ruinous and contributed to the almost unprecedented early resignation of the pontiff. His successor, Pope Francis, building on his personal charisma but also aware of the necessity to tackle the issue of command and control in the Vatican, has embarked on a more ambitious reform agenda, recognizable as part of a standard managerialist repertoire. Strategies have included enlisting leading management consulting firms to assess and oversee the reformation process (Winfield 2013) and the appointment of a council of high-calibre businesspeople under the aegis of a politically and administratively astute cardinal, George Pell, to head a new Secretariat for the Economy (Kahn 2015). Points of pressure are thus being developed for the incursion of new discourses preciously excluded.

While this attempt is still ongoing, leaked internal secret documents published as the basis of two bestselling journalistic investigation books (Nuzzi 2014, 2015) show that the opposition to change is stronger than ever. The high-profile change management team (whose authority would be irresistible in most organizational contexts) is frequently frustrated in its attempts to bring about even modest reforms. Even requests backed by full papal authority for information and data on assets, account ledgers, procurement practices are typically met with mellifluous messages expressing sentiments of brotherhood and collegiality, full support for the intent of preserving the assets of the church, together with wishes for a successful completion of the enterprise while at the same time avoiding offering any concrete information or support. The 'dance' of pious and courteous demands and indirect denials can be tracked in several examples of correspondence exchanges that became public after the 'Vatileaks'. The chasm between the form and the substance of this communication is evident in this extract from a letter sent by the prelate in charge of one of the reform commissions, Mons. Vallejo Balda, to the new Secretary of State, Mons. Pietro Parolin, requesting collaboration in guaranteeing access to essential accounting information:

> We were pleased to find, almost everywhere, a cordial reception and concrete collaboration, a sign of profound awareness of and loyal adherence to the desiderata of His Holiness. Pursuant to the dictated of the Pontifical Chirograph by which this Commission was established, I would therefore like to cordially request that you provide instruction for our operators to be provided with all the documentation. (Cited in Nuzzi 2015, p. 53)

The suave and courteous tone of the request makes this passage much mellower than the most diplomatic of corporate memos, yet it is permeated with oblique intimidations and remonstrations. 'Almost everywhere' is a clear hint that sometimes requests were met with hostility; moreover, most of the text is intent at highlighting that the request is highly authoritative, first by mentioning the pontiff's wishes, then by means of the reference to the papal decree (the 'chirograph') which bestows its legal mandate. Even more remarkable is the list, attached to the message, which enumerates the missing information that is the object of the request: "we have not yet received: the list of bank accounts, held or managed by the Secretariat of State and a full vision of the management of funds collected" (cited in Nuzzi 2015, p. 54). The data so politely requested are not ancillary technical documents but basic information that would be in the public domain in any legal-rational organizations!

A phronetic lens helps to reflect on the intersection between individual agency expressed in the use of language and structural and material elements. A superficial reading of the dynamics of power at play in this case would merely concentrate on the sources of agentic power that become available to some actors thanks to the areas of uncertainty that spring from a bureaucratic void (Crozier and Friedberg 1980). However, this issue would be resolved in an explicit power struggle, with the likely victory of the discursive forces of 'rationalization' drawing strong support from the global Discourses of managerialism, legality, modernity. The current way of acting, characterized by intrigue, favouritism, dissipation, appears unconscionable from the perspective of devout Catholics who should view wastefulness and profligacy as a sin, especially considering that the Church should invest its energies in pastoral and charitable activities. It is patent that a crisis of legitimacy is present but the potential protagonists of this discursive wave appear to be very timid and irresolute.

What is interesting in this case is not the presence of a political struggle but the lengths to which the challengers go to appear not to be in conflict and to avoid disturbances, behaviour that cannot be explained simply by the desire to present an external image of harmony since these communications were meant to be internal, secret documents. To comprehend this circumspect, hesitant, power play it is necessary to consider the 'horizons of meanings' that characterize the system as well as the complex array of supporting institutional forces and material elements.

The contemporary Catholic Church is a hybrid of legal-rational and of traditional, value-rationality-based principles. For instance, its hierarchy is now based on a 'merit' system in which higher positions are assigned to long-serving members who have distinguished themselves for their qualities and competence: bishops and cardinals are – at least on the surface – all mature clergymen with a distinguished career. At the same time, the Church's structure of domination and authority is still based on "a monopoly of the legitimate use of hierocratic coercion", that is, "psychic coercion by distributing or denying religious benefits" (Weber 1922 [1978], p. 52). Grace and absolution cannot be dispensed according to a conventional set of formal rules, since this would defy the essential interpretive and mediating role performed by the Catholic clergy (the alternative would mean turning into Protestants). As a consequence, the members of the hierarchy must remain endowed with a high level of discretionary power, with the system resting on a strong social contract based on trust and personal relationship. Social capital is pivotal in supporting the system and cannot be disrupted. For instance, the current supply network is based on a 'court' of providores, contractors and cronies operating on the basis of a personal fiduciary relationship. Trust is not predicated on their quality and honesty as purveyors but mostly on their demonstrated ability to guarantee privacy and personal loyalty to their clients. The introduction of bureaucratic rationalization would compromise this indulgency system (Gouldner 1954, 1955) creating dangerous ripples in the social network that enables hierocratic coercion.

Another central role is played by the way in which change is managed in the context of the Catholic Church. As one of the oldest, most enduring organizations in the world, its inherent conservatism is not surprising; yet its resilience as an institution demonstrates its ability to adapt to different conditions. Change in the Church appears typically to follow a model that has been defined as "enclaving". This is a "carefully controlled integration of learning within the existing structure, its 'capture' [...] from a particular enclave" (Mintzberg and Westley 1992, p. 52). Innovation attempts are, at first, tolerated but isolated to avoid challenges or contamination to other activities. The change can become accepted, legitimized and allowed to infuse the rest of the organization only if and when (typically after several years) two conditions are met: the transformative enclave must have moderated its radicalism; and the organization is going through a crisis which requires it to effect some reform (Mintzberg and Westley 1992). As a consequence, change happens but always at a glacial pace, eschewing jolts and with a very long time horizon.

Another material, non-discursive aspect, interferes with the pace of this transformation and assumes a particular relevance in the case of the botched rationalization attempts: the advanced age of the most influential members of the curia, the cardinals. Any conservative cardinal can block change by stalling it for a short period of time, before changes in the governing body, caused by the 'natural' turnover of the decision-makers, takes care of the reformist efforts. Paradoxically, one concession to modernity is hindering the adoption of other legal-rational principles: senior clergymen are so old because they must demonstrate their qualities by serving proficiently in the ranks of the organization for many decades. Doing so is quite different from what was customary in past centuries when purple clothes and Bishop's rings were bestowed by virtue of lineage, and juvenile cardinals were unexceptional.

The same rhetoric used by some to justify the need for transparency and efficiency in the management of the Church's mission is used by others to thwart change, by discursively justifying conservation as prudence and timidity of efforts as disinterest in mundanity. Analogously, the need to uphold values of fraternal communion and spiritual union can hamper transformation, since overt oppositions cannot be manifest, and decisions are constantly postponed. Communication is "systematically distorted" by self-referential systems, which "attempt[s] to reproduce themselves by subordinating all changes into a maintenance of their own set of imaginary relations" (Deetz 1992, p. 182), thus blocking the possibility of meaningful debate. The practical consequence is the anaemic flow of data that, in turn, disempowers otherwise influential actants: accounting reports and financial statements.

The example above shows how the multiple agencies that operate in an organization are not simply manipulated by discursive forces but are integrating a complex flow of material and symbolic forces. At the same time different discourses produce (and are sustained by) organizing and rationalizing structures that empower or disempower different agencies, thus enabling or thwarting their 'translation' attempts.

In conclusion, in this chapter I have argued that, while symbolic practices have a pivotal role in producing and preserving social patterns and organizational settings, it would be problematic to equate discourse and organization, since the latter requires more than mere talk to be substantiated. It is more useful to consider discourses as organizing devices that operate in conjunction with material elements. For this reason, it is useful to employ text-focused methodologies in conjunction with approaches, such as actor-network theory, that can take into account both the role of non-human actants and the performative unfolding of the mesh of associations that are then crystallized in textual representations. At the same time, we cannot imagine that this spinning of social webs happens in a void: existing structures of power/knowledge, embedded in discourse, constrain and enable these associations and it is therefore important to apply a phronetic critical perspective to the analysis. In

Chapter 6 I will further expand these themes, showing that discourses affect actants not simply by virtue of the meaning they produce but also through their emptiness.

REFERENCES

Ahrne, G. and Brunsson, N. 2005, 'Organizations and Meta-organizations', *Scandinavian Journal of Management*, vol. 21, no. 4, pp. 429–49.

Alcadipani, R. and Hassard, J. 2010, 'Actor-Network Theory, Organizations and Critique: Towards a Politics of Organizing', *Organization*, vol. 17, pp. 419–35.

Alvesson, M. and Kärreman, D. 2011, 'Decolonializing Discourse: Critical Reflections on Organizational Discourse Analysis', *Human Relations*, vol. 64, pp. 1121–46.

Alvesson, M. and Spicer, A. 2012, 'A Stupidity-Based Theory of Organizations', *Journal of Management Studies*, vol. 49, no. 7, pp. 1194–1220.

Ashcraft, K.L., Kuhn, T.R. and Cooren, F. 2009, 'Constitutional Amendments: "Materializing" Organizational Communication', *The Academy of Management Annals*, vol. 3, no. 1, pp. 1–64.

Barad, K. 2003, 'Posthumanist Performativity: Toward an Understanding of How Matter Comes to Matter', *Signs*, vol. 28, pp. 801–31.

Bauchspies, W.K., Restivo, S.P. and Croissant, J. 2006, *Science, Technology, and Society: A Sociological Approach*, Blackwell Publishing, Malden, MA.

Bisel, R.S. 2009, 'On a Growing Dualism in Organizational Discourse Research', *Management Communication Quarterly*, vol. 22, no. 4, pp. 614–38.

Boje, D.M. 1991, 'The Storytelling Organization: A Study of Story Performance in an Office-Supply Firm', *Administrative Science Quarterly*, vol. 36, pp. 106–26.

Boje, D.M., Oswick, C. and Ford, J.D. 2004, 'Language and Organization: The Doing of Discourse', *Academy of Management Review*, vol. 29, no. 4, pp. 571–7.

Bourdieu, P. 1977, *Outline of a Theory of Practice*, trans. R. Nice, Cambridge University Press, Cambridge, UK.

Brown, A.D., Clarke, C.A. and Hailey, V.H. 2009, 'Working Identities?: Antagonistic Discursive Resources and Managerial Identity', *Human Relations*, vol. 62, pp. 323–52.

Bryan, D. 2000, *Orange Parades: The Politics of Ritual, Tradition and Control*, Pluto Press, London.

Burns, T. and Stalker, G.M. 1966, *The Management of Innovation*, vol. SSP 6, Tavistock, London.

Butler, J. 1988, 'Performative Acts and Gender Constitution: An Essay in Phenomenology and Feminist Theory', *Theatre Journal*, vol. 40, pp. 519–31.

Cairns, G. and Śliwa, M. 2008, 'The Implications of Aristotle's Phronēsis for Organizational Inquiry', in D. Barry and H. Hansen (eds), *The SAGE Handbook of New Approaches in Management and Organization*, SAGE, Thousand Oaks, CA, pp. 318–28.

Callon, M. 1986, 'Some Elements of a Sociology of Translation-Domestication of the Scallops and the Fishermen of St-Brieuc Bay', in J. Law (ed.), *Power, Action and Belief: A New Sociology of Knowledge?*, Routledge, London, pp. 196–223.

Callon, M. 2002, 'Actor Network Theory', in N.J. Smelser and P.B. Baltes (eds), *International Encyclopedia of Social & Behavioral Sciences*, Elsevier Ltd, Amsterdam, pp. 62–6.

Castor, T. and Cooren, F. 2006, 'Organizations as Hybrid Forms of Life: The Implications of the Selection of Agency in Problem Formulation', *Management Communication Quarterly*, vol. 19, no. 4, pp. 570–600.

Chia, R. 2000, 'Discourse Analysis as Organizational Analysis', *Organization*, vol. 7, no. 3, pp. 513–18.

Chia, R. 2002, 'Essai: Time, Duration and Simultaneity: Rethinking Process and Change in Organizational Analysis', *Organization Studies (Walter de Gruyter GmbH & Co. KG.)*, vol. 23, pp. 863–8.

Chouliaraki, L. 2008, 'Discourse Analysis', in T. Bennett and J. Frow (eds), *The SAGE Handbook of Cultural Analysis*, SAGE, London, pp. 674–98.

Clegg, S.R. 1989, *Frameworks of Power*, SAGE Publications, London.

Clegg, S.R., Kornberger, M. and Rhodes, C. 2005, 'Learning/Becoming/Organizing', *Organization*, vol. 12, pp. 147–67.

Cooren, F. 2000, *The Organizing Property of Communication*, vol. 65, John Benjamins Publishing, Amsterdam.

Cornelissen, J.P. 2005, 'Beyond Compare: Metaphor in Organization Theory', *The Academy of Management Review*, vol. 30, pp. 751–64.

Corradi, G., Gherardi, S. and Verzelloni, L. 2010, 'Through the Practice Lens: Where is the Bandwagon of Practice-based Studies Heading?', *Management Learning*, vol. 41, pp. 265–83.

Crozier, M. and Friedberg, E. 1980, *Actors and Systems: The Politics of Collective Action*, University of Chicago Press, Chicago, IL.

Czarniawska, B. 2004a, 'Metaphors as Enemies of Organizing, or the Advantages of a Flat Discourse', *International Journal of the Sociology of Language*, vol. 166, pp. 45–65.

Czarniawska, B. 2004b, 'On Time, Space, and Action Nets', *Organization*, vol. 11, pp. 773–91.

Czarniawska, B. 2008, 'Organizations as Obstacles to Organizing', paper presented to the *Nobel Symposium Foundations of Organization August 28–30, 2008 Stockholm*, accesssed 1 March 2012 at http://bit.ly/Zo2fcx

Czarniawska, B. 2011, *Cyberfactories: How News Agencies Produce News*, Edward Elgar Publishing, Cheltenham, UK and Northampton, MA, USA.

Czarniawska, B. 2014, *A Theory of Organizing: Second Edition*, Edward Elgar Publishing, Cheltenham, UK and Northampton, MA, USA.

Czarniawska, B. and Gagliardi, P. (eds) 2003, *Narratives we Organize By*, John Benjamins, Amsterdam.

Deetz, S.A. 1992, *Democracy in an Age of Corporate Colonization: Developments in Communication and the Politics of Everyday life*, SUNY Press, New York.

DiMaggio, P.J. and Powell, W.W. 1983, 'The Iron Cage Revisited: Institutional Isomorphism and Collective Rationality in Organizational Fields', *American Sociological Review*, vol. 48, pp. 147–60.

Donaldson, L. 2001, *The Contingency Theory of Organizations*, SAGE, Thousand Oaks, CA.

Ezzy, D. 1998, 'Theorizing Narrative Identity: Symbolic Interactionism and Hermeneutics', *The Sociological Quarterly*, vol. 39, pp. 239–52.

Faggioli, M. 2015, 'The Roman Curia at and after Vatican II: Legal-Rational or Theological Reform?', *Theological Studies*, vol. 76, no. 3, pp. 550–71.

Fairclough, N. 1989, *Language and Power*, Longman, New York.

Fairhurst, G.T. and Putnam, L. 2004, 'Organizations as Discursive Constructions', *Communication Theory*, vol. 14, no. 1, pp. 5–26.

Feldman, M.S. 2000, 'Organizational Routines as a Source of Continuous Change', *Organization Science*, vol. 11, pp. 611–29.

Flyvbjerg, B. 1998, *Rationality and Power: Democracy in Practice*, University of Chicago Press, Chicago, IL.

Flyvbjerg, B. 2001, *Making Social Science Matter: Why Social Inquiry Fails and how it can Succeed Again*, Cambridge University Press, Cambridge, UK.

Flyvbjerg, B. 2004a, 'A Perestroikan Straw Man Answers Back: David Laitin and Phronetic Political Science', *Politics & Society*, vol. 32, pp. 389–416.

Flyvbjerg, B. 2004b, 'Phronetic Planning Research: Theoretical and Methodological Reflections', *Planning Theory & Practice*, vol. 5, no. 3, pp. 283–306.

Flyvbjerg, B., Landman, T. and Schram, S. 2012a, 'Important Next Steps in Phronetic Social Science', in B. Flyvbjerg, T. Landman and S. Schram (eds), *Real Social Science: Applied Phronesis*, Cambridge University Press, Cambridge, pp. 285–96.

Flyvbjerg, B., Landman, T. and Schram, S. 2012b, *Real Social Science: Applied Phronesis*, Cambridge University Press, Cambridge, UK.

Fox, S. 2005, 'An Actor-Network Critique of Community in Higher Education: Implications for Networked Learning', *Studies in Higher Education*, vol. 30, pp. 95–110.

Gabriel, Y. 2000, *Storytelling in Organizations: Facts, Fictions, and Fantasies*, Oxford University Press, Oxford, UK.

Gabriel, Y. 2004, 'Narratives, Stories and Texts', in D. Grant, C. Hardy, C. Oswick and L.L. Putnam (eds), *The SAGE Handbook of Organizational Discourse*, SAGE, London, pp. 61–78.

Gherardi, S. 2000, 'Practice-Based Theorizing on Learning and Knowing in Organizations', *Organization*, vol. 7, pp. 211–23.

Gherardi, S. 2006, *Organizational Knowledge: The Texture of Workplace Learning*, Blackwell, London.

Gherardi, S. 2012, *How to Conduct a Practice-based Study: Problems and Methods*, Edward Elgar Publishing, Cheltenham, UK and Northampton, MA, USA.

Giddens, A. 1984, *Constitution of Society: Outline of the Theory of Structuration*, Polity Press, Cambridge, UK.

Gouldner, A.W. 1954, *Wildcat Strike*, Antioch Press, Yellow Springs, OH.

Gouldner, A.W. 1955, *Patterns of Industrial Bureaucracy*, Routledge & Kegan Paul, London, UK.

Grant, D., Hardy, C., Oswick, C. and Putnam, L.L. 2004, 'Organizational Discourse: Exploring the Field', in D. Grant, C. Hardy, C. Oswick and L.L. Putnam (eds), *The SAGE Handbook of Organizational Discourse*, SAGE, London, pp. 1–35.

Grant, R.M. 1996, 'Toward a Knowledge-based Theory of the Firm', *Strategic Management Journal*, vol. 17, no. S2, pp. 109–22.

Greenwood, R., Oliver, C., Sahlin, K. and Suddaby, R. (eds) 2012, *Institutional Theory in Organization Studies*, SAGE, London, UK.

Higgins, E.T. 1987, 'Self-Discrepancy: A Theory Relating Self and Affect', *Psychological Review*, vol. 94, no. 3, p. 319.

Holt, R. and Sandberg, J. 2011, 'Phenomenology and Organization Theory', in H. Tsoukas and R. Chia (eds), *Philosophy and Organization Theory*, Emerald Group Publishing Ltd, Bradford, UK, pp. 215–50.

Jacques, R. 1995, *Manufacturing the Employee: Management Knowledge from the 19th to 21st Centuries*, SAGE, London.

Jarvis, W.P. 2009, 'Moral Accountability in the MBA: A Kantian Response to a Public Problem', University of Technology Sydney, Australia.

Jasanoff, S., Markle, G., Petersen, J. and Pinch, T. (eds) 1995, *Handbook of Science and Technology Studies*, SAGE, Thousand Oaks, CA.

Kahn, J. 2015, 'Pope Revamps the Scandal-Wracked Vatican Bank', *Bloomberg Business*, 6 May 2015.

Kitzinger, J. 2000, 'Media Templates: Patterns of Association and the (Re)Construction of Meaning over Time', *Media, Culture & Society*, vol. 22, pp. 61–84.

Knorr-Cetina, K. 1981, *The Manufacture of Knowledge: An Essay on the Constructivist and Contextual Nature of Science*, Pergamon Press, Oxford, UK.

Kogut, B. and Zander, U. 1992, 'Knowledge of the Firm, Combinative Capabilities, and the Replication of Technology', *Organization Science*, vol. 3, no. 3, pp. 383–97.

Kuhn, T. 2006, 'A "Demented Work Ethic" and a "Lifestyle Firm": Discourse, Identity, and Workplace Time Commitments', *Organization Studies*, vol. 27, pp. 1339–58.

Lancione, M. 2013, 'Truthful Social Science or How we Learned to Stop Worrying and Love the Bomb', *Journal of Political Power*, vol. 6, pp. 147–55.

Latour, B. 1996, *Aramis, or, the Love of Technology*, Harvard University Press, Cambridge, MA.

Latour, B. 1999, 'On Recalling ANT', *The Sociological Review*, vol. 47, no. S1, pp. 15–25.

Latour, B. 2005, *Reassembling the Social: An Introduction to Actor-Network-Theory*, Clarendon, Oxford, UK.

Latour, B. and Woolgar, S. 1979, *Laboratory Life: The Social Construction of Scientific Facts*, vol. 80, SAGE Publications, Beverly Hills, CA.

Law, J. 1987, 'On the Social Explanation of Technical Change: The Case of the Portuguese Maritime Expansion', *Technology and Culture*, vol. 28, pp. 227–52.

Law, J. 2009, 'Actor-Network Theory and Material Semiotics', in B.S. Turner (ed.), *The New Blackwell Companion to Social Theory*, Wiley-Blackwell, Hoboken, NJ, pp. 141–57.

Lawrence, T.B., Suddaby, R. and Leca, B. 2011, 'Institutional Work: Refocusing Institutional Studies of Organization', *Journal of Management Inquiry*, vol. 20, pp. 52–8.

Markus, H. and Nurius, P. 1986, 'Possible Selves', *American Psychologist*, vol. 41, no. 9, p. 954.

Markus, H. and Ruvolo, A. 1989, 'Possible Selves: Personalized Representations of Goals', in L.A. Pervin (ed.), *Goal Concepts in Personality and Social Psychology*, Erlbaum, Hillsdale, NJ.

McCabe, D. 2016, '"Curiouser and Curiouser!": Organizations as Wonderland – A Metaphorical Alternative to the Rational Model', *Human Relations*, vol. 69, no. 4, pp. 945–73.

McDaniel, C.J. 2015, *Civil Society and the Reform of Finance: Taming Capital, Reclaiming Virtue*, Routledge, Abingdon, UK.

Mintzberg, H. and Westley, F. 1992, 'Cycles of Organizational Change', *Strategic Management Journal*, vol. 13, no. S2, pp. 39–59.

Moran, D. 2000, *Introduction to Phenomenology*, Routledge, London.

Morgan, G. 2006, *Images of Organization*, SAGE, Thousand Oaks, CA.

Mumby, D.K. and Clair, R.D. 1997, 'Organizational Discourse', in T.A. van Dijk (ed.), *Discourse Studies – A Multidisciplinary Introduction: Vol. 2 – Discourse as Social Interaction*, SAGE, Newbury Park, CA, pp. 181–205.

Nayak, A. and Chia, R. 2011, 'Thinking Becoming and Emergence: Process Philosophy and Organization Studies', in H. Tsoukas and R. Chia (eds), *Philosophy and Organization Theory*, Emerald Group Publishing Ltd, Bradford, UK, pp. 281–310.

Nuzzi, G. 2014, *Ratzinger was Afraid: The Secret Documents, the Money and the Scandals that Overwhelmed the Pope*, Adagio eBook.

Nuzzi, G. 2015, *Merchants in the Temple: Inside Pope Francis's Secret Battle Against Corruption in the Vatican*, Macmillan, London.

Oliveira, J. and Clegg, S.R. 2015, 'Paradoxical Puzzles of Control and Circuits of Power', *Qualitative Research in Accounting & Management*, vol. 12, no. 4, pp. 425–51.

Orlikowski, W.J. 2007, 'Sociomaterial Practices: Exploring Technology at Work', *Organization Studies*, vol. 28, no. 9, pp. 1435–48.

Orr, J.E. 1990, 'Talking about Machines: An Ethnography of a Modern Job', Cornell University Press, Ithaca, NY.

Peters, T.J. and Waterman, R.H. 1982, *In Search of Excellence: Lessons from America's Best-run Companies*, Harper & Row, New York.

Pfeffer, J. and Salancik, G.R. 1978, *The External Control of Organizations: A Resource Dependence Approach*, Harper & Row, New York.

Pina e Cunha, M., Rego, A. and Clegg, S. 2011, 'Beyond Addiction: Hierarchy and Other Ways of Getting Strategy Done', *European Management Journal*, vol. 29, no. 6, pp. 491–503.

Powell, W.W. and DiMaggio, P.J. 1991, *The New Institutionalism in Organizational Analysis*, University of Chicago Press, Chicago, IL.

Raelin, J.A. 2007, 'Toward an Epistemology of Practice', *Academy of Management Learning & Education*, vol. 6, p. 495.

Robertson, B.J. 2015, *Holacracy: The Revolutionary Management System that Abolishes Hierarchy*, Penguin, London.

Schatzki, T.R. 2005, 'Peripheral Vision: The Sites of Organizations', *Organization Studies*, vol. 26, pp. 465–84.

Schatzki, T.R. 2006, 'On Organizations as they Happen', *Organization Studies*, vol. 27, no. 12, pp. 1863–73.

Senge, P.M. 1994, *The Fifth Discipline: The Art and Practice of the Learning Organization*, Doubleday/Currency, New York.

Silverman, D. 2010, *Doing Qualitative Research: A Practical Handbook*, SAGE, London.

Silverman, R.E. 2012, 'Who's the Boss? There isn't One', *The Wall Street Journal*, 19 June 2012.

Swann, W.B., Johnson, R.E. and Bosson, J.K. 2009, 'Identity Negotiation at Work', *Research in Organizational Behavior*, vol. 29, pp. 81–109.

Taylor, J.R. 2011, 'Organization as an (Imbricated) Configuring of Transactions', *Organization Studies*, vol. 32, no. 9, pp. 1273–94.

Useem, J. 2015, 'Are Bosses Necessary?', *The Atlantic*, October.

Weber, M. 1922 [1978], *Economy and Society: an Outline of Interpretive Sociology*, University of California Press, Berkeley, CA.

Weick, K.E. 1969 [1979], *The Social Psychology of Organizing*, 2nd edn, Addison-Wesley, Reading, MA.

Weick, K.E. 1990, 'The Vulnerable System: An Analysis of the Tenerife Air Disaster', *Journal of Management*, vol. 16, pp. 571–93.

Wilkins, A.L. 1983, 'Organizational Stories as Symbols which Control the Organization', in L. Pondy, P. Frost, G. Morgan and T. Dandridge (eds), *Organizational Symbolism*, JAI Press, Greenwich, CT, pp. 81–92.

Willmott, H. 1994, 'Theorizing Human Agency: Responding to the Crises of (Post)Modernity', in J. Hassard and M. Parker (eds), *Towards a New Theory of Organizations*, Routledge, London, pp. 44–60.

Winfield, N. 2013, 'Vatican Enlists McKinsey and KPMG to Oversee Communication and Financial Reforms', *Huffington Post*, 19 December 2013.

Wood, G. 2015, 'What ISIS Really Wants', *The Atlantic*, March.

6. Discourse as a mask: silence, emptiness and ambiguity in discourse

DISCOURSES AND MASQUERADES

The images of discourse considered in the previous chapters are characterized by a plenum of meaning: identifying discourses with maps and
organizing devices emphasizes their capacity to generate and convey
meanings. However, organizational discourses can also suppress communication and can be built around a central void, a fundamental
emptiness. Corporate and managerial discourses are often characterized
by grandiosity, in the attempt to produce a superficial status-enhancing
image:

> Grandiosity gilds the lily by lending a golden haze to various phenomena.
> Since this involves considerable doctoring of a world that is not always
> beautiful, it also involves the application of smoke screens [...] In working
> life, bureaucracy and mass production have had to make way for so-called
> knowledge-intensive companies, dynamic networks, and flexible, customer-
> steered operations. And people are employed for 'value creation processes'
> rather than for the production of goods and services. Small businesses are
> now run by 'entrepreneurs', at least according to researchers and policy-
> makers. Maybe one or two bicycle repairers or hairdressers have failed to
> keep up with the times and still regard themselves as small business owners?
> Managers and supervisors are increasingly labelled as 'leaders' [...] There is
> considerable inflation of job titles: more and more people have become
> 'managers' and 'executives', and it is not particularly exclusive to have 'vice
> president' on your business card these days. (Alvesson 2013, pp. 9–10)

Ambiguity, superficiality, silence result from both local and global
discourses, and these 'negative' outcomes can be as significant and
influential as their 'positive' (in sense of generative) effects. To account
for these 'hollow discourses' I will now introduce an alternative metaphor, discourse as a mask. The concept conjures the image of a physical
object (as in a ritual or theatrical mask) but also that of cosmetic
make-up. In both cases, masquerading implies altering one's features, to

embrace and communicate an alternative, ideal, fictional or symbolic identity. Thinking of a mask evokes different ideas: the first is about performance, and the fact that a mask can be used to conceal the true 'identity' of the wearer, offering (or imposing) a particular role. This particular meaning reiterates two concepts that we have already examined: discourse is generative of subjectivity, and discourse is (re)produced in performances. We are cognizant of the artificial nature of masks, and yet this awareness can be lost in a masquerade, as happens when both actors and the audience identify with fictional characters, or when we are seduced by the effects of well-applied make-up. Similarly, discourses can produce meaning, identity and action both in visible and explicit ways, and in implicit, paradigmatic ways.

However, a mask can be also seen as a means to deny communication, muzzling voices or even hiding someone's existence, as in the story of *The Man in the Iron Mask*, fictionalized by Alexandre Dumas but based on an actual political prisoner who, during the reign of Louis XIV of France, was forced to wear a velvet cloth mask to keep his identity secret. Like this mysterious mask, discourses can overtly or stealthily suppress voices. The distinction between the two types of silencing is not straightforward: on the one hand there are organizational situations in which it is possible to recognize explicit acts performed by certain actors with the intent of silencing others. At other times it is possible to identify situations in which actors are implicated in self-censoring, self-alienating behaviours in which they suppress their capacity to actively contribute to the formation of discourse. As a consequence, a collective phenomenon of 'organizational silence' can emerge from a combination of individual agencies and contextual and structural issues.

To say that a mask works only by repressing its wearer's identity would be one-sided. Masks can also be seen as liberating, at least when employed in particular social contexts, such as the carnival, where they can produce a subversion of the current status quo, liberating energies that lead to change and transformation: "The mask is connected with the joy of change and reincarnation, with gay relativity and with the merry negation of uniformity and similarity; it rejects conformity to oneself. The mask is related to transition, metamorphoses, the violation of natural boundaries, to mockery and familiar nicknames" (Bakhtin 1965, p. 40).

There is an interesting contradiction in this idea: how could a standardized, artificial mask liberate its wearers? Is it possible to conceive of discourses that while constraining their speakers into rigid interpretive categories could at the same time offer opportunities to express difference and transformation? This paradoxical concept finds a concrete application in fashions. The theme of fashion is very relevant for organizational discourse, considering the prevalence of ideological and conceptual vogues and fads in the field of management. The mask metaphor, with its paradoxical compresence of uniformity and trans-formative value, offers a good introduction to a discussion on management fashions.

Finally, masks do not necessarily conceal an existing identity. They sometimes act as simulacra, conferring personality to an empty vessel.

> The transition from signs which dissimulate something to signs which dissimulate that there is nothing, marks the decisive turning point. The first implies a theology of truth and secrecy (to which the notion of ideology still belongs). The second inaugurates an age of simulacra and simulation, in which there is no longer any God to recognize his own, nor any last judgement to separate truth from false, the real from its artificial resurrection, since everything is already dead and risen in advance. (Baudrillard 1994, p. 6)

Baudrillard suggests that a symbolic façade can cloak an essential void: discourse can be wrapped around entities that are so indistinct that the signifier lacks any connection with a real signified. Organizational discourses can be structured around such emptiness, giving semiotic substance to objects that lack ontological essence because they are rhetorical inventions, or because they attempt at capturing a miscellany of diverse or equivocal phenomena (think of the notion of leadership, or the idea of the entrepreneur).

In sum, the metaphor of the mask allows the introduction of three new aspects of organizational discourse: silence, fashionability and hollowness.

SILENCE IN DISCOURSE

It is counterintuitive to think of organizations in terms of silence. The symbolic performances that give them substance (meetings, reports, policies, proposals, business cases, discussions, etc.) produce a constant chatter, an overabundance of voices and texts where silence has no domain. Yet silence is not simply the absence of sound; it can represent the exclusion of certain voices, topics or views from the conversation. A silence of the first kind, as a form of speechlessness or reticence, can be interpreted as a "weapon for the less powerful participant, particularly as a way of being noncommittal about what more powerful participants say" (Fairclough 1989, p. 136). This evasive strategy can be easily defused where power imbalance is present, since "the latter may again be able to force participants out of silence and into a response by asking do you

understand? or do you agree? or what do you think?, for example"
(Fairclough 1989, p. 136).

At the same time, organizational discourse can be the result of various
censoring and editing processes, silencing voices. Many different 'hands'
are involved in this censoring activity and as a consequence 'tacitness' in
organizations can assume different forms. Blackman and Sadler-Smith
(2009), who focus on the role of silence in knowledge management,
differentiate between a knowledge that is "silent" (i.e. tacit or pre-
conscious) because it cannot be articulated or codified and one which is
"silenced": repressed from conscious awareness, suppressed by organizational norms, or consciously not articulated (as a strategic or social
acquiescence choice).

This simplified taxonomy shows the many forms that silence can
assume in organizational discourse. It can be the result of an explicit
agentic strategy (operated by some 'silencers' or by the 'silenced'
themselves) or it can be the outcome of structural conditions that are both
ignoring, suppressing, or repressing voices and information.

Various works on the topic of organizational silence have focused on
undesired structural circumstances producing breakdowns in the
bottom-up transmission of information that has been defined as organizational silence. In this case fear of negative feedback and a set of
implicit beliefs creates a collective "climate of silence: [the] widely
shared perceptions among employees that speaking up about problems or
issues is futile and/or dangerous" (Morrison and Milliken 2000, p. 708).
These conditions emerge from a combination of cultural factors (the
belief that employees' views are self-interested and ill-informed and that
only consent is positive) and structural elements (low-cost strategies,
high-power distance, casualization etc.) and are exacerbated by the
characteristics of personnel and by some organizational processes and
practices. This situation has negative consequences both on organizational morale and on organizational performances and adaptability,
producing a sense of cynicism that is difficult to change (Morrison and
Milliken 2000).

The frequently cited Morrison and Milliken's perspective on organizational silence considers that the collapse of communication is the
outcome of repeated patterns of individual mistakes, such as managers'
inability to lend an ear to their employees (Morrison and Milliken 2000,
2003). These studies presume that it is possible to engineer an ideal
communication flow. Some form of editing is an essential component of
sensemaking (see Chapter 5) and it is necessary to put in place processes
aimed at filtering irrelevant information, safeguarding decision-makers
from the "dysfunctional" impact of unrestricted voice (Morrison and

Milliken 2003, p. 1567). A limitation of these views is that they ignore the fact that principals, managerial agents and employees might have contrasting interests. For instance, management could decide to design voice mechanism aimed at serving exclusively corporate or managerial interests, with the consequence that employees realize that it is not necessarily in their best interest to participate in this communication exchange (Donaghey et al. 2011). Employees can also decide to withhold information and opinions to pursue parochial interests; for instance to enhance their capacity to influence other actors through the control of some strategic areas of uncertainty, as in the case of maintenance workers intentionally destroying repair manuals to maintain their knowledge monopoly (Crozier 1964; Crozier and Friedberg 1980).

The requisite organizational filtering devices can also be distorted and put at the service of specific interests. In this case the avoidance of discussion is instrumental to protecting the dominant group's interests and represents a tacit expression of power (Bachrach and Baratz 1962). Not discussing issues, negating their importance and subtracting them from open debate becomes an effective strategy to maintain the status quo. "Power is also exercised when A devotes his energies to creating or reinforcing social and political values and institutional practices that limit the scope of the political process to public consideration of only those issues which are comparatively innocuous to A" (Bachrach and Baratz 1962, p. 948). Not including issues in the discussion agenda is only one of the forms of filtering that can be found in organizational discourse. Talk, action and decisions can be separated and treated as separate products that can be managed independently instead of being part of a tightly coupled chain, with the purpose of managing inconsistencies between "what can be said but not done and what can be done but not said" (Brunsson 1993, p. 490). For instance this happens when stake-holders who cannot be satisfied are appeased by means of ritual consultations, or by being offered future promises, in an exercise of "organizational hypocrisy" (Brunsson 1989, 1993). In this case these audiences are not expressly silenced, since they can express opinions and positions which are duly recorded, but in practice their voice will have no impact on a parallel decisional process: this is often the way in which popular consultations are treated in political decisions that also involve powerful interest groups.

The exercise of power through silence has been highlighted in various contexts: for instance the idea of female leadership (Callás and Smircich 1991) exhibits a suppression that starts in business education, where mainstream pedagogical models tend to marginalize female MBA students (Sinclair 1995). In other cases, it is not subjects but topics that are excluded from the discourse. A typical example is the silence surrounding critical management perspectives in business education, aimed at presenting management as an ideology-free technique (Grey 2002; Jarvis and Amann 2011). These 'oppressive' forms of silence are not mere absence of communication. "Certain forms of discourse act to distort power relations, disguise inequity, sequester resistant discourses, and ultimately close emancipatory forms of communication. In short, communication can be silencing" (Clair 1998, p. 38).

Filters can operate at a more unconscious level. In this case it is not the explicit denial of avenues to express divergent positions, rather making it particularly costly or threatening to express ideas of subjectivities that are different from the accepted templates of normalcy. This engenders "spirals of silence" in which invisible minority groups, for instance those who do not share mainstream sexual orientations, do not feel able to talk about their personal identity and are thus inhibited in making a meaningful contribution to the group (Bowen and Blackmon 2003). The absence of adequate incentives to 'speak up' and also the need to be accepted and to be in control both play a role. Linstead and Thomas (2002) describe how female middle managers end up wearing gendered managerial masks in order to perform their professional role, since their "'female-ness' becomes a phenomenon that they must manage, as it can be used to undermine or deny women's authority, silence their voices and restrict their involvement in decision-making" (Linstead and Thomas 2002, p. 4). The need to wear masks suppressing one's 'authentic voice' is not something that applies exclusively to oppressed groups. Many people choose to don corporate masks that can be taken off at the end of the day, in the belief that this is an effective strategy to preserve and demarcate their authentic self, as in the case of the management consultants studied by Costas and Fleming (2009). However, this underlying authenticity is illusory, since they realize that their true identities are practically unattainable, because work overloads all aspects of their lives, the relative weakness of their alternative source of subjectivity and the phoney nature of the corporate attempts to offer sources for 'self-actualization' and engagement. Consequently, employees become aware that they are self-entrapped in an alien corporate self to which they must cling even if they suffer its unauthenticity, in a process of self-alienation (Costas and Fleming 2009).

BEYOND SILENCE: HEGEMONY AND CONSTRUCTION OF MEANING

The idea of muffling voices or refusing characters a place on stage implies that these issues and subjectivities will not extinguish a fire that still burns under the ashes; however, sometimes the silence on some issues is deafening and cannot be explained by the absence of channels for its expression. One episode which recently hit the news is emblematic. At the beginning of 2016 a temporary worker employed as a receptionist at PwC in London was allegedly turned away from the job because she was not willing to wear high heels, which apparently is a legitimate request since it is included in the enforceable dress code for employees. The disgruntled employee made the issue known to the media, generating global interest, and started a petition to make it unlawful for companies to impose high heels on female employees. In an attempt to minimize the PR fallout, PwC immediately distanced itself from the decision, attributing it to a decision of the third-party supplier to whom they outsource their front-of-house services. In turn, the contracting company assured that they are now in the process of reviewing their dress code policies (Lytton 2016).

What makes this story remarkable is not the fact that an employee decided to voice her grievance in the face of such an obviously discriminatory and sexist policy, but rather the fact that such an event only happened recently. Obviously such policies are neither unique nor bizarre (hence the global media interest and widespread discussion fuelled by the case) and it is also very likely that many other female employees have not felt completely at ease at having to wear high heels in the office. Yet the issue did not surface before.

This clearly indicates that we need to "consider the question of political quiescence: why grievances do not exist; why demands are not made; and why conflict does not arise, since such inaction may also be the result of power" (Hardy and Clegg 1996, p. 627). Power can be expressed in subtle forms, locking up people's "perceptions, cognitions, and preferences in such a way that they accept their role in the existing order of things" (Lukes 1974, p. 24). Lukes identifies a form of exercise based on cultural and discursive manipulation that silences interests whose legitimation is denied because they are hidden from the sight of their own holders. Based on Lukes' claims, Mumby and Clair state that "the most effective use of power [...] is exercised through a set of interpretive frames that each worker incorporates as part of his or her organizational identity" (1997, p. 184). The notion of interest manipulation is compelling and resonates with the experience of seeing oppressed individuals eagerly take part in reproducing practices and behaviours that are degrading and self-destructive, such as wearing 'sexy shoes' not because one wants to impress a potential partner, but because one is obliged to be accommodating to an objectifying, male-dominated culture that requires females to always be attractive and seductive.

At the same time, Lukes' idea is also problematic. First because it assumes the possibility of the observer assuming a transcendent position, making it possible to determine what the 'real interests' of someone are (there are indeed people who enjoy and who gain advantage from presenting a sexualized self-image). Moreover, it appears to consider the 'occult persuaders' immune to the same power effects: image management can be a very demanding business, even for dominant males (see Clegg, Courpasson and Phillips 2006, pp. 213–22 for a summary of the criticisms to Lukes' account).

Gramsci (1971), writing in the 1930s, while imprisoned by the Fascist regime in Italy (therefore a few decades before Lukes), provided a more sophisticated idea of 'cultural manipulation', one that is not explicitly based on indoctrination of the masses but rather on a dialectic relationship. Hegemonic domination, in Gramsci's view, results from a rational acceptance on the part of the subjects of the supremacy of a dominating class. Hegemony is predicated on the capacity of the ruling class to persuade the subordinate classes to acknowledge both its economic superiority and its intellectual and moral leadership.

> What we can do, for the moment, is to fix two major superstructural 'levels': the one that can be called 'civil society', that is, the ensemble of organisms commonly called 'private', and that of 'political society' or 'the state'. These two levels correspond on the one hand to the functions of 'hegemony' which the dominant group exercises throughout society and on the other hand to that of 'direct domination' or command exercised through the state and 'juridical' government. (Gramsci 1971, p. 12)

The consent of the dominated population is maintained by means of a continuous process of positive and negative reinforcement, produced by a variety of actors (teachers, priests, police, politicians, etc.) performing both ideological and moral suasion. The ideological process is supported and endorsed by the use of force and coercion to isolate and punish 'deviant' elements. As a consequence of these symbolic and material practices, the status quo, which favours certain interests and is harmful to others, is accepted by the majority as common sense. The foundations of hegemony are therefore based on "the ability of one class to articulate the interests of other social groups to its own" (Mouffe 1979, p. 183). The concept of hegemony not only has a sociological relevance, but also offers an important interpretive key to understanding the phenomenon of organizational control: in contemporary organizations these dynamics are also at play (Clegg and Dunkerley 1980).

The notion of hegemony has been expanded and framed into a post-structuralist worldview by Laclau and Mouffe (1985), who helped clarify that the notion of 'real interests' is fallacious because subjectivity emerges from the interplay of contingent discursive possibilities. As a consequence discourse also shapes 'ruling class' interests, with not even the Hegemon being immune from the discourse's hegemonic qualities. While despots can impose statements that legitimize and reinforce their rule, they also end up becoming encumbered by the trappings that embody that discourse: a divine king must constantly maintain a God-like performance. The paradox is that an approach that aims to unveil how existing inequities and domination are maintained through ideological manipulation risks treating both oppressors and oppressed as 'prisoners of discourse'.

Hegemonic oppression can emerge also in the absence of a definite strategy but as a side-effect of the competition between different discourses, different forms of knowledge. "Dominant knowledges pretend to rest on their own essence, or self-identity, while being nothing more than a play of differences over the voices they deny or silence" (Callás and Smircich 1991, p. 579). In this, context discourses become oppressive actants that suppress any attempts to be different.

While this perspective appears to negate the possibility of transformation, prefiguring an irresistible descent into subjugation, resistance can assume unexpected forms. Even silence can become an act of rebellion to oppressive discourses: Clair (1998, p. 147) cites the example of an Australian Indigenous woman who, at the end of a two-year period of mourning silence that was imposed on her by her community's customs, decided to keep her peace for another 24 years. This act of defiance demonstrates how even silence can become a gesture of insubordination, confirming the pragmatics of communication principle that every action (including keeping quiet) can be interpreted as a communicative act, making it impossible not to communicate (Watzlawick, Jackson and Bavelas 1967). While this might be a weak form of rebellion it still constitutes the demonstration of a continuing resistance to the discursive attempts to produce docile subjectivities.

Another opportunity of transformation and renovation, opposing the hegemonic tendencies of discourse, can stem from another unlikely source: fashion. Here it is the ephemeral and whimsical nature of organizational discourses that can offer an opportunity to escape stagnation.

FADS AND FASHION IN DISCOURSES ON ORGANIZATIONS

The existence of modes, fads, rages and vogues is testament to the centrality of signs and symbols in cultural and social life, a further demonstration of the influence of non-verbal communication and discourses on individual and collective action. Simmel (1904 [1957]) argued that fashion is linked both to discourse and identity: 'following fashions' entails engaging in a form of social relationship, conforming to the norms of a particular group. In Simmel's view this behaviour is strongly connected with modernity, which explains why people living in metropolises are 'trendier': in a traditional, small-circle setting, fashion is both less necessary because every individual is widely known and less possible because the visibility of their being there helps to confine them to the limits of what the community expects of and from them. On the other hand, modern individuals tend to be detached from traditional anchors of social support, with fashion being instrumental to signalling social identity: think of punks, goths and other contemporary cultural 'tribes'. Such types of symbolic behaviour also affect those who choose to be 'unfashionable', since they engage in an inverse form of imitation: even those who try to be seen as mavericks are positioning themselves in relation to the conformist groups and to declare their belonging to another clique, that of the 'non-conformists'.

This is not the only contradiction that is interesting about being in vogue: fashionability requires novelty since distinction is lost when a particular style, initially adopted to mark sophistication and discernment, is adopted by a large section of the population (Simmel 1904 [1957]). A paradoxical tension ensues: for the trend-setter "being and staying ahead of the style pack promises belonging – being approved and included" (Bauman 2008, pp. 144-5).

The contradictory nature of fashion is not limited to the 'spatial' relationship between conformity and alterity but concerns also the temporality of its process: "fashion is created even as it is followed [...] fashion stands for change, but as fashion is also repetitive, in a long-range perspective it stands for tradition as well" (Panozzo and Czarniawska 2008, p. 8). Fashion becomes the material embodiment of the central ambiguity of the oxymoronic idea of 'individual identity', in which two contradictory concepts are associated: individual (which stands for distinctiveness, difference) and identity (which represents commonality, sameness). Inconsistency is at the root of any discursive process, since any sign and idea must be defined in relation to others (from which they differ), thus postponing the achievement of meaningfulness through an endless chain of signifiers, an idea encapsulated by Derrida (1982) in the label *différance*. The subjects produced by discourse are always incomplete, because they are defined in relation to other subjects that, in turn, necessitate them to preserve sense and intelligibility.

There is more to fashion than meets the eye: complex sets of symbolic performances are tangible manifestations of discourse. The concept of 'management fads and fashions', often used dismissively, assumes therefore a much richer and nuanced connotation. A management fashion can be described as a "relatively transitory collective belief, disseminated by management knowledge entrepreneurs, that a management technique leads rational management progress" (Abrahamson 1996, p. 257). Similar to aesthetic fashions they are influenced by psychological factors, such as the desire to appear progressive, or to mark one's own status, as well as by social expectations, which in the specific case of management fashions are the norms of rationality and progress. In addition, there are techno-economic forces influencing management fashions' demand. These are macroeconomic fluctuations (e.g. global recessions), political forces (e.g. labour strife), and unsolvable contradictions originating from within organizations, such as the tensions between control and learning (Abrahamson 1991, 1996). In Abrahamson's view it is important to transcend the purely 'symbolic' dimension of fashion, since style can become imbued with function (and vice versa) producing artefacts that by means of "cultural-technological fusions" can deliver "beautiful technologies" and "efficient beauties" (Abrahamson 2011).

Fashions play a pivotal role in the diffusion of ideas, to the extent that even academics, whose research endeavours should be informed by methodological rigour and by a thoughtful consideration of validated prior findings, are demonstrably subject to the influence of the way in which concepts are constructed by 'lay' discourses. For instance a thorough investigation of the literature on organizational culture allowed Barley, Gordon and Gash (1988) to show how "the rubric of practitioners' discourse remained stable over time, while the pragmatics of academics' discourse changed" (1988, p. 52). The longitudinal analysis of the data reveals an academic literature moving from an anthropological viewpoint that considered cultures as something that organizations 'are' to one that ends up embracing the dominant practitioners' rhetoric, centred on the commoditization of culture. As a consequence, an approach that represented a departure from the dominant functionalist tradition of organizational theory had been (at least by the mid-1980s) colonized by the instrumental perspective promoted by management gurus who seized the opportunity of selling a novel tool to influence people towards performative outcomes.

Even studies on discourses (whose authors are supposedly highly sensitized to the issue) are not immune from discursive influences. Researching, writing and publishing about organizational discourse is itself a symbolic practice, which operates both at a grand Discourse level, in the context of the 'publishing game' (Broad 1981; Starbuck 2003; Alvesson and Gabriel 2013), but is also influenced by local discursive conditions (e.g. how relevant is a particular publishing achievement in the context of a specific research community or institution). It is a discourse typically relying on indefinite lacks, such as the notion of research 'gaps' (Alvesson and Sandberg 2011; Sandberg and Alvesson 2011), an idea predicated on an imaginary landscape of coherent and flat 'knowledge' fabric that ideally can be filled to achieve a more perfect coverage of a given fundamental reality. The assumption that studies which offer an 'original theoretical contribution' (which might concretely mean a totally abstract addition to a dialogue known only to a handful of specialists) are preferable to those which might have the capacity (thanks to their intelligibility or situated relevance) to influence the practices of a myriad of practitioners represents an example of the hegemonic characters of this academic Discourse on organizational studies.

As discussed in Chapter 1, every time we conceptualize, reflect or communicate complex thoughts we engage in symbolic behaviour. Yet most scholars appear to be oblivious of this phenomenon: "in almost all empirical research, the research design and the research text are developed and written as if language is strictly controlled by the researcher, a simple tool through which she or he mirrors the world" (Alvesson and Kärreman 2000, p. 138). Empirical and theoretical studies of organizational discourse are particularly affected: the only conceivable way for researchers to situate themselves completely 'outside' an observed discursive phenomenon would be to investigate a completely alien and unintelligible symbolic behaviour.[1]

It appears that fashions and fads are discursive influences from which no one is immune. Therefore, the question that must be asked is whether this is a positive influence or a negative phenomenon, to be resisted.

---

[1]   From this perspective, perhaps the only 'pure' discourse analysis comprises those ethologists studying animal communication.

Abrahamson (1991, 1996, 2011) sees it as a neutral institutional process that is connected with the diffusion of innovation, and that combines psychological and social desires with elements of rationality. The idea of fashion emerging from isomorphic pressures does not appear to find strong evidence and quantitative studies have failed to identify clear patterns or determinants in the spreading of fashions in the organizational discourse (Carson et al. 2000). A more promising approach could be the one suggested by Røvik (2011) who proposes to overcome the idea of fashion, associating the diffusion and adoption of management ideas to viral infections.

Regardless of their mode of spreading, various voices are highly critical of fads and vogues in management, and "fashion has been portrayed as an irrational deviation from rational managerial behaviour" (Panozzo and Czarniawska 2008, p. 4). Kieser (1997) describes them as rhetorical devices, creating mythologies that confound fact with fiction and which have a negative impact on the critical capacities of their users. Certain concepts, techniques and ideas prosper not by virtue of their demonstrated economic impact but because of their interpersonal reproductive capacity, operating as memes, the units of memory that are culture's analogue of genes (Williams 2004). An important role in spreading these self-reproducing myths is played by consultants and management gurus, who are sometimes then vilified as organizational snake oil vendors who apply cheap tricks to win over naïve (or unconfident) practitioners (Kieser 1997, 2002). Similarly, Clark and Salaman (1996) associated management gurus with witch doctors or the kind of people who resort to illusions assisted by smoke and mirrors.

In the face of such views we should not be surprised that various academics have devoted their energies to opening the eyes of the beguiled practitioners, separating true scientific knowledge from the chaff of managerial fads (Hilmer and Donaldson 1996; Pfeffer and Sutton 2006). Nevertheless, empirical studies have shown that the idea of managers as dopes is unwarranted. On the one hand the demand side of the market for management fashion is not homogeneous (Rossem and Veen 2011); on the other hand the consumers of management fashions are not passive recipients but are taking part in the production of fashions (Mazza and Alvarez 2000; Clark 2004).

This is particularly true when fads convey the template of ideal selves. In this case the relationship between the statements uttered in the context of managerial fashions and the emerging professional identities of practitioners is complex, and is confounded by double hermeneutic effects (Giddens 1984). For instance, emotional intelligence (Goleman

1995, 1998), a manipulation technology which fits well with post-bureaucratic organizational contexts (Clegg and Baumeler 2010), has become a requisite skill for successful executives, with the consequence that numerous managers have striven to re-craft (or at least re-brand) themselves as 'emotionally intelligent leaders'.

It is not just a matter of overcoming the simplistic assumption according to which these fashions are mere trinkets offered by wizards to gullible and ignorant savages. In fact even magical remedies can sometimes prove to be vital for the welfare of an organized group, while in the same context an application of technical rationality would be detrimental. Weick provides an effective illustration of this concept, describing how the Naskapi Indigenous of Labrador successfully managed game hunting for centuries by resorting to a 'magical device', the use of cracks formed on caribou shoulder bones as a map, with which to locate game. By randomizing their hunting practices, this strategy prevented stock depletion and contemporarily made hunting more efficient because it made hunters' behaviour unpredictable, avoiding the game becoming sensitized to human actions (Weick 1969 [1979], p. 262). This is a case in which an 'irrational' model works as an effective sensemaking device, precisely *because* of its ambiguous and mysterious logic. The nonsensical and random nature of the decision-making device offers an effective solution to the problem of the "tragedy of the commons" (Hardin 1968) since it defies the possibility of actions informed by a short-term, individual rationality which would cause resource depletion.

Similarly unplanned, 'magical', side-effects to the adoption of fashion have been identified in organizational contexts. One example is the case of the implementation of ISO 9000 quality standards. Typical examples of a management fad, these standards have been adopted by innumerable organizations (with a peak in the 1990s) in the questionable belief that they would improve sales or product qualities. Indeed, these methodologies have often developed positive outcomes, but by means of unintended organizational consequences ranging "from achieving decentralisation to creating arguments in the internal dialogue of a profession" (Larsen and Häversjö 2001, p. 472), rather than through branding.

Another even more relevant (and surprising) positive effect of the faddishness of management thinking is offered by ten Bos (2000). He argues that, not only are fashions in management theory unavoidable, but they are highly preferable to 'utopianism', the single-minded pursuit of absolute, scientific truths about management. Fashionability becomes for ten Bos an allegory of a pluralist, constructivist and reflexive way of making sense of reality, of producing a socially accepted set of coherent representations that can be as valid and rigorous as the proposition of positivist science. It serves as an antidote to a myth of rationality that annihilates individuality and pluralism, and that ends up producing only a travesty of the truth, since this is far too complex to be captured by a single reductionist model. Acknowledging fashion means becoming aware of the idiosyncratic, fleeting, superficial qualities of our representations, maintaining a more balanced and inquisitive stance, enabling "managers to become sensitive to their own roles in a turbulent and ever-changing environment which belies reason" (ten Bos 2000, p. 187).

EMPTY DISCOURSES

Reality is impossible to represent since "we are not confronted with a fully completed world out there (or in the head) waiting to be labelled" (Iedema 2007, p. 342). However, this can lead to an apotheosis of Discourse, pictured as an 'unmoved mover' from which ontological substance flows: in other words, the idea that discourse operates as a script that some mysterious agency has produced in the past and is determining our social roles and actions. However, discourses can be as bereft of a seminal identity as the subject they create, being spun around a hollow core of signification. Signifiers do not pre-exist the signified and therefore do not come first to cast reality from an inchoate matter: "the effect of meaning is always produced backwards" (Žižek 1989, p. 113). Žižek accepts that our inchoate experience is assembled in a meaningful frame by hegemonic systems of representation and reproduction; these however cannot fully inscribe experience and it is in this slack that resistance is still possible. Discursive constructions such as ideology are not "an illusion masking the real state of things but … an (unconscious) fantasy structuring our social reality itself" (Žižek 1989, p. 33). In this structuring of an ineffable reality a pivotal role is assumed by "signifiers without a signified", words that do not refer to any clear and distinct concept or demonstrable object, but which draw their potency from being ambiguous and void of meaning: they are "sublime objects". As a consequence, "a shared lie is an incomparably stronger bond for a group than the truth" (Žižek 1997, p. 22)

One familiar example in the organizational discourse of an object that is rich in meaning but empty of distinct substance is the concept of the 'entrepreneur'. This subject "is indefinable, and necessarily so; the entrepreneur is an 'absent centre'" (Jones and Spicer 2005, p. 236). It is problematic to answer the question 'what makes an entrepreneur an entrepreneur' not simply because our understanding of the attribute of this subject is incomplete and provisional but because, as a socially constructed object, the content of this signifier is radically contingent:

> For instance, the entrepreneur may be described as self-reliant or overly prone to take risks. These words carry with them a specific meaning with which we can map our understanding of the entrepreneur. Yet, these characteristics are by no means exhaustive and, even more important, they remain dubious and contestable. And since it is not possible to symbolize what it is that lies beyond these positive characteristics – at a deeper level – these characteristics will tend to fall short in determining the nature of the entrepreneur [...] The entrepreneur may be characterized by certain activities, relations and motives. But following a post-foundational reading, all these activities, motives and relations associated with an entrepreneur are held together and given meaning through the unsymbolizable lack. (Cederström and Spicer 2014, p. 188)

The empty, ambiguous notion of entrepreneur can, by virtue of its indefiniteness, hold together a discourse that is neither coherent nor stable and that is instead characterized by paradoxes, providing "a narrative structure to the fantasy that coordinates desire" (Jones and Spicer 2005, p. 237).

Another case of an organizational discourse that is rich in imagery and symbols but empty of substantive content is that of leadership. In this case the availability of hundreds of definitions and dozens of theories (Kellerman 2012, p. xxi) does not equate to an abundance of meaning; on the contrary, it generates a noise that ensconces the obscurity and vagueness of the concept. An example of the indistinct and arbitrary nature of the concept is the list of the 'World's 50 Greatest Leaders' published by *Fortune* magazine:[2] the top five places on this list include characters as different as two successful companies' CEOs (Jeff Bezos of Amazon and Tim Cook of Apple), Pope Francis, the German Chancellor Angela Merkel and a Nobel Peace Prize winner, Aung San Suu Kyi. The only thing that these disparate characters have in common is the fact that the compilers of the list see them as people who "are transforming the world and inspiring others to do the same". However, as Alvesson (2013) observes, the reality rarely corresponds to the epic narrative of the leader who can single-handedly transform organizations and cultures.

An alternative to this aggrandizing discourse could be to "emphasize the relational and process aspects of leadership [...] Leadership is, here, linked to ordinary and sometimes perhaps even trivial acts, but may nevertheless be significant for the commitment and engagement of employees" (Alvesson 2013, p. 174). This unorthodox view of leadership

---

[2]   See http://fortune.com/worlds-greatest-leaders/

implies that "(1) mundane act carried out by (2) a manager and (3) labelled leadership means (4) an expectation of something significant, even 'magical' being accomplished" (Alvesson and Sveningsson 2003, p. 1455). The leader is akin to a witch doctor or a wizard: individuals who do not really have extraordinary powers but whose status is based on the belief that the perfectly ordinary acts they perform have magical power. It is a perfect example of circular reasoning which can, however, produce concrete effects: a wizard (leader) is whoever can perform a magic act (of leadership); what makes the act magic is the fact that it is performed by a wizard/leader. The emptiness of the subject and the uncertainty of the attributes of leadership are not problematic but are instrumental in enabling this social attribution of meaning. With this perspective, leaders can be seen as empty vessels on which an organizational audience projects desires and needs, as happens to the character of Chance the Gardener in Hal Ashby's movie *Being There*. Here, a simple-minded and naïve character, magnificently impersonated by Peter Sellers, is mistaken for a visionary leader by people, who see great meaning, hope and wisdom in his most banal and inane utterances. Chance is misunderstood because people see in him what they want to.

An important difference with the reality of organizations is that, while the character of Chance is totally guileless, executives/leaders are extremely cunning. These leaders are adept at seducing their followers, building their mythology through an erotic process. This idea is explored by Harding et al. (2011), who shows that this is an eroticism deprived of physicality, with "the leader as a penetrative but disembodied perpetrator", guaranteeing that "the libidinal energies are not turned towards hedonistic pleasures but to production" (Harding et al. 2011, pp. 17–18). Again, it is all smoke and mirrors, arousal and promises, rather than factual action and performance: "managers' theory of leadership is therefore of the leader's desire: a desire to be desired" (Harding et al. 2011, p. 17).

The discourse of leadership is therefore built around another semantic void, from which it paradoxically draws energy and power. The capacity of 'empty' symbols to have performative consequence can be explained considering the processes through which social patterns and structures are recursively constructed: Schütz (1932) explicates how individuals recur to memory and ideal types to make sense of and share experiences. Since meaning "is not a quality inherent to certain experiences emerging within our stream of consciousness but the result of an interpretation of a past experience looked at from the present" (Schütz 1945, p. 535), our amorphous and malleable memory can construct a 'sensible' understanding: "meaning is the tension between what becomes and what is passing"

(Schütz 2013, p. 51), explaining why it is possible to create meaningful and performatively consequential discourses around empty concepts. Even if it is true that "the leadership ideal is espoused rather than enacted" (Alvesson 2013, p. 184), this espousal becomes the stage that gives coherence and significance to the antics of strutting and fretting leaders.

This discussion shows that the metaphor of the mask is useful to elaborate our understanding of organizational discourse because while reasserting the generative powers of discourse it also shows that this construction can take place even in the absence of a well-defined, meaningful centre, that it can at times silence voices and that at times it can kindle alterity and transformation. Organizational discourse is a veritable carnival that incorporates and appropriates fragments of multiple social discourses (Rhodes 2001). We return to where we started, back to the notion of carnival. We have seen how, in Bakhtin's view (1965), the masquerade enables one to overcome the rigid boundaries imposed by social roles, and bring in the possibility of transformation. However, this happens within a framework of social institutions, and the apparently anarchic release of energy during the carnival is paradoxically meant to confirm and reinforce these same institutions. The traditional carnival reaffirmed the same social rules that it was momentarily suspending and parodying, since "without a valid law to break, carnival is impossible" (Eco 1984, cited in Rhodes 2001, p. 381). Similarly, many 'alternative' organizational discourses (e.g. post-bureaucracy, non-hierarchical organizations, open collaboration, sustainability) are often evoked to reaffirm the centrality of the traditional dominant discourses: bureaucracy, hierarchy, control and shareholders' interest.

It is a performance of transformation and change that maintains the illusion of openness and innovation in organizational discourses that are built on control. Here, the emptiness of central meaning becomes a powerful straightjacket, since it denies the possibility to the less powerful of denouncing a lack of actual correspondence between, for instance, the practices of a manager and a concrete model of leadership (or entrepreneurship, innovation, empowerment, etc.). It is difficult to proclaim that the king is naked when fashion requires clothing to be transparent.

REFERENCES

Abrahamson, E. 1991, 'Managerial Fads and Fashions: The Diffusion and Rejection of Innovations', *The Academy of Management Review*, vol. 16, pp. 586–612.

Abrahamson, E. 1996, 'Management Fashion, Academic Fashion, and Enduring Truths', *The Academy of Management Review*, vol. 21, pp. 616–18.

Abrahamson, E. 2011, 'The Iron Cage: Ugly, Uncool, and Unfashionable', *Organization Studies*, vol. 32, pp. 615–29.

Alvesson, M. 2013, *The Triumph of Emptiness: Consumption, Higher Education, and Work Organization*, Oxford University Press, Oxford, UK.

Alvesson, M. and Gabriel, Y. 2013, 'Beyond Formulaic Research: In Praise of Greater Diversity in Organizational Research and Publications', *Academy of Management Learning & Education*, vol. 12, pp. 245–63.

Alvesson, M. and Kärreman, D. 2000, 'Taking the Linguistic Turn in Organizational Research: Challenges, Responses, Consequences', *The Journal of Applied Behavioral Science*, vol. 36, pp. 136–58.

Alvesson, M. and Sandberg, J. 2011, 'Generating Research Questions Through Problematization', *Academy of Management Review*, vol. 36, no. 2, pp. 247–71.

Alvesson, M. and Sveningsson, S. 2003, 'Managers Doing leadership: The Extra-ordinarization of the Mundane', *Human Relations*, vol. 56, no. 12, pp. 1435–59.

Bachrach, P. and Baratz, M.S. 1962, 'Two Faces of Power', *The American Political Science Review*, vol. 56, pp. 947–52.

Bakhtin, M. 1965, *Rabelais and His World*, trans. H. Iswolsky, Indiana University Press, Bloomington, IN.

Barley, S.R., Gordon, W.M. and Gash, D.C. 1988, 'Cultures of Culture: Academics, Practitioners and the Pragmatics of Normative Control', *Administrative Science Quarterly*, vol. 33, pp. 24–60.

Baudrillard, J. 1994, *Simulacra and Simulation*, University of Michigan Press, Ann Arbor, MI.

Bauman, Z. 2008, *Does Ethics Have a Chance in a World of Consumers?*, Harvard University Press, Cambridge, MA.

Blackman, D. and Sadler-Smith, E. 2009, 'The Silent and the Silenced in Organizational Knowing and Learning', *Management Learning*, vol. 40, no. 5, pp. 569–85.

Bowen, F. and Blackmon, K. 2003, 'Spirals of Silence: The Dynamic Effects of Diversity on Organizational Voice', *Journal of Management Studies*, vol. 40, no. 6, pp. 1393–417.

Broad, W.J. 1981, 'The Publishing Game: Getting More for Less', *Science*, vol. 211, pp. 1137–9.

Brunsson, N. 1989, *The Organization of Hypocrisy: Talk, Decisions and Actions in Organizations*, Wiley, Chichester, UK.

Brunsson, N. 1993, 'Ideas and Actions: Justification and Hypocrisy as Alternatives to Control', *Accounting, Organizations and Society*, vol. 18, no. 6, pp. 489–506.

Callás, M.B. and Smircich, L. 1991, 'Voicing Seduction to Silence Leadership', *Organization Studies*, vol. 12, no. 4, pp. 567–601.

Carson, P.P., Lanier, P.A., Carson, K.D. and Guidry, B.N. 2000, 'Clearing a Path through the Management Fashion Jungle: Some Preliminary Trailblazing', *Academy of Management Journal*, vol. 43, no. 6, pp. 1143–58.

Cederström, C. and Spicer, A. 2014, 'Discourse of the Real Kind: A Post-foundational Approach to Organizational Discourse Analysis', *Organization*, vol. 21, no. 2, pp. 178–205.

Clair, R.P. 1998, *Organizing Silence: A World of Possibilities*, SUNY Press, New York.

Clark, T.A.R. 2004, 'The Fashion of Management Fashion: A Surge Too Far?', *Organization*, vol. 11, pp. 297–306.

Clark, T. and Salaman, G. 1996, 'The Management Guru as Organizational Witchdoctor', *Organization*, vol. 3, pp. 85–107.

Clegg, S.R. and Baumeler, C. 2010, 'Essai: From Iron Cages to Liquid Modernity in Organization Analysis', *Organization Studies*, vol. 31, pp. 1713–33.

Clegg, S.R. and Dunkerley, D. 1980, *Organization, Class and Control*, Routledge/Kegan Paul, Boston, MA.

Clegg, S.R., Courpasson, D. and Phillips, N. 2006, *Power and Organizations*, SAGE, London.

Costas, J. and Fleming, P. 2009, 'Beyond Dis-identification: A Discursive Approach to Self-alienation in Contemporary Organizations', *Human Relations*, vol. 62, no. 3, pp. 353–78.

Crozier, M. 1964, *The Bureaucratic Phenomenon*, University of Chicago Press, Chicago, IL.

Crozier, M. and Friedberg, E. 1980, *Actors and Systems: The Politics of Collective Action*, University of Chicago Press, Chicago, IL.

Derrida, J. 1982, 'Différance', *Margins of Philosophy*, University of Chicago Press, Chicago, IL, pp. 1–28.

Donaghey, J., Cullinane, N., Dundon, T. and Wilkinson, A. 2011, 'Reconceptualising Employee Silence: Problems and Prognosis', *Work, Employment & Society*, vol. 25, no. 1, pp. 51–67.

Eco, U. 1984, 'The Frames of Comic "Freedom"', in T.A. Sebeok (ed.), *Carnival!*, Gruyter, Berlin, pp. 1–10.

Fairclough, N. 1989, *Language and Power*, Longman, New York.

Giddens, A. 1984, *Constitution of Society: Outline of the Theory of Structuration*, Polity Press, Cambridge, UK.

Goleman, D. 1995, *Emotional Intelligence*, Bantam Books, New York.

Goleman, D. 1998, *Working with Emotional Intelligence*, Bloomsbury, London.

Gramsci, A. 1971, *Selections From the Prison Notebooks*, International Publishers, New York.

Grey, C. 2002, 'What are Business Schools for? On Silence and Voice in Management Education', *Journal of Management Education*, vol. 26, pp. 496–511.

Hardin, G. 1968, 'The Tragedy of the Commons', *Science*, vol. 162, no. 3859, pp. 1243–8.

Harding, N., Lee, H., Ford, J. and Learmonth, M. 2011, 'Leadership and Charisma: A Desire that Cannot Speak its Name?', *Human Relations*, vol. 64, no. 7, pp. 927–49.

Hardy, C. and Clegg, S.R. 1996, 'Some Dare Call It Power', in S.R. Clegg, C. Hardy and W. Nord (eds), *Handbook of Organization Studies*, SAGE, London, pp. 368–87.

Hilmer, F.G. and Donaldson, L. 1996, *Management Redeemed: Debunking the Fads that Undermine Corporate Performance*, Simon and Schuster, New York.

Iedema, R. 2007, 'On the Multi-modality, Materially and Contingency of Organization Discourse', *Organization Studies*, vol. 28, no. 6, pp. 931–46.

Jarvis, W.P. and Amann, W. 2011, 'Restoring Public Trust in the MBA: A Road Tested Kantian Approach', in W. Amann, M. Pirson, C. Dierkmeir, E.v. Kimakowitz and H. Spitzeck (eds), *Business Schools Under Fire: Humanistic Management Education as the Way Forward*, Palgrave Macmillan, Hampshire, UK, pp. 147–70.

Jones, C. and Spicer, A. 2005, 'The Sublime Object of Entrepreneurship', *Organization*, vol. 12, no. 2, pp. 223–46.

Kellerman, B. 2012, *The End of Leadership*, HarperCollins, New York.

Kieser, A. 1997, 'Rhetoric and Myth in Management Fashion', *Organization*, vol. 4, pp. 49–74.

Kieser, A. 2002, 'Managers as Marionettes? Using Fashion Theories to Explain the Success of Consultancies', in L. Engwall and M. Kipping (eds), *Management Consulting: Emergence and Dynamics of a Knowledge Industry*, pp. 167–83.

Laclau, E. and Mouffe, C. 1985, *Hegemony and Socialist Strategy: Towards a Radical Democratic Politics*, Verso, London.

Larsen, B. and Häversjö, T. 2001, 'Management by Standards – Real Benefits from Fashion', *Scandinavian Journal of Management*, vol. 17, no. 4, pp. 457–80.

Linstead, A. and Thomas, R. 2002, '"What Do You Want from Me?" A Poststructuralist Feminist Reading of Middle Managers' Identities', *Culture and Organization*, vol. 8, no. 1, pp. 1–20.

Lukes, S. 1974, *Power: A Radical View*, Macmillan, New York.

Lytton, C. 2016, 'Temp Worker Sent Home Unpaid from PwC Job "For not Wearing High Heels"', *The Telegraph*, 11 May 2016.

Mazza, C. and Alvarez, J.L. 2000, 'Haute Couture and prêt-à-porter: The Popular Press and the Diffusion of Management Practices', *Organization Studies*, vol. 21, no. 3, pp. 567–88.

Morrison, E.W. and Milliken, F.J. 2000, 'Organizational Silence: A Barrier to Change and Development in a Pluralistic World', *Academy of Management Review*, vol. 25, no. 4, pp. 706–25.

Morrison, E.W. and Milliken, F.J. 2003, 'Speaking Up, Remaining Silent: The Dynamics of Voice and Silence in Organizations', *Journal of Management Studies*, vol. 40, no. 6, pp. 1353–8.

Mouffe, C. 1979, 'Hegemony and Ideology in Gramsci', in C. Mouffe (ed.), *Gramsci and Marxist Theory*, Routledge, London, pp. 168–204.

Mumby, D.K. and Clair, R.D. 1997, 'Organizational Discourse', in T.A. van Dijk (ed.), *Discourse Studies: A Multidisciplinary Introduction: Vol. 2 – Discourse as Social Interaction*, SAGE, Newbury Park, CA, pp. 181–205.

Panozzo, F. and Czarniawska, B. 2008, 'Preface: Trends and Fashions in Management Studies', *International Studies of Management and Organization*, vol. 38, pp. 3–12.

Pfeffer, J. and Sutton, R.I. 2006, *Hard Facts, Dangerous Half-Truths, and Total Nonsense: Profiting from Evidence-Based Management*, Harvard Business School Press, Harvard, MA.

Rhodes, C. 2001, 'D'Oh: The Simpsons, Popular Culture, and the Organizational Carnival', *Journal of Management Inquiry*, vol. 10, no. 4, p. 374.

Rossem, A.V. and Veen, K.V. 2011, 'Managers' Awareness of Fashionable Management Concepts: An Empirical Study', *European Management Journal*, vol. 29, pp. 206–16.

Røvik, K.A. 2011, 'From Fashion to Virus: An Alternative Theory of Organizations' Handling of Management Ideas', *Organization Studies*, vol. 32, pp. 631–53.

Sandberg, J. and Alvesson, M. 2011, 'Ways of Constructing Research Questions: Gap-spotting or Problematization?', *Organization*, vol. 18, no. 1, pp. 23–44.

Schütz, A. 1932, *The Phenomenology of the Social World*, Northwestern University Press, Evanston, IL.

Schütz, A. 1945, 'On Multiple Realities', *Philosophy and Phenomenological Research*, vol. 5, pp. 533–76.

Schütz, A. 2013, *Life Forms and Meaning Structure*, Taylor & Francis, London.

Simmel, G. 1904 [1957], 'Fashion', *American Journal of Sociology*, vol. 62, no. 6, pp. 541–58.

Sinclair, A. 1995, 'Sex and the MBA', *Organization*, vol. 2, no. 2, pp. 295–317.

Starbuck, W.H. 2003, 'Turning Lemons into Lemonade: Where is the Value in Peer Reviews?', *Journal of Management Inquiry*, vol. 12, pp. 344–51.

ten Bos, R. 2000, *Fashion and Utopia in Management Thinking*, John Benjamins, Amsterdam.

Watzlawick, P., Jackson, D.D. and Bavelas, J.B. 1967, *Pragmatics of Human Communication: A Study of Interactional Patterns, Pathologies, and Paradoxes*, Norton, New York.

Weick, K.E. 1969 [1979], *The Social Psychology of Organizing*, 2nd edn, Addison-Wesley, Reading, MA.

Williams, R. 2004, 'Management Fashions and Fads: Understanding the Role of Consultants and Managers in the Evolution of Ideas', *Management Decision*, vol. 42, pp. 769–80.

Žižek, S. 1989, *The Sublime Object of Ideology*, Verso, London.

Žižek, S. 1997, *The Plague of Fantasies*, Verso, New York, NY.

7. Organizational discourse analysis in practice: the case of business education discourse

THE NEED FOR AN EMPIRICAL ILLUSTRATION

Investigating how language impacts organizations involves various conceptual problems and opportunities. Rather than embarking into a detailed comparison of the specific methods that different perspectives on organizational discourse analysis entail, I prefer to offer a concrete example of the application of this approach. The choice of the empirical case, the 'Discourse of business education', is particularly significant because it is a phenomenon that is unescapably intertwined with many other local and global manifestations of organizational discourse. This is in part due to the influence that business schools have on the education of the contemporary managing class. The resulting financial and political relevance of this industry makes it a terrain that other dominant discourses attempt to colonize, as well as an arena of struggle and resistance for various counter-discourses.

An additional reason that gives illustrative value to this investigation is the fact it is based on data that are entirely available in the public domain, in the form of a rich academic literature debating the past, present and future of managerial education and the practice of organizational research. This enables readers to identify and verify sources and evidences, thus establishing the credibility of the analysis, offering at the same time the possibility to critique it and to identify its limitations.

Metaphorically, the field of management research and education is here considered a discursive landscape, and as such is examined both from a historical and geographical perspective, and contemplating both material and symbolic elements. First, I look at the history of the field, to understand how the current entanglements of discursive and material elements came into being. I will then consider a symbolic-material entanglement of forces that are driving decisions and transformations in the field: ranking and accreditation. Third, I look at another Discourse: managerialism. This represents a separate set of symbolic practices describing and constructing reality which is orthogonal to the discourse of business education, intersecting and strongly influencing it, producing both compliance and resistance. Further on, I consider the debate on other factors that combine discursive and performative components: the publishing game, the discursively constructed tension between rigour and relevance, and the wicked issue of interdisciplinarity. The results of this review are summarized in the form of a map of the contrasting life worlds that, potentially, can emerge from different configurations of ideological and social forces characterizing the field of management studies and education. As with any map it is not a faithful representation of a territory but rather a representation of 'possible worlds'. The actual local landscape that is experienced by most management academics is probably flatter and more even; this is because one of these alternative arrangements of ideas and practices often becomes dominant and, by exercising a powerful normalizing influence, much opposition becomes eroded.

A TALE OF BUSINESS EDUCATION

Describing the history of business education is not a simple task, especially considering Jacques' warning that "every story in the past tense is not history" (2006, p. 39) and that several pitfalls are possible: being purely anecdotal, succumbing to anachronisms or looking for 'evolutionary' tales (Jacques 2006). My aim is to trace transformations in conception(s) of business education rather than producing an authoritative chronicle of the birth and development of management education. In this regard what is offered is not a history of facts, people and deeds so much as an archaeology of ideas and representations, one that seeks to describe the development of current discourses (Foucault 1972). As a consequence I am more interested in comparing and contrasting different accounts of this history than in retracing primary sources, accepting that narratives can be discursively more powerful than facts (Bruner 1991).

I start by considering the orthodox account (the localized 'creation myth') of the rise and diffusion of business education. Epic narration will be criticized to show the existence of other interesting but subordinated stories underrepresented in mainstream narratives. In the context of a globalized academia, with international faculty and hyper-mobile professors, the most successful business schools have become similar to premier league soccer teams, having, for instance, Asian financiers, American management and a multi-ethnic faculty (Altman and Laguecir 2012). However, there is a lineage to be found in the genealogy of the different local varieties of business school and even in a globalized world evidence of diversity survives.

Once Upon a Time in America

During the 20th century, American business schools transformed their identity and practices in an attempt to gain respectability and stature as well as in response to various market and political pressures. Many different chroniclers of this historical process have depicted a remarkably similar plot. The 'invention' of the business school dates back to 1881, when the University of Pennsylvania established the Wharton School (Khurana 2007, p. 88). These seminal organizations were trade and practice oriented, but in the 1950s they repudiated their origins as trade schools for apprentice managers, to embrace the more appealing character of academic institutions devoted to the scientific study of management (Bailey and Ford 1996, p. 8). This happened in response to incentives and pressures from both large foundations and the federal government (Ghoshal 2005, p. 77; Khurana 2007, pp. 210–22). The 'scientific turn' in business education can be seen as an example of the spreading and consolidation of an ideology of modernity in the late 1950s in the USA (Latham 2000), and also as a special case of a rationalization of society, linked to the institutionalization of scientific and technical development (Habermas 1987, p. 81). Emblematic of these changes was the introduction and dissemination of behavioural science theories into the business schools, notably articulated through the agency of Cyert and March's (1963 [1992]) text.

Two main ideas imprinted the pedagogy of these reformed business schools: first, teaching had to be informed by positivistic scientific research and, second, it should be organized along disciplinary lines inspired by the functional areas of business administration (Clegg and Ross-Smith 2003, p. 88). The rigid separation of knowledge in specialized disciplines reflected the positivistic belief in the possibility of codifying knowledge by breaking it into parts (Raelin 2007, p. 498), and as such was a key tactic in the professionalization strategy aimed at legitimizing management as an academic discipline. It allowed rapid institutional legitimation, through the mimesis of established behavioural sciences in recruitment patterns: psychology, political science and, above all, economics, were sources of new graduate recruits.

According to Lorsch (2009), the transformation of disciplinary silos dominated by a positivistic epistemology was not immediate but happened in the decades following the structural changes initiated as a response to the reports from the Ford and Carnegie inquiries conducted in the late 1950s. The 'original' intent of producing novel knowledge about organizations that would improve the practice of management in general was to be achieved by generating a politically neutral account of organizations as systems. Conceiving of all organizations as systems meant that no attention needed to be paid to contentious issues of ownership, relations of production, and other issues raised by Marxist-influenced scholarship. Systems were either more or less efficient and were essentially impersonal and thus non-hierarchical in their relations. Relations occurred between sub-systems rather than between concrete entities such as capitalists and labourers. Academic careers ensued that were founded on the mass production of mono-disciplinary pieces of academic research, of the type that Kuhn (1962, p. 35) would describe as "puzzle-solving" normal science, in which the basic notions of behavioural science and system theory were taken for granted.

Systems theory, while regarded as scientifically legitimate, was highly abstracted: it was supposed to apply to all organizations, anywhere (Parsons 1951). In part, its abstraction fed its legitimacy. The systems paradigm was high-value cultural capital in the university but its abstractions were, in many respects, irrelevant to the everyday concerns of practical men – as almost all managers were. While the vested interests of academics pushed in the direction of 'practically irrelevant' knowledge, growing institutional and market pressures were reorienting the strategic priorities of business schools: MBA programmes progressively became 'cash cows' for universities (Zell 2001; Starkey, Hatchuel and Tempest 2004), a phenomenon that can be framed in the broader shift in the social function of education, to see it increasingly "as an industry, not as a mechanism for socializing and educating the young" (Pfeffer and Fong 2004, p. 1510). The falling public support for higher education, a process that started in the USA and spread to other countries, has made business schools more dependent on revenues from student tuition fees and corporate contributions, further reducing autonomy (Trank and Rynes 2003). Business schools are major means for the conversion and translation of capital: initially, they were arenas in which the economic capital of established family businesses in static or declining branches of industry could be translated into the intellectual capital necessary for access to dynamic areas such as consulting as means for getting better jobs and salaries (Thomas, Whitley and Marceau 1981). The cultural capital that accrued to established wealth, such as yachts, country houses and ski lodges, was of importance in these translations. For these elites, attending business education isn't so much an opportunity to inject 'rationality' and scientific analysis skills into the toolbox of practising managers, nor a vocational choice, so much as simply an investment of time and money aimed at career opportunities with higher salaries and bonuses (Pfeffer and Fong 2004).

More generally, as business school education spread out to encompass many more recruits than merely the sons and, increasingly, the daughters of established local elites, its intellectual production became part of the trend toward the "commodification of knowledge" (Trank and Rynes 2003), which involved the "segmentation of knowledge in discrete packages or qualifications which could be purchased [...] The MBA can be seen as one such package" (Sturdy and Gabriel 2000, p. 980). With a huge proliferation in the number of institutions offering MBAs, new forms of stratification occurred in the marketplace, signalled largely through cost and status measures, which were directly related. Originally based on notions of embedded expertise, stratification claims were increasingly made on the basis of a reification of the offerings of business schools though "the process of commensuration – or the transformation of qualities into quantities and the creation of common metrics" (Wedlin 2011, p. 203) represented by the introduction of MBA rankings in the 1990s.

All these trends are thought to be general; according to this account all business schools tend to display similar strategies and conducts. Institutional theory (DiMaggio and Powell 1983) highlights the role played by mimetic isomorphic behaviours, a thesis accepted, amongst others, by Khurana (2007). The fact that demand for managerial skills has for a long time exceeded supply has also moderated the selection potential of the market (Wilson and McKiernan 2011) and probably reduced incentives for developing innovation and diversification in the offerings of business education. Also, since MBA students were universally treated as 'paying customers' (Zell 2001) their preferences and idiosyncrasies became a driving force. One consequence is that "business schools, under pressure to make their students happy, succeed in the ratings and grow their enrolments, have begun to all follow essentially the same strategies and produce MBAs who look remarkably alike" (Pfeffer and Fong 2004, p. 1514).

The industry has thrived this past half-century. Business schools based around the reformed and academically oriented American model that developed in the 1960s spread around the world, making the MBA the first authentically global degree (Clegg and Ross-Smith 2003; Mintzberg 2004; Starkey et al. 2004). The number of graduate management programmes around the world has risen exponentially in recent decades and the spread of more condensed programmes than the traditional US two years' full-time MBA degree is a demonstration of the commercial success of a business education derived but evolved from the American business school model. MBAs are highly valued by employers: the MBA is regarded by industry as "the 'gold standard' and 'guarantee of quality' as well as a company's 'long-term investment'" (GMAC 2010, p. 14), guaranteeing a full return on investment for graduates.

This apparently successful strategy is now increasingly put in question. What now troubles most business schools are intensifying market pressures, caused by a combination of factors that include the excessive supply of business education, the reduction in demand due to the global financial crisis and the emergence of alternative business education providers (Datar, Garvin and Cullen 2010). Even the sustained success that business education has had until this day is, paradoxically, a potential threat. Universities have come to depend on it as a vital source of funds (Starkey et al. 2004; Starkey and Tempest 2008), and as a consequence business schools are subjected to increased corporate scrutiny and performative demands by their parent institutions.

An apparently complex plot can be reduced to a linear narrative: the attempt to legitimate management by taking a scientific turn in business education has gone awry – because of the combination of vested interests and a blind following of market logics – and the abandonment of the professionalization project has reduced legitimacy both with respect to the components of the managerial class and the practices of business education. Now, as it becomes more saturated by providers, the business education market is becoming highly competitive such that the lack of diversification and relevance of offerings poses strategic threats.

How the West was Won: Beyond America

While this tale of the rise and (possible) decline of business education is accorded credence by a large number of observers it seems too simple and linear to be entirely plausible. For instance, it is unlikely that thousands of organizations operating in different countries, with different local market, cultural and institutional pressures, all end up following the same models, under common mimesis. The reality is that the model of business schools, while generally based on the American prototype, has a number of regional variations.

European business schools' reality is "more loosely configured, more heterogeneous, and, therefore, more open, in principle, to design innovations" (Starkey and Tempest 2008, p. 386). Europe in the post-war period was not 'virgin terrain' ripe for colonization by American cutting-edge ideas of business education. A conspicuous number of commercial schools had been founded across Europe in the 19th century, actually predating by many decades the 'first' American-inspired European business schools (Antunes and Thomas 2007, p. 384) such as INSEAD and LBS. However, their development was slower and constrained by national (and linguistic) borders, and the diffusion of the American standard in the 1950s (also propelled by national interests) eclipsed – on a global scale – these alternative models.

Still important differences persist between European and American business schools. Some differences are 'institutional', given the high cultural and linguistic diversity of Europe versus the homogeneity of the USA, the much heavier European regulatory environment, as well as the smaller size of European business schools (Antunes and Thomas 2007). To this list relevant historically formed differences must also be added. In particular, a divorce between practice and theory in management studies together with the drive for disciplinary specialization never happened completely, thanks to the existence of strong nationally specific academic and intellectual traditions. For instance, in Germany management education remained anchored to a strong practical model (Clegg and Ross-Smith 2003); a similar attitude had been present in the UK but was later displaced with the American model finally becoming embraced in the 1980s (Wilson and McKiernan 2011). On the other hand, in France the market niche of education in administration was already occupied by an old, highly reputed and successful group of elite institutions – the *Grandes Écoles* – which, while providing their students with a level of accreditation and networking comparable or superior to those of the top American schools (Bourdieu 1996), were traditionally informed by a high degree of interdisciplinarity (Kumar and Usunier 2001). Beneath these were the regional schools run by regional Chambers of Commerce. The majority of managers in continental Europe always possessed a strong 'professional' identity, often having graduated either in engineering or in economics (Kumar and Usunier 2001), degrees that signified a level of status and prestige. As a consequence, in this context the symbolic value of a more 'professionalizing' MBA had less purchase.

Another set of factors setting American and European management education apart pertains to the 'competitive differences' between the two systems (Antunes and Thomas 2007), including different systems of governance and funding. In his recent work on the global state and perspectives of business education, Iñiguez de Onzoño identifies at least three different funding modes: subsidized business schools, endowment-funded business schools and tuition-based business schools (Iñiguez de Onzoño 2011, pp. 64–6). The second model, a normal feature of the US university system, is generally not available to its European counterparts outside of a few elite institutions such as Oxford and Cambridge.

Consequently, European schools that belong to public universities, together with those located in countries where education is largely state funded (such as China), belong to the first category. However, the trend, especially in the UK, is towards a reduction of public funding (Starkey et al. 2004) and this is pushing a number of schools towards the third funding option. The top-rated European business schools, which operate in an elite niche of the market for professional vocational education, do so largely through fee-based models where prestige and price are closely related.

Another type of competitive differences that set apart the Old and the New World is the fact that European management education appears to be more sensitive "to international business, languages, diversity and culture" (Antunes and Thomas 2007, p. 394). This higher flexibility is probably connected to its tendency to assume a more critical approach to the theories and models that it teaches, compared to American practice (Pfeffer and Fong 2004). A salient factor in this differentiation are the biographical experiences of many of the European elites in having been educated in a cognate social science rather than explicitly in business education: for the generation that rose to prominence in the post-war wave of growth the options of a highly developed undergraduate education in business were not available. One last difference noted by Antunes and Thomas (2007) concerns the type of media used to transmit knowledge: US business education traditionally relied more on discipline and research-based journals, while European institutions preferred books and practice-oriented publication outlets. However, these trends are converging on the US model in all those systems in which state rankings of research efforts have become the norm. Access to the privileges afforded the best-ranked schools drives behaviour towards the metaphorical Eden in which additional resources to tuition fees are plentiful, distributed on the basis of research profiles.

East of Eden

Looking beyond the 'Western axis' one of the most striking elements that differentiates Asian business schools is the difference in market conditions: while the competition seems to be stiffer in the USA and Europe, especially for lower-ranked schools, there is a steady growth in demand in Asia, especially in the Far East (Datar et al. 2010). Expansion is due both to the rapid development of Asian economies but also to national government commitments to increasing the capacity of local business education, attracting students that previously went overseas, mainly to English-speaking countries, to achieve their MBAs (Zammuto 2008).

The sheer number of institutions offering business education in Asia (by 2010 there were more than 1200 of these in China, the Philippines and India alone) illustrates the potential impact for local and global economies and business education discourse, even if, at the moment, the contribution of these new players is under-recognized because of post-colonial complexes and the hegemonic role of American and European business school models (Yeung and Kulwant 2011). Analysing the case of Malaysia, Sturdy and Gabriel (2000, p. 989) attribute a significant part of the success of foreign-validated MBA 'products' to their reputation for integrity and fairness in awarding degrees, and to the symbolic resonance of a prestigious 'brand', such that "students engage in seemingly obsessive comparison between the prestige of different institutions".

In Latin America, the hegemony of the 'American way' of business education is more apparent than real: Brazilian business schools, for instance, have adopted the acronym MBA, and some of the more prestigious ones, such as the Brazilian *Fundação Getulio Vargas*, were US-founded but the format, the content and the methodology have diverged from North American programmes as they slowly built a global reputation and profile developing their own educational model, adapting both local cultural, market and institutional conditions as well as building on traditions of critical thinking (Leme Fleury and Wood Jr 2011).

Another case altogether is that of developing countries, where the shortage of qualified managers can be a factor hindering development. However, rather than being educated to the same model and with the same methodologies used in mature economies, aspirant managers receive instruction more aligned with some of the specific challenges and opportunities that characterize developing countries (gender equity, difficult access to markets, the need to preserve local culture, the opportunity for technological leapfrogging, etc.), aiming at the development of 'micro-business' models, that is designing and managing systems of transactions that require minimal infrastructure and investment (Wood 2004). Another example relates to the transferability of training methodologies in different cultural contexts: case study methods – a centrepiece of the American approach to business education – are at odds with the educational customs and role expectations of students and trainers in Middle Eastern and North African countries (Gillespie and Riddle 2004).

When addressing the role of business education in emerging markets we are not only faced with the moral imperative to overcome post-colonial supremacy; the issue at stake is the need to understand the role that business education can and must play in steering the growth of economies that are forecast to become the leading global players in the next few decades (Cheng et al. 2007). It has been argued, for instance, that in emerging markets the need for the quantitative functional business skills typically developed by the 'standard' model of management education needs to be complemented by mental, interpersonal and cultural skills teaching to allow the graduated students to cope with the complex negotiating environments (Reeves-Ellington 2004). The diversity of experiences and perspectives is not well-represented in the critical literature on business education, probably because of the discursive predominance of North American research on management (Clegg and Ross-Smith 2003, p. 89). Also, American schools, or schools inspired by their model, dominate present rankings (Antunes and Thomas 2007, p. 395), creating a hegemonic scenario according to which elite US business schools are an absolute benchmark of quality that less developed countries should aspire to.

"We're Doing Fine in the Lucky Country": Australia

The teaching of management subjects in Australia had an early start: in 1916 a lecture in industrial psychology was delivered at Sydney University. The event, however, was an isolated instance such that before WWII vocational business education was almost absent in Australia (Pearse 2010, p. 128). It was only in the 1950s that the US model of business education, with its complement of case study analysis and scientific management models, was imported. By 1963 Melbourne, Sydney and Canberra had universities offering American style MBAs (Pearse 2010, p. 162).

Before the 1970s, Australia's academic production in the field of organizational sciences appeared to be marginal, even if the nation was a 'net exporter' of scientific talent. Eminent early authorities in the field of management sciences, such as Elton Mayo or Fred Emery, were born and trained in Australia but made their reputations and careers in the USA and the UK (Pearse 2010, pp. 156–8). In the late 1970s an elite institution explicitly modelled on US models was founded as the Australian Graduate School of Management at the University of New South Wales. At the time, policy saw no need for more than one national business school, designed and funded on an elite model.

The boom in the business education industry of Australia is a phenomenon that started in the 1990s after the end of the binary divide: the number of business students grew threefold between 1990 and 2007, often in what had been former Colleges of Advanced Education and Institutes of Technology that assumed university status. Between 2001 and 2005 the number of postgraduate business degrees doubled, with a dramatic increase (+126.7%) in master-by-coursework students (Pearse

2010, p. 223). As a result, according to an overseas observer, present day "Australia has 39 universities, of which two are private, and a further 70 business schools" (Iñiguez de Onzoño 2011, p. 83).

Expansion has been propelled both by domestic and international opportunities. Internally, apart from a constantly growing economy, driving forces have been the increased numbers of students enrolled on courses (engineering, information technology, accountancy and law) that put graduates on a managerial career path, as well as the proliferation of management education and training service providers, which came to include management consulting firms, recruitment firms, specialist training firms, professional and industry associations (Pearse 2010, p. 224).

The real catalyst for the development of the industry, however, has been the international market. Since the 1990s Australian universities, with diminishing levels of public funding, have joined other private education providers in aggressively recruiting international students paying higher fees (Zammuto 2008). By 2010, the number of overseas students enrolled in Australian higher education put Australia ahead of both the USA and the UK as the destination of choice for fee-paying international students (Iñiguez de Onzoño 2011, p. 87), and nearly half of these international students are enrolled on management and commerce courses (Norton 2012). The other side of the coin is that the success in attracting foreign students has made the sector highly dependent on this source of revenues, exposing Australian schools to the competition of a global market (Zammuto 2008). For instance, a strong currency has recently altered the path of international student education demand, increasing the demand for short-term (and lower-quality) training (Ross 2012).

A more relevant consequence for the organization of academic institutions in Australia is that rich market opportunities provided by the growth in demand for managerial labour in a booming regional economy, together with the progressive disengagement of government from education funding, created a very fertile environment for an increase in corporatization and commodification of business education. While market forces have mostly shaped the industry, with public policy initiatives lagging behind, the remarkable Australian success in attracting international business students has been attributed both to the role played by public–private partnership promotional initiatives and to immigration policies giving opportunities to students to remain in the country after they graduate (Iñiguez de Onzoño 2011, p. 88).

Inside Australian business schools, a progressive 'modernization' is reducing academic autonomy and causing tensions between academic and administrative staff. Ryan and Guthrie (2009) identified three forces shaping the progressive corporatization of Australian universities: 'hard managerialism', academic consumerism and fragmentation of work. The first is based on the principles of performance measurement, strong central management and cost reduction. The second indicates student empowerment, given their status as paying customers, which allegedly causes conflicts of interests and biases in the assessment processes. The third refers to various practices disrupting traditional academic prerogatives, such as the efforts to diminish disciplinary boundaries by increasing centralized control or through the casualization of academic jobs.

Summing up, business education in Australia in the second decade of the 21st century appears to be a dynamic industry where commercially aggressive semi-corporate identities compete – in a globalized market – to attract paying customers. Even their scientific output is increasingly commoditized with academics being pushed to increase their productivity. Moreover, mimetic forces are pushing them in an "accreditation rush" in order to increase reputational capital that can be quickly converted into higher incomes for their graduates (Zammuto 2008). The effects of ranking and accreditation are discussed in detail in the next section.

"TOP RANKING"

Zooming back to a global perspective, it is necessary to consider another twist in the tale of the evolution of business education: the rise (with no fall in sight) of accreditation and ranking systems. While this development can be seen as an essential step towards the professionalization of management, the definition and application of a set of standards has important political implications and repercussions. Such a system, instead of promoting excellence, can turn into a conservative force that maintains the status quo and preserves the prerogatives of the established elites (Lowrie and Willmott 2009). Accreditation in business education is bestowed mainly by three bodies, which have the declared intent of regulating the quality of MBA programmes: the Association to Advance Collegiate Schools of Business (AACSB), the European Quality Improvement System (EQUIS) and the Association of MBAs (AMBA) (Wilson and McKiernan 2011).

While the AACSB "is typically viewed as the most prestigious accreditation" (Zammuto 2008, p. 261) various concerns have been expressed about its neutrality, objectivity and leadership: colourfully, it has been compared to "a group of foxes guarding the MBA henhouses" (Navarro 2008, p. 120). According to Lowrie and Willmott (2009) the problem is the absence, in AACSB accreditation, of requirements for a core curriculum paired with ambiguity concerning the definition of either the 'quality' of education or its 'utility'. The 'hollow core' offers the impression that the accreditation system is flexible and capable of including a diversity of approaches, a factor that helped diffusion of its accreditation beyond US borders. However, these authors argue, the peer-reviewed process that it uses is inherently conservative and only those institutions that comply with the traditional education (and ideological) model of elite US schools can hope to achieve accreditation. Even if each school can set its vision, the criteria for establishing the quality of its achievement, such as number of active researchers, publications, PhDs etc., is largely US-inspired.

What accreditation systems have in common is their isomorphic drive: they tend to produce conformity within MBA programmes (Grey 2002; Pfeffer and Fong 2004), and at the same fail to mandate the presence in the curricula of essential professional competences, such as business ethics (Trank and Rynes 2003). 'Accreditocracy' has even been accused of reducing the capacity of business schools to cope with a more turbulent environment, by focusing on incremental improvement rather than innovation (Julian and Ofori-Dankwa 2006).

Zammuto (2008) is more optimistic about the value of accreditation as it provides legitimacy through quality certification and forces schools to formulate a clear mission and strategy. While the legitimating value of accreditation is evident, rituals of strategy rather than realities of practice can develop an unwarranted faith in accreditation as a strategy (Clegg, Carter and Kornberger 2004) that underestimates the specific challenges linked to the loosely coupled character of education organizations (Weick 1976, 1982; Orton and Weick 1990). Since accreditation standards do not differentiate between elite and non-elite schools (Julian and Ofori-Dankwa 2006), the need to distinguish providers in an increasingly competitive market stimulated the diffusion of ranking systems. In the case of business education, it is the economic press that arrogated the role of arbiter and assessor of the quality of management education programmes, focusing in particular on the MBA. These media rankings have been used now for more than three decades, the first one having been proposed by *Business Week* in 1988 (Devinney, Dowling and Perm-Ajchariyawong 2008). The system is highly selective, with no more than one-fifth of the AACSB-accredited schools making these rankings (Halperin, Hebert and Lusk 2009).

The metrics used to rank business schools are slightly different but the most influential ones (developed by the *Financial Times*, *The Economist*, *Business Week* and *The Wall Street Journal*) share a common model, based on five criteria (Wedlin 2007): programme features (curriculum, teaching), employability and career of graduates, school features (e.g. infrastructures, faculty), incoming class features, and research. The presence of different providers of ranking is not a demonstration of pluralism: a comparative study conducted by Halperin et al. (2009) shows that, regardless of apparent differences in methodology and metrics, all the major ranking systems appear to be measuring the same dimensions in the programmes.

The proliferation of media rankings is not a phenomenon restricted to business education (Wedlin 2007), and their function is not simply to help consumers make an informed decision. They can also "serve as rhetorical devices to construct and maintain legitimacy for organizations and their activities [... and] can be used to create, enhance or validate organizational reputation" (Wedlin 2011, p. 203). According to Gioia and Corley (2002) ranking systems can have a beneficial effect, by stimulating a competition that forces schools to become more reactive to changes in the business environment, more relevant, more accountable, and more strategic in defining their positioning and focus (even if the same reservation that I have expressed before when discussing the claimed strategic benefits of accreditation systems applies here). They also make available useful information for applicants who have to decide where to study, simplifying the otherwise daunting task of acquiring and comparing data from different providers (Iñiguez de Onzoño 2011, pp. 118–19).

Both accreditation and ranking systems produce a powerful reputational effect that has a clear influence on competition in the business school market, creating a clear elite category, compounded by the high brand loyalty that develops among a school's alumni, who have an interest in enhancing the symbolic value of their degree and therefore support and promote their alma mater, producing a virtuous circle (Antunes and Thomas 2007, p. 395). The reputational boost given by a positive ranking has an immediate effect on the financial return of a business school, thanks to significant increases in student intake and fees (Peters 2007).

A number of concerns have been expressed about the impartiality of the system and the consequences of 'ranking pressures' on business education. While the independence of the referees administering the system (media outlets) is not questioned, it has been suggested that these business schools are being measured against objective criteria skewed by the unequal distribution of symbolic capital in the field.

First, in the absence of agreed upon standards as to what constitutes an 'ideal business school' (Devinney et al. 2008), assessors need to legitimate their ranking system. Since their first goal is to attract their readers (Glick 2008) they are not overly concerned with preoccupations of epistemological rigour; their purpose is simply to provide a simple and credible (in the sense of convincing, plausible) source of information. The simplest way to do that is to make sure that the results "confirm, to some extent, previously held notions of the positions of leading business schools in the field" (Wedlin 2011, p. 212). Consequently, each player is confronted with a benchmark of excellence that a priori, in an uncritical fashion, has been attributed to a group of traditionally dominant American educational institutions. Such practice contributes to one negative outcome of rankings, which is their effect as a homogenizing force. As typically happens with accreditation systems, what was created to differentiate induces conformity as aspirant institutions seek to emulate the elites in a process of institutional isomorphism: thus, rankings induce business schools to become more alike (Wedlin 2007), thus conforming to a template dominated by US orthodoxy.

Apart from the prejudices embedded in the choice of metrics, doubts have been raised about the rigour and the quality of statistical methodologies used in these rankings. They are often based on simple aggregations of information: consequently, each of these can be expected to contain measurement errors (statistical 'noise') such that the overall ranking can be extremely 'noisy' (Dichev 2008). Moreover, the metrics used have been shown not to be mutually independent (Safón 2009). In any case it is not even clear what is the underlying construct that these metrics are measuring: is it reputation, performances, customer satisfaction, market positioning or something else (Devinney et al. 2008)? The limited focus of rankings that instead of assessing the overall offer of a business school are oriented primarily towards MBA programme assessment adds to the problem of their scarce methodological validity, which risks returning these institutions to their former status as "glorified vocational schools, training people for jobs, rather than educating them as professional managers" (Gioia and Corley 2002, p. 108).

It would be insufficient to improve the indicators and the methodologies used continuously to measure the quality of management education, as some ranking organizations reportedly do (Bradshaw 2007), because these rankings tend to produce a series of unintended consequences. Some critics have, for instance, alerted the market to the de-professionalizing effects induced by 'ranking pressure'. Trank and Rynes (2003) argue that the influence of metrics unrelated to educational content can distract schools from improving their pedagogy and even induce biases. They note, for instance, that the starting salary of the alumni (a typical metric in ranking) is much more strongly influenced by the geographical location of the school than by its 'quality'; moreover, it can induce schools to prefer students willing to pursue more lucrative careers (e.g. finance) over those who want to work in areas such as human resources or non-profit organizations. The tendency can bring about other inequalities, such as the discrimination of ethnic minorities (Gioia and Corley 2002, p. 113) whose cultural capital is widely perceived as deficient.

The fact that rankings are driven by structural factors that are difficult to change (Wilson and McKiernan 2011), together with the short tenure of deans and the frequent shift of criteria, induces a short-term strategic outlook in business schools. As a consequence they tend to focus on branding and image promotion, to create an impression of progress, at the expense of investments in substantive pedagogical improvements (Gioia and Corley 2002). These reflections appear to be confirmed by empirical data: a quantitative study on the relationship between reputation and ranking (Safón 2009) has revealed how ranking and student quality are the two key factors influencing business schools' reputations, while research, placement success and the learning outcomes have no effect on it. In other words these data suggest that the promise of quality embedded in the ranking is more important than actual performances.

Even the positive effects of the competition induced by ranking systems can be stifled by the presence of a virtuous circle which favours those American institutions on whose profile the ordering criteria have been created: being rated 'world best' allows them to attract top students and resources (in the form of alumni donations), while their alumni are sought by high-paying companies; consequently, elite business schools maintain their prominent rank, while it is extremely difficult for new players to enter among the chosen few (Corley and Gioia 2000). Clear demonstration of this is the fact that while operating in an apparently dynamic environment, "the majority of schools in the top 50 has tended to remain relatively stable over the years, with a small number of schools fighting each year over the bottom rungs" (Navarro 2008, p. 111).

The most important aspect of ranking as a phenomenon is that it is here to stay, and that it constitutes an essential feature of the discursive landscape in which management academics, together with their colleagues from other disciplines, operate. "Despite their failings, their ambiguity and their imprecision, business school rankings have become reified" (Wilson and McKiernan 2011, p. 462) and whether they like it or not business schools have to play the game (Corley and Gioia 2000; Peters 2007). As Gioia and Corley effectively summarize, "all the things wrong with the rankings matter considerably less than the plain fact that the rankings matter" (2002, p. 112).

A central feature of discursive normalization is that certain views become implicit assumptions. For instance, a characteristic of the reviewed debate is that the issue of ranking and accreditation is typically seen in the perspective of a 'natural' competition among business schools. The reason for this blind spot can be found in the powerful influence of other pervasive and connected discourses, founded on the belief that measurement is a "primary contributor to human knowledge" (Harzing and Adler 2009, p. 73), promoting an ethic of performativity and considering academic activity as something that can be rightfully commodified and subject to managerial control (Parker and Jary 1995; Parker 2014). What is left therefore is to reflect on the implication of the 'irresistibility' of this power/knowledge configuration, in particular the fact that, above all the rest, these measures of performativity appear to contrast (employing explicit and implicit silencing strategies) the development of ethical and social responsibility in management.

LONG LIVE MANAGERIALISM! BUSINESS SCHOOLS BETWEEN MORAL DEAFNESS AND OVERT PROPAGANDA

While the business model driving the industry still seems to be viable, many observers have expressed serious concerns about the loss of legitimation of business education. After the numerous scandals that rocked the corporate world in the early years of the 21st century, and especially in the aftermath of the economic meltdown that followed the 2007/2008 global financial crisis, it is unsurprising that business schools have been accused of propagating a morality based on a principle that, to paraphrase a line from Brecht's *The Threepenny Opera*, could be summed as: "stock options are the first thing, morality follows".

Khurana (2007) argues that, during the past few decades, the original professional ideals have been replaced by an ideology of market capitalism, one which students internalize. Grey (2002) agrees, critiquing MBA programmes which socialize students into 'managerialism' and 'turbo capitalism', reproducing one-sided thinking and problematic practices. Equally, according to Pfeffer and Fong, business schools seem to be concerned only with teaching how to maximize monetary returns for shareholders, "offering a value proposition that primarily emphasizes the career-enhancing, salary-increasing aspects of business education" (Pfeffer and Fong 2004, p. 1501). Such an attitude has harmful effects on the ethos of managers: "by propagating ideologically inspired amoral theories, business schools have actively freed their students from any sense of moral responsibility" (Ghoshal 2005, p. 76). As a negative trend this has been attributed to competitive pressure among business schools (Pfeffer and Fong 2004), to deficiencies in the theoretical apparatus supporting business education (Ghoshal 2005), or to a lack of professionalism in management practice (Bennis and O'Toole 2005).

The blind belief in the 'free market' ideologies which crept into the business schools' curricula has all but displaced ethical concerns over the last few decades. Managers turned from the Parsonian ideal of agents of stability whose mission was to build stronger and larger corporations (Khurana 2007, p. 363) becoming servants of the short-term interests of institutional shareholders who have no attachment either to the company or to the wider community. In fact, research shows that people attending business education tend to display selfish attitudes, even showing an inclination towards outright unethical and devious behaviours (Carter and Irons 1991; Cadsby and Maynes 1998; Schulze and Frank 2000; McCabe, Butterfield and Trevino 2006; Malhotra and Wang 2011). Moreover, people tend to replicate in the workplace the 'bad habits' (such as cheating) in which they were inculcated during their college years (Nonis and Swift 2001).

On top of the naturalized status of performativity and efficiency, the very idea of a 'rational division of labour' and specialization can produce perverse effects on the ethics of management. An excessive disciplinary specialization, for instance, risks producing moral desensitization, decoupling task from organizational outcomes, transforming managers into 'willing executioners' (Bauman 1989). The bureaucratic rationalization offers an alternative, petty morality, which appeases the sense of duty of the corporate golems, where, in Weber's words "The 'objective' discharge of business primarily means a discharge of business according to calculable rules and 'without regard for persons'" (cited in Bauman 1989, p. 14). It is likely that the collapse of companies such as Lehman Brothers is both a consequence of the unbridled greed of testosterone fuelled young executives (Currie, Knights and Starkey 2010) as well as "a product of routine bureaucratic procedures" (Bauman 1989, p. 17).

The sin of business education is not simply one of omission. If on the one hand business schools are not doing enough to counteract the perverse effects of the extension of managerialism throughout society, on the other hand they are also actively reproducing and perpetuating ideologies that are serving the interests of international business elites. Vaara and Faÿ (2012) have attempted to analyse this system of ideological reproduction by applying Bourdieu's perspective to conceptualize business schools as part of a global 'field' where the influence of ranking and accreditation systems combined with competition and the desire of the student to acquire symbolic capital drives them towards convergence and conformity. The set of values and discourses, *nomos* and *doxa* (Bourdieu 1977), underlying this field, summed up by the labels of managerialism, neoliberalism and instrumentalism, serve the interests of an elite as well as being ethically flawed and unsustainable, as the current financial and environmental crises demonstrate. The problem is that servile, uncritical acquiescence in such principles on the part of business schools, combined with pedagogical practices that reinforce problematic dispositions, such as short-term orientation, the attitude to exploitation and elitism, tend to reproduce and strengthen this *nomos* and *doxa* (Vaara and Faÿ 2012, p. 1036). Such reflections are in stark contrast with the "admiration of the scientific method, analytical tools, and precise testable models among business educators" (Steiner and Watson 2006, p. 423). The problem is that most studies tend to objectify managerial work, leading to a technicist, purportedly value-free understanding of management (Grey 2002). Any technique is always a value-laden activity; furthermore, the practice of management has particular ethical implications because it is necessarily based on the exercise of power (Grey 2002).

This use of power over other individuals is often uncritically accepted and taken for granted by most commentators, especially when it is cloaked in the noble idea of 'leadership'. As such, the power of managers is not only legitimized but even advocated by many as a solution to integrate the teachings of business schools, overcoming the 'banes' of functional silos-thinking and analytic rigidity (Bailey and Ford 1996; Datar et al. 2010; Iñiguez de Onzoño 2011). But as Khurana (2007, p. 362) noted, the notion of leadership is far less ethically constraining than that of professionalism.

The model of manager that management education reproduces is that of a technocrat, an agent who acquires methodologies helpful to solve narrowly defined problems but without any deontological concern. This breed of managers is not oriented "toward the realization of practical goals but toward the solution of technical problems" (Habermas 1987, p. 103). The traditional 'hands-on', practice-based model of management despised by the reformers of business education in the 1950s has been replaced now by a technocratic conscience built on "the elimination of the distinction between the practical and the technical" (Habermas 1987, p. 113). Business students are socialized through the routine application of discursive techniques, such as the use of case study analysis, that privilege a technical rationality over a critical reflection on goals, which fails to contemplate the political and relational character of practice (Roberts 1996).

The paradoxical consequence for managers is that the same techno-cratic paradigm that was supposed to enhance their status can become an oppressing force, reducing them to mere executors. In other terms, the rationalization of business education effectively de-professionalizes man-agement, whose "hired hands" (Khurana 2007) can cause harm to organizations not only because they are driven by their self-interest (Jensen and Meckling 1976) but also because they are not sufficiently self-empowered to tackle the complexity, uncertainties and moral ambi-guities of managerial actions. The process can be seen as part of a systematic strategy towards "the commodification of professional know-ledge that makes individual employees more expendable" (Trank and Rynes 2003, p. 193). It is quite ironic that managers are rewarded for making their peers, and ultimately themselves, disposable objects.

Nonetheless "modern management education has all but ignored the idea of a moral education" (Clegg and Ross-Smith 2003, p. 96). In fact, even today only about one-quarter of AACSB-accredited schools in the USA include in their curriculum a stand-alone business ethics course (Rutherford et al. 2012, p. 183). While the preoccupation about the role that business education should play in developing ethical behaviours in management is also shared by most AACBS deans, it is evident that their capacity (or willingness) to walk the talk is limited (Evans and Marcal 2005).

The decision to include a business ethics course does not seem to be a strategic choice motivated by an agenda of professionalization of man-agement or informed by a belief in critical management ideals. On the contrary its primary drivers appear to be the values and institutional setting of the organization (e.g. business schools with a religious affilia-tion will frequently include some form of moral education) and the characteristics of its leadership (gender and professional background), while the financial wealth of the institution appears to make it more conservative and unyielding to external entreaties, thus resisting the introduction of ethical courses (Rutherford et al. 2012).

On the other hand, it would not be sufficient simply to include in the programme of study a tokenistic course on ethics (Ghoshal 2005). What most commentators advocate is to make ethical training an essential part of the curriculum, as happens for other professions (Grey 2002; Trank and Rynes 2003) but with a caveat: "the process of socialization consists in the manipulation of moral capacity – not in its production" (Bauman 1989, p. 178). A major issue is that "academic attention to public accountability has focused on the legal aspects of compliance and regulation" instead of "cultivating reflective judgment on matters of moral accountability" (Jarvis 2009, p. viii). Future or current managers cannot be 'made moral' by feeding them normative ethics training; their moral standards can (and should) instead be probed, discussed, critically examined and nurtured all through the course of their training.

POWER IN NUMBERS: THE CASE OF ACADEMIC PUBLICATIONS

The apparently simple issue of providing publicity for research generates an intricate political jungle. To be influential, to have an impact, a study has to appear in a reputed journal. This requires following linguistic standards and templates that tend to be idiosyncratic to the discipline, the study stream, and the publication outlet. These conventions have an impact on the knowledge that is generated and transferred (Rhodes 2001).

To start with, the editorial review system is not perfect. It can reject useful papers that do not conform to the idiosyncrasies of the local interpretive community or the dominant paradigmatic views (Pfeffer 2007; Raelin 2008). Reviewing has been compared to a playground game, where actors interact on the basis of formal and informal rules, sometimes unfairly (Graue 2006). Institutional pressures to publish have produced veritable inflationary processes, especially in 'hard' sciences, with the emergence of the idea of the 'LPU', or 'least publishable unit', a euphemism with which to describe the practice of publishing to fragment the description in order to generate a higher number of peer-reviewed publications (Broad 1981).

Empirical research has shown that in the field of management studies the best predictor of the number of citations that a work may receive is the prestige of the journal in which it was published (Judge et al. 2007). A self-supporting loop is created, since the number of citations and journal ranking reinforce each other (Starbuck 2005). Moreover, articles do not contribute evenly to the reputation of a journal, as measured by citations, since a few highly cited articles ('big hitters') can propel a journal to the top tier (Mingers and Willmott 2013).

Editorial selection involves considerable randomness, because reviewers' assessment of the quality of a specific manuscript can differ, even if they agree on the ideal properties of 'good paper', an issue that becomes more serious as the number of reviewers-gatekeepers increases (Starbuck 2005). The presence of bias and randomness in reviews is a consequence of the fact that the audience to a communication is never passive and researchers can maximize their chances of publication by knowing the audience and adapting their style accordingly (Starbuck 2003). Despite the attention received, the dimensions of the problem of the inadequacy of peer-reviewed journal practices are undetermined. A comparative examination of hundreds of studies on the subject (Weller 2001) poses important questions (Is the best science published? Does the peer-review process help authors to improve their work?), yet most of these questions are left unanswered because of widely different findings. Consequently, despite the rhetoric on rigour, academics resort also to anecdotal evidence, personal experience or 'gut feeling' to 'win the publishing game'. Data on publication success show that, "in the case of non-empirical work, an article's impact was almost completely dependent on astute topic selection and adroit argumentation" (Judge et al. 2007, p. 503). In the presence of a multiplicity of political, aesthetical, historical and technical factors influencing the outcomes of the game, success requires the exercise of a set of practical skills embodied in particular researchers' capabilities.

One tangible example of how senior academics maintain a head start in the competition by virtue of their 'practical mastery' is seen in co-authorship. The increased number of competitors in the publishing arena, together with the unpredictable outcomes of the peer-review process, make focusing on the production of a single authored work a very risky investment. Authors 'hedge their bets' by contemporarily undertaking several team projects, as demonstrated by empirical studies showing a trend towards multiple authorships in business literature (English and Manton 2007). Such a phenomenon highlights the importance of the social and symbolic capital accumulated in the course of a successful career. The network of relationships developed by academics and their membership in a distinct 'tribe' are essential assets, determining the possibility of a sustained success.

As a consequence, an author who skilfully complies with the conventions and the editorial policy of top journals, who builds a good collaboration network and who sticks to 'safe' and fashionable topics can have a successful career even without providing any significant contribution to scholarship or practice. The unfairness and whimsicality of the game affect not only individual academics but also universities and society at large. The ranking system is based on a series of purely arbitrary and arguable rules, including the focus on English-written articles published in a small number of 'prestigious' journals. This situation has a number of negative consequences, such as delayed, culturally biased and often practically irrelevant knowledge (Harzing and Adler 2009).

The crisp clarity of a ranking based on a numerical rank ordering produces a strong disciplinary effect, driven by a *habitus* awed by quantification, which any modern, educated individual is trained to recognize as a mark of veracity and undisputed authority. However, this exactitude, this reification and extreme reduction of a complex phenomenon to a single cipher, is achieved by means of a practice made up of multiple power effects constituting the production of academic prestige. An example of these is the choice of how to weight contributions in the case of multi-authored papers, or of papers published by scholars with multiple affiliations (Harzing and Adler 2009). The choices of institutional bodies producing ranking systems and the presence of an established elite of gatekeepers (in the form of editors and reviewers) shape the rules of the game, producing various pragmatic consequences. First, they reproduce domination and inequalities, especially at the cost of researchers who do not belong to the 'white Anglo-Saxon male' dominant group (Özbilgin 2009). Second, they induce individual academics to adopt strategies which can be detrimental for the originality, relevance or innovativeness of contributions (Harzing and Adler 2009; Gabriel 2010). Third, they create damaging forms of insecurity and anxiety in individual academics, impairing their potential contributions. While monitoring and measuring affect almost everyone in contemporary society, academics' performances are routinely scrutinized by "a myriad of different constituencies [who] legitimately stand in judgement" of their work (Knights and Clarke 2014, p. 350), including students, managers, colleagues, reviewers, etc.

Regardless of the objectivity and equity of the adopted measuring system, the emphasis on performativity and quantifiable outputs supports the reification and commodification of knowledge (Sturdy and Gabriel 2000; Radder 2010), producing it as an object with an exchange value: thus, its ability to understand, question and transform social reality is diminished or increased according to the extent that its exchange value is lower or higher. Moreover, it conspicuously alters the practices of academics, an important point from the perspective of my enquiry.

The publication game affects scholarly practices in various ways, from the tendency to read and write articles rather than books, which produces an inflation of available sources, leading to a superficial approach to knowledge, often based on reading abstracts, picking up what has been cited by others or has surfaced in electronic searches, and considering writing more important than reading (Gabriel 2010, p. 762). The way in which information and knowledge is acquired, the manner in which findings and ideas are articulated, even the places where the work is performed (and, consequently, the opportunities for meeting, exchange and socialization), are all transformed. Furthermore, the fierce competition for accessing the limited space offered by high-ranking publication outlets has relevant consequences on work practices. The competition to be published in a prestigious journal is such that "submitting to a 'quality' journal these days appears to have become virtually a trial by ordeal [...] involving numerous revisions, citing authors one does not care for, engaging with arguments one is not interested in and seeking to satisfy different harsh masters" (Gabriel 2010, pp. 763–4). Researchers have to submit themselves to this 'ordeal' because their careers depend on it (Starbuck 2005); as a consequence of the trend towards managerialism and the "McDonaldization" of universities (Parker and Jary 1995) there is increased emphasis on standards, measures, rankings.

The challenge for contemporary academics is closer to that of a salesperson who is only paid on commission than to that of a piecework labourer, since there is no way for the researcher who is producing a paper to predict if, when, and where it will be published, thus becoming able to 'cash in their bets'. Also, the proliferation of journals, which could at least provide more opportunities to find a stage for academic works, paradoxically becomes another source of pressure and exploitation for individual researchers, since the growth of publications is fuelled by a huge amount of unpaid academic labour (Gabriel 2010).

Critical management students tend to attribute the responsibility of this state of things to corporatized universities, represented as arenas of class warfare, in which neoliberal politicians and managerialist administrators are set against freethinking and collegial academics. The defeat of the latter at the hand of the former determines a commodification of academic labour, replacing production of use value with that of exchange value (Willmott 1995). In addition, the Tayloristic reliance on mono-thematic performance measures, based on journal metrics, causes a reduction of heterogeneity and a marginalization of innovation in management research (Mingers and Willmott 2013). The power landscape underlying this dynamic is more complex, though, than this analysis suggests. Academics are not just victims of an imposition of computable performativity, but they are engaged in the mutual reproduction of this managerialist discourse (Keenoy 2005), as they try to "make out" colleagues, not dissimilar to the shop-floor blue-collar workers described by Burawoy (1979). While the corporate university is probably exploiting academics' passion for their job (Clarke, Knights and Jarvis 2012), 'unwholesome' emotions such as narcissism also play an important role in supporting the replacement of scientific publication use value ('Does this work contribute to knowledge and practice?') with their exchange value ('Will it improve my reputation and career?') (Fellman 1995). As a consequence, administrators and researchers find themselves allied, and this association is particularly amenable to the interests of the elites of both groups, whereas the "aspirations to publish in highly ranked journals ensure a harmony with the demands of the institution" (Knights and Clarke 2014, p. 350). The two groups simply use different 'legal tenders' to represent the exchange value of their work output. What university administrators' compute in financial terms is calculated, in academic terms, in publication credits, citations and H-indices.

Not only are 'perpetrators' and 'victims' roles' blurred in these processes, as described, but non-human elements also play a critical role in shaping this scenario. While measurement has been considered a cornerstone of scientific enquiry since the Enlightenment (Harzing and Adler 2009), the digital revolution has made possible extraordinarily sophisticated systems of metrics, ease of access to an unprecedented abundance of sources to organize, use and reuse a wealth of information efficiently, thus enabling the 'game' (Weller 2011). Non-human actants (search engines, digital databases, citation and indexing software, word processors, etc.) are as important as the decision of any human actor in shaping the practices of researchers attempting to produce 'publishable material'. Such a representation of the determinants of the publishing game provides a vivid illustration of how the phenomenon of power transcends any trivialization as a mere form of domination of the strong over the weak and that it is better understood as a process of the mutual constitution of meaning and social disparities, whereas "power produces rationality and truth; rationality and truth produces power" (Flyvbjerg 2001, p. 124). The fact that this unfair system is justified by the need for "fairness in universities' hiring, promotion, and tenure decisions, and accountability and value-for-research-dollars in the grant-awarding processes" is demonstrative of this mutual implication (Harzing and Adler 2009, p. 74)

TOWARDS A COMPLEX NOTION OF RELEVANCE

Business schools frequently have been accused of producing and dispensing irrelevant knowledge. Their research is too abstract or circumscribed such as to be of little consequence for practitioners (Bennis and O'Toole 2005); management researchers carry out prevalently descriptive, rather than prescriptive, studies (Bazerman 2005), producing theories that have little connection to practice (Peters and Bogner 2002), cladding their findings in a specialist language which, although rigorous, is often so obscure and esoteric as to defy the efforts of the most open-minded and educated practitioner (Kieser and Leiner 2011). Despite the plea for research to "focus on persistent problems that real-world executives and leaders need to solve" (Lorsch 2009, p. 113) empirical evidence suggests a constant decline in the last half-century of the number of publications containing actionable and practically relevant knowledge (Pearce and Huang 2012).

The lack of practical grounding led Mintzberg (2004, p. 5) to state that "pretending to create managers out of people who have never managed is a sham". The need to develop practice-based programmes has been strongly advocated by various scholars (Starkey et al. 2004; Raelin 2007; Tushman et al. 2007). Even the attempt to simulate reality with the use of business games and case studies falls short of expectations, because these methods oversimplify reality, producing overconfident but fundamentally incompetent wannabe managers (Mintzberg 2004). The problem, therefore, is not the reliability of the data or the validity of research findings but the nature of managerial decisions. Despite the presence of calls to the contrary (Donaldson 1996, 2010), "statistical and methodological wizardry can blind rather than illuminate" (Bennis and O'Toole 2005, p. 99), since management operates in rapidly transforming contexts dominated by uncertainty, where decisions sometimes must be made with incomplete data.

Decision-makers who have to deal with the condition of bounded rationality (Simon 1957) or, worse, with 'garbage can' decisional situations (Cohen, March and Olsen 1972; Olsen and March 1976) are unlikely to find elegant models or theories useful. Moreover, practising managers have little exposure to the evidence gathered by management scientists, often because it fails to find its way to the business schools' classrooms (Rousseau 2006). However, the concept of relevance is not easy to pin down. Trying to find a minimum common denominator between relevance and rigour based on concepts such as interestingness and justification of research findings (Baldridge, Floyd and Markóczy 2004) does not seem to be very useful, since it attributes too much importance to the perception of novelty and importance: "perceived usefulness is not tantamount to factual usefulness" (Kieser and Leiner 2011, p. 893).

Indeed, practitioners have a limited, situated and idiosyncratic understanding of the nature of the managerial tasks: "the much lamented 'relevance gap' is as much a product of practitioners wedded to gurus and fads as it is of academics wedded to abstractions and fundamentals [...] Practitioners forget that 'the' real world is actually 'a' world that is idiosyncratic, egocentric and unique to each person complaining about relevance" (Weick 2001, p. S71). Augier and March (2007, p. 138) agree, stressing that "the definition of relevance is ambiguous, its measurement imprecise, and its meaning complex", and that "the pursuit of relevance is often myopic in practice". The real issue is that "judgements about the relevance of something learnt are subjective, time-bound and context dependent; relevance and irrelevance depend very much on our intellectual 'readiness' to see possible connection" (Paton, Chia and Burt 2013, p. 2).

The 'applicability of knowledge' conundrum is further aggravated by the fact that practitioners do not simply face problem-solving but also problem-setting issues (Nicolai and Seidl 2010, p. 1261), which reveals the inescapably political nature of knowledge applied to social systems. Practitioners are not always seeking knowledge for making better-informed choices but use it as a political device to legitimize their decisions and to reinforce their identities (Knights and Willmott 1997). Even the motivations that drive academic interest in relevance have been questioned, since the declared noble intent (producing useful knowledge) could in reality conceal more mundane desires for recognition and rewards, with the risk of becoming enslaved to the interests of business (Knights 2008).

Given that the idea of relevance is context and observer dependent, any decision about what is 'relevant' assumes strong political undertones. It entails discarding other elements as non-significant, removing viewpoints as not pertinent: it is a form of "mobilization of bias" (Bachrach and Baratz 1962, p. 952) that exercises power by blocking issues and silencing voices. Various forces attempt to drive research agendas instrumentally, usually putting them at the service of managerialism (Mitev 2009). While many different ideas of relevance can be congenial to particular interests, it is not possible neutrally and impartially to determine which idea of relevance has a superior status (Wensley 2010).

A critical approach to the issue requires assuming a complex, composite idea of relevance, one that can encompass differences in viewpoint, interests and ideological stances. Moving in this direction, Nicolai and Seidl (2010) have proposed to distinguish, in practical terms, between *instrumental* relevance (comprising schemes, technological rules and forecasts that can be used by practitioners to make better decisions), *conceptual* relevance (concerning conceptual tools to reinterpret reality) and *legitimative* relevance (the capacity of academic research to provide practitioners with credentials and with rhetorical devices to justify and gain support for their decisions). Such an approach points to the fact that a given set of information conveyed by management education can assume a different form of relevance for different audiences and in different contexts. Hence, relevance is not linked uniquely to the capacity of a work to state something correct about an ontologically fixed world. However, even this laudable attempt to build an empirically based and 'pluralist' definition of relevance is hindered by an ideological flaw. It is based on a taken-for-granted assumption about the role and nature of management education, the idea that its social function is uniquely that of enhancing economic growth and production. Such a 'performative teleology' of management research should be recognized as a social construction, not as a natural, unavoidable essence. This Tayloristic-inspired ideology, one that considers the increase of productivity or the maximization of profit as the only legitimate task for managers, is an implicit tenet of the offering of any business school. The recent debate on the need to address the ethical aspect of business (Grey 2002; Ghoshal 2005; Khurana 2007; Wilson and Thomas 2012) seems to have developed as an afterthought, in an attempt to create a buffer to protect against an excessive focus on greed.

The hegemonic view is perfectly portrayed in the words of the 'neoliberal prophet' Friedman: "there is one and only one social responsibility of business – to use its resources and engage in activities designed to increase its profits so long as it stays within the rules of the game" (1962, p. 133). According to this received wisdom, making business education more relevant is 'simply' a matter of establishing which knowledge can support more effective decision-making and implementation on the part of the managers. But what if we actually ask "the hoary question: what is the primary goal of business education?" (Bennis 2010, p. 23). Questioning the precept that the only function is to provide knowledge that helps to improve performances would lead us to ask *which kind of relevance is actually relevant* for business schools.

If we want to consider the whole range of the potential aims of business education, we should start by taking into account the fact that their offering can serve the needs of many different stakeholders. Accepting that "stakeholders in business schools have differing views of what business schools should be doing" (Starkey and Tempest 2008, p. 379) would allow embracing a richer and more plural conception of relevance. This multiple paradigm of relevance is needed not just for the love of difference and complexity but because of a practical consideration. The needs and expectations of each of the different beneficiaries of business school offerings is for them significant, since they are sources both of material resources and of legitimation.

Identifying all the stakeholders who are significant for business education is a difficult exercise and if we choose a fine-grained level of analysis we risk ending up with a taxonomy that is too vast to be of any practical utility. Iñiguez de Onzoño (2011) identifies 14 different types of stakeholders of some relevance for business schools, both internal (as faculty members, students, corporate partners, etc.) and external (accreditation bodies, publishing industry, government, etc.). In order to simplify this complex network, it is possible to borrow the concept of 'scale' introduced by Spicer (2006) as a spatial level factor influencing organizational logic. From this perspective it is possible to identify three spatial perspectives of relevance that can be of consequence for business schools, ranging from a micro-scale (that of the individual students-consumers of management education), to a meso-scale (the organizations that employ managers), and then up to a macro-level (that of the system-nation in which individual organizations are embedded or based).

A first group is that of the paying customers of business education, students and executives attending courses in order to be instructed how to perform their managerial task better but also to get better job positions (Pfeffer and Fong 2004; Khurana 2007, p. 348) or to maintain their status in society (Thomas et al. 1981). Even without entering into the debate between agency and stewardship theory in management (Donaldson and Davis 1991), we can safely assume that the interests of the non-executive students (those who are not currently occupying a management position) will be different from the interests of their potential employers. More-over, executives who are drawn to business school by the desire to learn techniques that maximize their efficacy as managers will also be inter-ested in acquiring a useful cachet in terms of symbolic, intellectual or social capital (Vaara and Faÿ 2011). The opportunity to improve their market value as 'managerial labour supplier', that is increasing their career opportunities by acquiring relevant skills, will certainly be con-sidered an important source of relevance. These skills are usually conceived in the form of practical know-how rather than complex intellectual, ethical and relational skills: "Students expect a 'turnkey' education when they major in business. They want prescriptions" (Gutek 1997, p. 35).

One should not assume that business school students' idea of relevance is oriented uniquely to performative concerns. For instance, students will deem the maximization of relational and political capabilities an import-ant feature of a 'relevant' business education course. This outcome is produced by business schools via the supply of networking opportunities, for instance by promoting and supporting alumni networks (Crainer and Dearlove 1999; Vaara and Faÿ 2011), and also by setting high access standards and barriers that, in the words of James March, help in "establishing that you're one of the very smart folks" (reported in Khurana 2007, p. 348). The fact that these networks can also have negative side effects, such as corruption and conflicts of interests (Mintzberg 2004), is a further demonstration that one cannot assume an overlap between students of management and companies' interests and ideas of relevance.

Finally, one should not discard the possibility that some of the students will be sensitive to the allure of management as a profession (Iñiguez de Onzoño 2011). This implies acknowledging that professionalization involves not only expert knowledge and societal accreditation but also entails a complement of values, responsibilities and conduct standards. In this case the provision of ethical instruction and the discussion of ethical issues and dilemmas pertaining to managerial practice would be highly relevant, helping to build an ethos and a sense of identity in the graduated managers (Jarvis 2009; Clegg, Jarvis and Pitsis 2013). Just taking into consideration one of the possible stakeholders illustrates how the notion of what is relevant knowledge of business and management can vary depending on the 'functional' focus of attention (or main value proposition), be it performativity, relation building and politics, or ethical issues.

Considering a different viewpoint, that of organizations which employ managers, another set of criteria for relevance will be contingent on the functional focus. The capacity to solve problems pertaining to increases in productivity, profitability or shareholders' returns is frequently taken for granted as the paradigmatic function of managers (Mintzberg 2004), and consequently becomes a key metric for the relevance of the knowledge developed and imparted by business schools (Syed, Mingers and Murray 2010). However, they also have a social role in inculcating practices and values (*habitus*) and in reproducing legitimated and thus dominant Discourses (*doxa*) on the social organization of labour and the desirable outcomes of managerial and corporate work (Vaara and Faÿ 2011, 2012). The capacity to discipline aspirant managers into prescribed role expectations is certainly useful in order to maintain the current structures of domination and can therefore constitute, from the perspective of a conservative organization, another relevant function of business education, while, conversely, the decision to impart a critical perspective and to develop critical analysis within management could be seen not only as irrelevant but even harmful to corporate harmony and integration.

The capacity to impart ethical education can be valuable also from the firm's perspective, since it can contribute to enhancing the reputational value of the company (Jackson 2006), a concept that includes considering and balancing the interests of all groups affected by the organization, building long-term trust and relationships. Even if this does not seem to be a concern in most business schools (Pfeffer and Fong 2004), there are strong institutional pressures to incorporate business ethics courses in MBA curricula (Wilson and McKiernan 2011).

Another perspective that can enrich our collection of alternative models of relevance is that of the broader political-economic system in which both business schools and companies are embedded. If we assume the perspective of the nation state, then we must acknowledge that – in order to be performatively relevant – business education needs to help improve the productivity and competitiveness of the industrial system, fostering growth and promoting the discourse of the 'knowledge-based economy'. In this sense it is possible to conceptualize "business education as part of an ecology of learning, knowledge production and circulation involving both the spaces of business education and the spaces of corporate practice within business service firms" (Hall 2009, p. 600). History shows how this 'ecology of learning' has been actively promoted and steered by private institutions (such as foundations) and governments which have exerted various pressures on business education providers to enhance the perceived quality of their output in order to preserve the economic and national welfare (Khurana 2007, pp. 232–5).

Nation states can also have an interest in exporting their ideological models and projecting soft power by means of educational colonization: the implementation in Europe of the American model of business education based on the MBA after WWII has been described as an example of this discursive hegemony (Djelic 2001; Clegg and Ross-Smith 2003, p. 88). Many business schools have also been accused of ethnocentrism and neocolonialism because of the cultural hegemony of the North American business model in their curricula and approaches (Vaara and Faÿ 2011). The capacity to contribute to the spread and upholding of this dominant discourse (or of an alternative one) is certainly a factor of relevance in a national perspective. Ethics concerns are also relevant from this standpoint, since business education can help in developing professional standards and codes for management (Pfeffer and Fong 2004), which could reduce the risk of corporate scandals and malpractices, limiting the occurrence of corruption, all phenomena that hinder economic growth and national welfare (Mo 2001; Méon and Sekkat 2005). Doing this requires assuming a 'critical' approach to business education, adopting a pluralist and dialectical approach that is akin to the study of politics rather than that of techniques (French and Grey 1996).

One does not aspire to a comprehensive view of all possible ideas about the 'relevance' of management sciences' contributions but simply to highlight a number of relevance constructs (summarized in Table 7.1).

Table 7.1　Alternate relevance constructs

| | Stakeholder focus (scale) | | |
	Individual	Organization	Nation
Value proposition			
Enhance performance	Career; higher salary through accreditation (Khurana 2007)	Improve shareholders' revenues (Mintzberg 2004)	Improve productivity and competitiveness (Hall 2009)
Build relations; political effectiveness	Building networks; increase influence (Crainer and Dearlove 1999)	Reinforce disciplinary control over staff (Vaara and Faÿ 2011)	Spread ideology across borders (Clegg and Ross-Smith 2003)
Promote ethical behaviour	Professionalism (Bennis and O'Toole 2005)	Improve reputational capital (Jackson 2006)	Develop professional standards and codes (Pfeffer and Fong 2004)

An example of the limit of this simplified taxonomy is the fact that it considers business school students as a single stakeholder, sharing the same needs and desires, thus misrepresenting an increasingly more heterogeneous student population (Hodgkinson and Rousseau 2009). However, this only confirms the central thesis that the crux of the matter is the multiplicity of possible views on what constitutes relevant knowledge for business practitioners.

The important strategic choice for any business school – beyond paying lip service to a simplistic view of relevance – is to decide explicitly which of the different criteria should be put at the centre of its research and teaching agenda, and to manage the trade-offs between incompatible views of practical relevance. Doing so means openly and transparently engaging with the fact that "relevance issues are masks for issues of political power and that the obscuring of interests and their importance is not innocent in a struggle among interests" (Augier and March 2007, p. 136).

On a more practical and implementation-oriented note, business schools can embrace this pluralistic approach by turning the noun 'relevance' in a verb, 'to *relevate*' in an approach proposed by Paton et al. (2013), who suggest that business schools could provide an ideal ground to help practitioners, in collaboration with academics, to reflect critically on their deeply held assumptions, thus discovering what is really relevant in the specific context in which they are operating. Assuming this view also reduces the risk of management studies becoming purely instrumental to the pursuit of performance enhancement. It might be true that business schools have not been particularly successful in influencing business practices (Pfeffer and Fong 2004; Pfeffer 2007), but devoting all their intellectual potential to the service of managerialist performativity would mean sacrificing the critical, moral and social responsibility of the university to the altar of surplus value production. However, the relative significance of different views on 'what is relevant for management' is determined by the dominance of the constituency supporting them and by the pervasiveness of the discursive spaces in which they emerged. Again, power/knowledge is at play, making managerialism, and its specific discourse on relevance, 'normal' and natural, so that it is acritically taken for granted by most that the goal of management theory is to maximize performances. Yet, these 'minority ideas' about ethics, social and environmental sustainability, and improving employees' well-being are also present and are kept alive by dedicated and active groups. Consequently, all these different notions of 'what is relevant' become salient features of the conceptual landscape in which management academic identities and practices emerge.

INTERDISCIPLINARITY OF HETEROGLOSSIA?

One of the critical hurdles to more relevant business education appears to be the separation of the academic field into a series of intellectual silos. Numerous commentators (Hamilton, McFarland and Mirchandani 2000; Latham, Latham and Whyte 2004; Mintzberg 2004; Athavale, Davis and Myring 2008) have argued that the lack of integration and the excessive focus on specialized knowledge are to blame for the disconnection between academic theorizing and concrete challenges encountered by practising managers. The problem of interdisciplinarity in science is a complex one and its historical origins, current connotations and future trends are more comprehensively treated in the specialized literature on the subject (see for a review Jacobs and Frickel 2009; Frodeman, Klein and Mitcham 2010); however, here I will focus exclusively on the organizational implications of interdisciplinarity in the context of business schools.

Curricula that are based on functional areas rather than on a holistic perspective (Weber and Englehart 2011) and especially the silo-mentality that results from excessive departmentalization of disciplines and subjects (Latham et al. 2004), are reputed to damage the potential of education in management. Business schools' "lack of a synthetic/integrative analysis of the cross-functional and interdisciplinary nature of management leaves little room for engaging with the variety of social and political facets of managing in the context of organizational life" (Antonacopoulou 2010, p. s8).

While serving a reductionist research agenda focused on the heuristic fascination of identifying an Aristotelian 'efficient cause', capable of producing and explaining the current state of affairs, the artificial divisions of business studies into separate branches of learning produces a cacophony of epistemological standpoints, interests, methodologies and disciplinary jargon that renders management studies confusing and less than transparent to the uninitiated practitioner. The problem is both one of knowledge application and of knowledge production. On the application side the new managerial challenges brought by globalization, ICT diffusion and 'glocalization' of knowledge (Iñiguez de Onzoño 2011) require a flexible, multidisciplinary approach. But, also, the "new institutional landscape of knowledge production is marked by academic disciplines showing increasing fuzziness at their boundaries" (Gibbons et al. 1994, p. 138). To help consolidate the contribution of different disciplines most business education programmes rely on 'capstone experiences', requiring students to combine learning from different disciplines (Athavale et al. 2008), while others recur to more specific pedagogies, such as the use of service learning projects (Godfrey, Illes and Berry 2005). The most 'revolutionary' approach is the one proposed in a small number of business schools, led by the Rotman School of Management, which are advocating the adoption of 'design thinking', which involves approaching managerial problems as designers (Boland and Collopy 2004; Dunne and Martin 2006; Boland et al. 2008; Martin 2009; Cross 2011), and 'integrated thinking', "the capacity to take a cross-functional, multidisciplinary approach to the solution of unstructured business problems" (Latham 2000, p. 4).

The agenda of integration has great rhetoric potential and an obvious market appeal. The attractiveness of general management and the fact that most business school students aim (at least ideally) to become not mere technical specialists but top executives, bolsters an educational approach tailored to the need of a prospective CEO (Starkey and Tempest 2008). Moreover, since the 1990s management discourse has become dominated by ideas of flexibility, horizontal integration and knowledge management capabilities (Knights and Willmott 1997; ten Bos 2000). Consequently, the push towards integrated, interdisciplinary business schools appears to be irresistible but interdisciplinary integration is easier preached than practised. First, the declared drive towards interdisciplinarity is hindered by the division of labour within academia: the espoused values of open-mindedness and a self-critical spirit clash with the disciplinary closeness sanctioned by academic culture and career paths (Knights and Willmott 1997, p. 10).

The division of labour in business schools also emerged as part of the strategy to confer scientific respectability to a discipline that was tainted by its 'humble' origins as a technical and trade-related field (Knights and Willmott 1997; Clegg and Ross-Smith 2003; Khurana 2007). But, paradoxically, the pedagogical consequences of this division are that it ends up reinforcing the same 'trade-driven' outlook that business schools have shunned for a long time. This effect is also compounded by the practice of relabelling – within business schools – established academic disciplines with functional names (such as 'accounting', 'marketing', 'human-resource management') that are supposed to sound more relevant to the potential customers (Knights and Willmott 1997). As a consequence a strategy that is supposed to overcome academic silos ends up replacing them with functional ones: these might sound more 'relevant' but they do little to integrate the field and they are probably even less useful in educating reflexive managers.

The fact that management and organizational studies' researchers have been typically rewarded for producing original, distinctive and provocative approaches (Hodgkinson and Rousseau 2009) has further driven fragmentation. Faculty members appear to be subject to two divergent directives: as researchers they are disciplined to stick to their narrowly defined epistemological universe, while as educators they are required to provide a big picture outlook, in order to train impartial general managers. Beyond the espoused values and integration rhetoric, a political wedge is driven between research and educational practices.

Baunsgaard and Clegg argue that differentiation has discursive and political implications, and that meaning is constantly produced and reproduced in the form of local 'truths' emerging from power relations and professional identities, and inscribed in members' categorization devices (MCDs), those linguistic practices and codes that are used by individuals and groups to organize meaning and produce sense. Such a conceptualization is well suited to illustrate the political and ideological nature of disciplines in academia, which can be described "as different constellations of professional identity communities constituting diverse ideological arenas of struggle" (Clegg and Baunsgaard 2013, p. 41). Each discipline plays its own 'language game', whereby word meanings are not simply derived from the actions or objects that they denote but from

the historical discursive context in which they have developed (Wittgenstein 1958). Therefore communication and collaboration between disciplines is problematic, since any real attempt to cross disciplinary
boundaries risks being regarded as a form of defection (Knights and
Willmott 1997). Starkey and Madan (2001) highlight how both the
organizational structure and the primary institutional function (training
specialist in established research areas) of the majority of higher education organizations favour a mono-disciplinary research culture.

These reflections show that to cross the disciplinary barriers is not
simply difficult but constitutes a 'wicked problem' (Rittel and Webber
1973). This means that it is an issue that is not just ambiguous or
inadequately described but for which it is impossible to provide a
definitive formulation, since its interpretation can be disputed. In fact, if
we approach the concept of interdisciplinarity in epistemological terms,
as a statement of the necessity to bridge and connect the knowledge
domains of different branches of learning in order to produce a more
comprehensive understanding of the universe, we are paradoxically
reinforcing the same silo mentality that we are ostensibly opposing. By
talking of *inter*disciplinarity, one is implicitly acknowledging the ontological validity of what is in reality just a historically produced, contingent social construction, the 'discipline'. Those scientific disciplines that
we regard as natural fields of study, a logical subdivision of the
constantly swelling sphere of scientific knowledge, only emerged in the
19th century as a consequence of the 'scientification' of knowledge, of a
general trend towards specialization propelled by industrial revolution
and by the development of sophisticated and expensive research instru-
mentation (Klein 1990, p. 21). The rise of disciplines was consolidated in
particular by the emergence of communities of specialized scientists, by
the remodelling of the communication system on which such knowledge
communities were based, with the introduction of modern scientific
publications and an overall reorganization of the scientific production
process aligned to the new imperative of the search for novelties
(Stichweh 2001). Transformation of the knowledge production processes
and practices was inescapably accompanied by a restructuring of the
labour organization and of the institutional field. In the nineteenth
century, career patterns of academics completely changed, from a traditional hierarchical succession, whereas the progression of positions
(chairs) happened within the same organization, so that "one could, for
example, rise from a chair in the philosophical faculty to an (intellectually unrelated) chair in the medical faculty" (Stichweh 2001, p. 13729),
to a modern 'disciplinary' scientific career, a progression of position
inside a discipline and across different universities.

Because of the genealogy of disciplines, scientific researchers, unlike other members of the workforce who are uniquely assessed by the organizations that employ them, are primarily assessed by other members of their disciplinary community, while their employers are merely adopting performance metrics that have been externally determined. A consequence of this arrangement is the limited appeal of efforts aimed at integrating disciplinary work put in place by single institutions: in fact if a tertiary education organization decided to promote strongly an agenda of integration by explicitly assessing the level of interdisciplinary research output of its faculty members, this would be tantamount to forcing researchers into a 'double bind' situation (Bateson 1972).

Asking academics to be 'valuable interdisciplinary researchers' is a paradoxical injunction, since they know they can only attain recognition as 'proper' researchers within the strict boundaries of a discipline, a community which has a conservative and disciplining nature (Syed et al. 2010, p. 75). In the specific case of business education, Bennis and O'Toole (2005) highlight the influence of recruiting and promotion systems rewarding specialization and academic accomplishments such as the number of publications in peer-reviewed journals. They also provide some anecdotal evidence that this trend is penalizing those who pursue an agenda of interdisciplinarity in research and teaching. Likewise, Knights and Willmott (1997) stress how organizational and resourcing arrangements can constitute a barrier to any form of interdisciplinarity, alongside institutional arrangements linked to the publishing industry and research funding.

Disciplines are not static silos: they are agitated by an internal competition that makes them dynamic and are connected by a network of intellectual and material exchanges (Jacobs 2014). New specialties are constantly emerging, propelled by technological advances that offer new means of perceiving, translating and inscribing phenomena (Latour and Woolgar 1979), or as a result of institutional pressures, as in the case of a reallocation of public funding along different priorities. In addition, disciplinary boundaries constantly change also because of "an expansionary strategy in which the discipline attacks and takes over parts of the domain of other disciplines" (Stichweh 2001, p. 13730). In the specific field of management studies it has been noted that the typical responses to the appeal for interdisciplinary research involve either fabricating "an appearance of interdisciplinarity through the selective borrowing of concepts or ideas from another discipline [... or] a single discipline extending the sphere over which it claims some expertise" (Knights and Willmott 1997, p. 10). Cooperation among the different competing "tribes" is discouraged because it threatens their sense of identity, since

178 *Elgar introduction to organizational discourse analysis*

belonging to a discipline provides academics with a sense of security and a 'script' (Knights and Willmott 1997).

Jacobs and Frickel (2009) sum up the barrier to interdisciplinary collaboration in three categories: epistemic (different thought styles, methods and languages), structural (specialized journals, departmental organization, funding arrangements) and administrative (bureaucratic arrangements keeping disciplines separated); however, it is quite evident that all these differences are not just typical of academia but are similar to the cultural and pragmatic separations that emerge as the physiological consequences of any organizational differentiation process.

According to some commentators, integration efforts are hindered by institutional forces that spring from a neoliberal and managerialist political agenda (which often goes under the label of NPM, 'new public management'). The emphasis on 'practical' research seems destined to break down those disciplinary silos but this intent is completely undermined by two other central tenets of NPM: accountability and performativity (Clarke et al. 2012). The distrust in individual work ethics, the assumed centrality of market relationships, and an aversion for anything 'public' leads to an obsession with measuring individual outputs. This focus on demonstrating achievement ends becomes translated into the widespread adoption of centrally administered 'performance-based research funding systems' (Hicks 2012) which oblige academics to concentrate on demonstrating research achievements through publication in high-ranked journals (Ryan and Neumann 2011) and to devote considerable energies to the acquisition and administration of research funds (Herbert, Barnett and Graves 2013). Journal-based metrics have been identified as factors inhibiting interdisciplinarity in research (Rafols et al. 2012) and performance-based research funding can restrict autonomy by enhancing the control capacity of disciplinary elites (Hicks 2012). In addition to this, the exclusive emphasis on research outputs reduces the relevance, and therefore the disciplinary integration potential, of teaching.

All these sophisticated discussions tend to portray a mono-dimensional discourse, dominated by a single factor that determines business academic behaviour and subjectivities, be it the NPM metrics, the quest for methodological purity or the existence of different subcultures and local discourses. Such a reductionist view leads to an underemphasis on how academics perform multiple roles, across different sites, interfacing different stakeholders and are thus exposed to contradictory requests. The organizational space they inhabit can be defined as *heteroglossic*; that is, characterized by multiple voices and forms of knowledge, constituting a multi-discursive nexus. The idea of heteroglossic organization is proposed by Rhodes (2001, pp. 29–32), who borrows the term from Bakhtin, to expound the thesis that organizational contexts can be characterized not just by multiple stories and narratives but also by multiple languages and ways of representing and constructing reality, which makes any attempts to reduce them to a single interpretative model in vain.

Business schools appear to be an ideal exemplar of heteroglossia, since they are situated at the crossroads between academia and industry, public and private interests, research and teaching. Disciplinary differences are not the only ones producing different languages. A source of different language in the organization is the presence of a large, growing and increasingly dominant bureaucratic administration. In addition to the increased emphasis on performance management and formal accountability, this growth is propelled by the need to obtain and manage competitive grants that have become a vital source of income for the institution. Similar considerations apply for the accreditation and ranking pursuits, which require the maintenance of a hefty bureaucracy. As prophesied by Weber, bureaucracies tend to be autopoietic and expand "until the last ton of fossilized coal is burnt" (Weber 1920 [2005], p. 123), or at least until they literally choke themselves, their organizational learning capacities suffocated by the numbing effect of rules (Schulz 1998). Universities appear to be following a similar trajectory: the traditional dualism between the academic 'collegium' and the hierarchy/bureaucracy has been transformed by the increasing power and dimension of the latter over the former (Kogan 2007).

In addition to this large administrative and managerial body the "full-time academic bureaucrat is becoming more common" (Kogan 2007, p. 171). In fact, one can assume that this role is a possible career alternative for a number of lecturers and professors and even attractive from a remuneration perspective. A bureaucratized university tries to breed administratively inclined academic-managers, capable of conferring the sacraments of conformity and standardization.

Another source of heteroglossia derives from the presence of another category of 'strangers'. Business schools often 'enrich' their faculty with practitioners, with the intent of demonstrating that they provide relevant know-how, but also in order to manage the shortage of faculty with doctoral degrees (Clinebell and Clinebell 2008). Tenured faculty members, who have to play the scientific research game before the executive training one, can feel challenged by the fact that adjunct professors, thanks to their real-world experience and their freedom from other research commitments, can raise the bar of teaching standards and customer care, putting them in a negative light (Zell 2001, p. 329). The role of adjunct faculty (or in the AACSB's definition, 'clinical faculty members') is often ambiguous: an example of this ambiguity is provided by a study of innovation in a business school where the issue of the level of 'academic freedom' to be granted to executive professors (i.e. autonomy in deciding their syllabus) was often left undecided (Thompson and Purdy 2009).

Another alternative set of voices which can be heard in the institution is that of students. The way in which they are seen and conceptualized plays a role in defining the behaviours and attitudes of the faculty (Azaddin Salem 2009). Knights and Willmott (1997) have argued that the desire to maintain a social distance between student and academic, combined with the idea that teaching is secondary to research or consulting, explains some didactic choices that are then rationalized in terms of the necessity of maintaining scientific rigour. Such decisions are compounded by the fact that the choices and behaviours of management academics are – despite their best efforts to declare the opposite – often driven by ideological and political forces that have little to do with the uninterested desire to advance human knowledge. Research fund allocation for instance plays a major role (Clegg and Dunkerley 1980), with the fact that research patterns are subject to fads and fashions being empirically demonstrated (Barley, Gordon and Gash 1988). Even the translation of the theoretical knowledge acquired by research into praxis through the pedagogical intermediation of management educators is problematic since complex theories are often trivialized and misrepresented in the process of being transformed into recipes for managerial action (Weatherbee, Dye and Mills 2008).

In this Tower of Babel, some silences can be deafening. As seen in Chapter 6, silence on important themes or identities can be an outcome of discourse, and one such silenced subject in the discursive context of business education is that of emotions. The central role of emotions in decision-making is now well acknowledged by psychology (see Lerner et al. 2015 for a review) but is scarcely discussed in business schools. Contemporary business education puts much emphasis on concepts such as flexibility, capacity to adapt to turbulence, and the need to adopt post-bureaucratic structures and practices. While the Weberian model of rational authority was based on de-personalization, logic and subtraction of passions and emotions, in the new flexible capitalism the emotional side of workers has to be recruited in order to harness their creativity and adaptability to turbulent conditions. However, only emotion that can be used productively in the pursuit of organizational aims, such as enthusiasm or stress management, is given right of citizenship. The use of concepts such as 'emotional intelligence' can be seen as the application of a disciplinary regime of emotional conduct (Baumeler 2010), a situation reflected in business education's growing interest in the application of models of emotional intelligence (Boyatzis, Stubbs and Taylor 2002; Myers and Tucker 2005) despite other 'pre-rational' aspects being suppressed or ignored, such as anxiety linked to learning and teaching, even if such emotion is physiological and can have a productive dimension (Vince 2010). Indeed the decision to engage or not with emotional aspects appears not to be determined by an epistemological bias towards rationalism but rather driven by an implicit political agenda.

This is not the only silence that can be heard in the context of business education: various authors lamented the lack of discussion on fundamental topics such as the role of power/knowledge (Clegg and Ross-Smith 2003); the problem of oppressive and dangerous work conditions (Grey 2002); gender and sexuality (Sinclair 1995); female leadership (Callás and Smircich 1991); the social purposes of business (Kiyatkin, Reger and Baum 2011); and even those identities (of students and academics) which do not conform with the dominant normativity (Vaara and Faÿ 2012).

The multiple differentiations that characterize business education do not produce a pleasing rainbow of diverse hues and colours, offering a rich tapestry of knowledge sources. In contrast they generate a boisterous sound landscape in which many strong voices, speaking various tongues, compete for attention, while other relevant issues become silenced.

SUMMING UP: A MAP OF THE MOST RELEVANT DISCURSIVE ELEMENTS

This broad review of the principal issues, concepts and dynamics which affect the world of management research and education can be summarized in the form of a map of the discursive 'terrain' in which the observed academic practices and identities operate. The presence of dialectically opposed 'imagined life worlds', alternative conceptions of the purpose, essence, nature, of management research and education, should make this discursive territory very rugged.

The unevenness of the landscape is not always manifested; each thesis and antithesis represents a configuration of power/knowledge relationships more than an abstract idea. These dialectic alternatives, often presented as alternative philosophies that agents are free to choose depending on their inclinations and desires, are enacted as more or less powerful arrangements of ideas, bodies, resources, institutions. In a specific spatial-temporal site a thesis (and its complement of power relations) can become hegemonic, completely erasing the possibility of its antithesis, through processes of power-driven rationalization and normalization. As a consequence, dialectic relationships are not easily 'resolved' by actors in a synthesis. Sometimes one thesis will become congealed in their *habitus*, veiled by the *illusio* that they stolidly accept as the only conceivable form of the life world, becoming an element of stability in practices and identity but also forcing individual differences in a dystopian homogeneity (ten Bos 2000). In other cases the less powerful alternative will remain visible, haunting the tranquillity of the actors, sometimes stimulating their active resistance and stirring conflicts. The principal dialectic contrasts, presented as opposing 'force fields', are presented in Table 7.2.

Table 7.2   Alternative force fields shaping the discursive landscape

PERFORMATIVITY	REFLEXIVITY
The function of management education and research is to increase profits and production. Relevant interlocutors are managers and shareholders. The model is aligned with neoliberal ideologies, NPM-inspired models of research funding, and with the current accreditation and ranking metrics.	The purpose of management science is to reflect critically on organization phenomena that are characteristic of modernity, making practitioners aware of their ethical, social and environmental responsibilities. Management scholarship should engage with all stakeholders affected by production systems.
Associated contrasts:	
Training	*Educating*
Management is a technical skill: students are customers who invest their time and money to receive usable knowledge and expertise that they will be able to sell on the market recouping their investment.	Management implies ethical responsibilities: students must be made critically aware of the consequences of their acts and decisions. The ultimate purpose of education is to improve society and reduce inequities.
Know that/know how	*Know why*
The focus of research and education is on improving operational capabilities in individuals, organizations, industries and economies through the development of theoretical (know that) and applied (know how) knowledge.	The focus of research and education is to increase public awareness of the moral and material consequences of action. The focus is on questioning the current and 'normalized' views.

Quantitative/financial metrics	*Social impact*
All performances must be quantified and tested for their 'utility', measured in financial terms (return on investment). Metrics are used to rank contributions and distribute rewards. Success is equivalent to career advance.	The value of academic contribution is the capacity to produce debate and discussion in the field, produce new ways to interpret the social world, even bring about a positive change in practices (that is, one that reduces inequities and improves well-being).

STANDARDIZATION	PLURALITY
Strong drive toward a globalized and uniform set of 'best' practices in teaching, researching, managing. The focus is on control and supervision of individual efforts. Academic activity requires a relevant amount of 'tick-boxing' aimed at demonstrating conformity. This approach produces, feeds and is championed by a strong academic bureaucracy and management.	Drive towards variety and pluralism, adapting to and being inspired by local conditions and issues. The focus is on learning, innovation and diversity of interests, approaches and interpretations, catering for the needs of a variety of stakeholders. Non-academic functions should operate as internal services in support of academic enterprises.

Associated contrasts:

Accreditation/ranking	*Innovation*
The achievement of accreditation and of a high standard in rankings is considered as unavoidable, or is even considered an end in itself. A strong identity comes from complying with institutional isomorphism.	The capacity to produce truly original and unique results, and to be acknowledged for the capacity to create an impact in a specific context. Novelty of contribution and originality are the basis for a strong identity.

Publishing	*Influencing*
Acknowledgement through publication is, more than a means to ensure publicity to ideas, an end in itself. Success, motivation, self-efficacy are functions of the literary output. This generates and is reproduced by a complex industry, based on a 'non-monetary' economy built on conspicuous contributions of unpaid labour. Activities that do not lead to publication outputs are shunned.	Motivation and drive come from the capacity to 'leave a mark' through teaching, social activism, researching and writing. Teaching, mentoring, engaging with industry and other stakeholders are as relevant as publishing. The choice of the communication medium (e.g. a book, a journal article, a blog) is motivated by the desire to reach different audiences or by the type of method or findings.

USA model hegemony	*Pedagogic and heuristic pluralism*
The US model of business education represented by the top-ranked business schools is considered a benchmark of quality and an ideal to be emulated. The approaches of these 'sacred cows' are always looked at with awe and considered a source of inspiration.	Different models of management education, born of different academic and cultural traditions are to be included in a dialogue aimed at the development of a plurality of approaches in research and teaching. The creation of an international non-hegemonic network of collaboration is envisioned.

Table 7.2   (continued)

REDUCTIONISM	HOLISM
Model that privileges the production of strong, clear and linear narratives that reduce complexity by excluding elements that do not fit a specific, actor-network made of specific methods, languages, viewpoints, interests. Since cogency, consistency and accuracy are trumpeted as ultimate measures of truthfulness this approach tends to produce, and to be reproduced by, a strong *disciplinary arrangement*, both in the sense of a systematic set of instructions on correct behaviour and as a well-delimited field of scholarship.	Based on the acknowledgement of the complex, interconnected and constructed nature of the social world, this field accepts that it is necessary to employ a vast array of conceptual lenses and forms of knowledge to make sense and operate on it. It privileges cross-disciplinary and interdisciplinary collaborations and considers 'contamination' essential to produce useful knowledge. Epistemological differences are considered opportunities for learning rather than causes for contraposition.

Associated contrasts:

Disciplinary differentiation	*Cross-disciplinary integration*
The only possible form of organization of academic work is based on differentiation along disciplinary lines, with each discipline striving to achieve orthodoxy and correctness.	Integration across disciplines is considered essential – despite difficulties in communication – in order to produce valuable and actionable knowledge.

Normal science	*Science that matters*
The production and distribution of knowledge happens mostly within the boundaries of 'normal science' (Kuhn 1962).	Aim of researchers is to conduct enquiries which, through cross-disciplinary integration and collaboration with practitioners, can produce practical wisdom.

These contrasts can be visible more or less in a specific context, such as in a particular department of a business school at a given moment in time.

However, before moving on, it is important to exploit fully the problematizing potential of this map. The presence of these differences exposes that universities, usually regarded as extremely stable institutions, characterized by centuries' old practices, and dominated by intellect and rigour, are in fact agitated by strong currents. This is not just the consequence of human weaknesses (captured in witty quips such as 'academic politics are so vicious precisely because the stakes are so small'[1]). It appears instead to be a physiological characteristic of a field where the multiplicity of stakeholders and the presence of multiple objectives tend to generate deep paradigmatic divisions. These rifts transcend theoretical diatribes and denote the presence of alternative teleologies and the persistence of different power/knowledge structures. Consequently, individual academics are subject to multiple discourses, a factor that can allow a great variance in behaviours and attitudes.

This map is also interesting for what it does not show, for the remarkable absence of an expected fact. It is extraordinary that scholars who are devoted to the study of management methods devote so little of their immense scholarly production to the consideration of the forms of management most fitting to organize their own activities. There is a deafening silence on 'positive' recommendations on this topic. The literature seems to offer plenty of ideas on what should be taught or researched in business schools but little discussion is given to how to coordinate, direct or systematize the efforts of individual academics. The only stream of studies that consistently addresses the issue of academic management is critical management studies. However, the stance taken by most authors who engage in this discussion is distinctively anti-managerialist (notable examples include Parker and Jary 1995; Willmott 1995; Clarke et al. 2012; Knights and Clarke 2014; Parker 2014). An otherwise well-informed and well-argued critique of the way in which business schools and universities are currently managed risks losing its transformative potential by jettisoning the very possibility of management.

In the literature (or talking to senior academics) it is often possible to come across an undisguised nostalgia for a lost golden age of collegiate management. This lost utopia was certainly not free of contradictions and oppression (Trounson 2012); however, this nostalgia probably represents the projection of current fears and problems (Ylijoki 2005). Nostalgia or resistance are not necessarily negative and could provide narratives that help in designing alternative futures. Nonetheless, there is the need for an open discussion of how to provide a form of accountability that is neither bureaucratic compliance nor the self-regulation performed by an incontestable elite; on how to guarantee the return on the social investment on education and research and protect the rights of the 'consumers' of business education; on how to represent the voices and the interests of

---

[1] This sentence, apparently coined by Wallace S. Sayre, has become a trope and has been used in various forms by a number of commentators, and it is routinely attributed to Henry Kissinger (Clegg 1979 [2013]).

the myriad of stakeholders who are affected by 'bad' management theories and practices.

The rare attempts to propose models of management that could replace the despised NPM ones (an example is Ryan and Guthrie 2009) suffer from another limit, the fact that they focus uniquely on the academic personnel. In contemporary corporate universities the size and influence of the non-academic staff are such that this personnel outnumbers faculty members. These actors are not mere sidekicks. In this regard universities increasingly resemble Major League Soccer clubs: the footballers are those who score the goals, determine the results and get the press attention but they represent only a fraction of the staff (and they are hardly the ones who determine the governance of their clubs). It becomes necessary to consider forms of management which, while considering the central role of the 'players/academics', allowing them to shine and compete at the best of their abilities, also take into account the activities of the entire set of professionals who contribute to run these institutions.

A VERY SHORT, AND VERY OPEN, CONCLUSION

Why did I choose to close this work with an extensive discussion on a specific case of organizational discourse? There are three reasons that are connected with my fundamental intent in writing this volume. First, a conceptual book aimed at introducing a complex and at times esoteric literature; a major risk was to be too theoretical. Many discussions on organizational discourse appear concerned with hair-splitting debates on ontology and epistemology, rather than with the everyday reality of working organizations, and the practical consequence of discourse for flesh and blood individuals. For this reason I wanted to follow the advice to "get on with it" (Bisel 2009, p. 628), engaging with data and observation rather than getting entangled in endless philosophical disputes.

Second, in coherence with the need to avoid a reductionist approach, I did not wish to offer the reader a set of detailed 'routing' instructions, favouring instead a concrete exemplification of how to perform an analysis of organizational discourse. The idea was to present a study which, while focusing on the ways in which reality is constructed and interpreted by means of narratives and symbolic practices, could go beyond the texts, including in the analysis also the observation of the performances of human actors and of non-human actants, as elements that both carry and interact with symbols.

Third, the case of management education represents both a para-digmatic and an extreme case (Flyvbjerg 2006) of organizational dis-course. This is both because this is an organizational setting where symbolic practices are fundamental: academic work is all about linguistic representations and use of language to construct subjects, and because few organizations are so heteroglossic. The great diversity of languages and genres that business schools incorporate makes them an ideal setting to illustrate the importance of considering the concrete impacts of different discourses on a variety of stakeholders.

In essence, this case endorses my call for 'opening up' organizational discourse analysis. This implies associating, rather than considering in isolation, different 'varieties of discourse': global Discourses are main-tained and reproduced by local discourses, and meaning is neither pre-existent nor magically generated by linguistic performances, but instead dialectically emerges from a negotiation between interpretation and material affordances. Moreover, 'opening' concerns the necessity to integrate the consideration of 'textual' aspects with that of material, tacit and embodied components, thus linking linguistic modes of discourse analysis to other theories and perspectives, in the firm belief that, as any symbol is meaningless in isolation, so any reductionist or 'methodo-logically pure' description of complex social phenomena is totally useless.

REFERENCES

Altman, Y. and Laguecir, A. 2012, 'Leadership in the Academic Field of Business and Management and the Question of Country of Origin: A Commentary on Burgess and Shaw (2010)', *British Journal of Management*, vol. 23, no. 4, pp. 589–97.
Antonacopoulou, E.P. 2010, 'Making the Business School More Critical: Reflexive Critique Based on Phronesis as a Foundation for Impact', *British Journal of Management*, vol. 21, no. s1, pp. s6–s25.
Antunes, D. and Thomas, H. 2007, 'The Competitive (Dis)Advantages of European Business Schools', *Long Range Planning*, vol. 40, pp. 382–404.
Athavale, M., Davis, R. and Myring, M. 2008, 'The Integrated Business Curriculum: An Examination of Perceptions and Practices', *Journal of Education for Business*, vol. 83, pp. 295–301.
Augier, M. and March, J.G. 2007, 'The Pursuit of Relevance in Management Education', *California Management Review*, vol. 49, p. 129.
Azaddin Salem, K. 2009, 'Student-as-Aspirant: Strategic Implications for Business Education', *European Business Review*, vol. 21, pp. 172–90.
Bachrach, P. and Baratz, M.S. 1962, 'Two Faces of Power', *The American Political Science Review*, vol. 56, pp. 947–52.

Bailey, J. and Ford, C. 1996, 'Management as Science Versus Management as Practice in Postgraduate Business Education', *Business Strategy Review*, vol. 7, pp. 7–12.
Baldridge, D.C., Floyd, S.W. and Markóczy, L. 2004, 'Are Managers from Mars and Academicians from Venus? Toward an Understanding of the Relationship Between Academic Quality and Practical Relevance', *Strategic Management Journal*, vol. 25, pp. 1063–74.
Barley, S.R., Gordon, W.M. and Gash, D.C. 1988, 'Cultures of Culture: Academics, Practitioners and the Pragmatics of Normative Control', *Administrative Science Quarterly*, vol. 33, pp. 24–60.
Bateson, G. 1972, *Steps to an Ecology of Mind: Collected Essays in Anthropology, Psychiatry, Evolution, and Epistemology*, Intertext, Aylesbury.
Bauman, Z. 1989, *Modernity and the Holocaust*, Polity, Cambridge.
Baumeler, C. 2010, 'Organizational Regimes of Emotional Conduct', in B. Sieben and A. Wettergren (eds), *Emotionalizing Organizations and Organizing Emotions*, Palgrave Macmillan, Basingstoke, pp. 272–92.
Bazerman, M.H. 2005, 'Conducting Influential Research: The Need for Prescriptive Implications', *The Academy of Management Review*, vol. 30, p. 25.
Bennis, W.G. 2010, 'Comment on "Regaining Lost Relevance"', *Journal of Management Inquiry*, vol. 19, pp. 22–4.
Bennis, W.G. and O'Toole, J. 2005, 'How Business Schools Lost their Way', *Harvard Business Review*, vol. 83, p. 96.
Bisel, R.S. 2009, 'On a Growing Dualism in Organizational Discourse Research', *Management Communication Quarterly*, vol. 22, no. 4, pp. 614–38.
Boland, R.J. and Collopy, F. 2004, 'Design Matters for Management', in R. Boland and F. Collopy (eds), *Managing as Designing*, Stanford University Press, Stanford, CA, pp. 3–18.
Boland, R.J., Collopy, F., Lyytinen, K. and Yoo, Y. 2008, 'Managing as Designing: Lessons for Organization Leaders from the Design Practice of Frank O. Gehry', *Design Issues*, vol. 24, pp. 10–25.
Bourdieu, P. 1977, *Outline of a Theory of Practice*, trans. R. Nice, Cambridge University Press, Cambridge.
Bourdieu, P. 1996, *The State Nobility: Elite Schools in the Field of Power*, Polity Press, Cambridge.
Boyatzis, R.E., Stubbs, E.C. and Taylor, S.N. 2002, 'Learning Cognitive and Emotional Intelligence Competencies through Graduate Management Education', *Academy of Management Learning & Education*, vol. 1, pp. 150–62.
Bradshaw, D. 2007, 'Business School Rankings: The Love–Hate Relationship', *Journal of Management Development*, vol. 26, pp. 54–60.
Broad, W.J. 1981, 'The Publishing Game: Getting More for Less', *Science*, vol. 211, pp. 1137–9.
Bruner, J. 1991, 'The Narrative Construction of Reality', *Critical Inquiry*, pp. 1–21.
Burawoy, M. 1979, *Manufacturing Consent: Changes in the Labor Process under Monopoly Capitalism*, University of Chicago Press, Chicago, IL.
Cadsby, C.B. and Maynes, E. 1998, 'Choosing between a Socially Efficient and Free-riding Equilibrium: Nurses versus Economics and Business Students', *Journal of Economic Behavior and Organization*, vol. 37, pp. 183–92.

Callás, M.B. and Smircich, L. 1991, 'Voicing Seduction to Silence Leadership', *Organization Studies*, vol. 12, no. 4, pp. 567–601.
Carter, J.R. and Irons, M.D. 1991, 'Are Economists Different, and if So, Why?', *Journal of Economic Perspectives*, vol. 5, no. 2, pp. 171–7. American Economic Association, Nashville, TN.
Cheng, H.F., Gutierrez, M., Mahajan, A., Shachmurove, Y. and Shahrokhi, M. 2007, 'A Future Global Economy to be Built by BRICs', *Global Finance Journal*, vol. 18, pp. 143–56.
Clarke, C., Knights, D. and Jarvis, C. 2012, 'A Labour of Love? Academics in Business Schools', *Scandinavian Journal of Management*, vol. 28, pp. 5–15.
Clegg, S.R. 1979 [2013], *The Theory of Power and Organization*, Routledge, London.
Clegg, S.R. and Baunsgaard, V.V. 2013, 'Walls or Boxes: The Effects of Professional Identity, Power and Rationality on Strategies for Cross-functional Integration', *Organization Studies*, vol. 34, pp. 1299–1325.
Clegg, S.R. and Dunkerley, D. 1980, *Organization, Class and Control*, Routledge and Kegan Paul, Boston, MA.
Clegg, S.R. and Ross-Smith, A. 2003, 'Revising the Boundaries: Management Education and Learning in a Postpositivist World', *Academy of Management Learning & Education*, vol. 2, p. 85.
Clegg, S.R., Carter, C. and Kornberger, M. 2004, 'Get Up, I Feel like Being a Strategy Machine', *European Management Review*, vol. 1, pp. 21–8.
Clegg, S.R., Jarvis, W.P. and Pitsis, T.S. 2013, 'Making Strategy Matter: Social Theory, Knowledge Interests and Business Education', *Business History*, vol. 55, no. 7, pp. 1247–64.
Clinebell, S.K. and Clinebell, J.M. 2008, 'The Tension in Business Education Between Academic Rigor and Real-World Relevance: The Role of Executive Professors', *Academy of Management Learning & Education*, vol. 7, p. 99.
Cohen, M.D., March, J.G. and Olsen, J.P. 1972, 'A Garbage Can Model of Organizational Choice', *Administrative Science Quarterly*, vol. 17, pp. 1–25.
Corley, K. and Gioia, D. 2000, 'The Rankings Game: Managing Business School Reputation', *Corporate Reputation Review*, vol. 3, pp. 319–33.
Crainer, S. and Dearlove, D. 1999, *Gravy Training: Inside the Business of Business Schools*, Jossey-Bass, San Francisco, CA.
Cross, N. 2011, *Design Thinking: Understanding How Designers Think and Work*, Berg, Oxford, UK.
Currie, G., Knights, D. and Starkey, K. 2010, 'Introduction: A Post-Crisis Critical Reflection on Business Schools', vol. 21, pp. s1–s5.
Cyert, R.M. and March, J.G. 1963 [1992], *Behavioral Theory of the Firm*, Wiley, New York.
Datar, S.M., Garvin, D.A. and Cullen, P.G. 2010, *Rethinking the MBA: Business Education at a Crossroad*, Harvard Business Review Press, Boston, MA.
Devinney, T., Dowling, G.R. and Perm-Ajchariyawong, N. 2008, 'The Financial Times Business Schools Ranking: What Quality is this Signal of Quality?', *European Management Review*, vol. 5, no. 4, pp. 195–208.
Dichev, I.D. 2008, 'Comment: The Business Schools Ranking: What Quality is this Signal of Quality?', *European Management Review*, vol. 5, no. 4, pp. 219–24.

DiMaggio, P.J. and Powell, W.W. 1983, 'The Iron Cage Revisited: Institutional Isomorphism and Collective Rationality in Organizational Fields', *American Sociological Review*, vol. 48, pp. 147–60.

Djelic, M.-L. 2001, *Exporting the American Model: The Postwar Transformation of European Business*, Oxford University Press, Oxford, UK.

Donaldson, L. 1996, *For Positivist Organization Theory: Proving the Hard Core*, SAGE Publications, Thousand Oaks, CA.

Donaldson, L. 2010, *The Meta-analytic Organization: Introducing Statistico-organizational Theory*, M.E. Sharpe, Inc., Armonk, NY.

Donaldson, L. and Davis, J.H. 1991, 'Stewardship Theory or Agency Theory: CEO Governance and Shareholder Returns', *Australian Journal of Management*, vol. 16, pp. 49–64.

Dunne, D. and Martin, R. 2006, 'Design Thinking and How it Will Change Management Education: An Interview and Discussion', *Academy of Management Learning & Education*, vol. 5, p. 512.

English, D.E. and Manton, E.J. 2007, 'The Trend Toward Multiple Authorship in Business Journals', *Journal of Education for Business*, vol. 82, pp. 164–8.

Evans, F.J. and Marcal, L.E. 2005, 'Educating for Ethics: Business Deans' Perspectives', *Business and Society Review*, vol. 110, pp. 233–48.

Fellman, G. 1995, 'On the Fetishism of Publications and the Secrets Thereof', *Academe*, vol. 81, no. 1, pp. 26–35.

Flyvbjerg, B. 2001, *Making Social Science Matter: Why Social Inquiry Fails and How it Can Succeed Again*, Cambridge University Press, Cambridge, UK.

Flyvbjerg, B. 2006, 'Five Misunderstandings about Case-Study Research', *Qualitative Inquiry*, vol. 12, pp. 219–45.

Foucault, M. 1972, *The Archaeology of Knowledge*, vol. TB 1901, Harper & Row, New York.

French, R. and Grey, C. 1996, 'Rethinking Management Education: An Introduction', in R. French and C. Grey (eds), *Rethinking Management Education*, SAGE, London, pp. 1–16.

Friedman, M., with Friedman, R.D. 1962, *Capitalism and Freedom*, University of Chicago Press, Chicago, IL.

Frodeman, R., Klein, J.T. and Mitcham, C. 2010, *The Oxford Handbook of Interdisciplinarity*, Oxford University Press, Oxford, UK.

Gabriel, Y. 2010, 'Organization Studies: A Space for Ideas, Identities and Agonies', *Organization Studies*, vol. 31, no. 6, pp. 757–75.

Ghoshal, S. 2005, 'Bad Management Theories are Destroying Good Management Practices', *Academy of Management Learning & Education*, vol. 4, p. 75.

Gibbons, M., Limoges, C., Nowotny, H., Schwartzman, S., Scott, P. and Trow, M. 1994, *The New Production of Knowledge: The Dynamics of Science and Research in Contemporary Societies*, SAGE, London.

Gillespie, K. and Riddle, L. 2004, 'Case-Based Teaching in Business Education in the Arab Middle East and North Africa', in I. Alon and J.R. McIntyre (eds), *Business Education and Emerging Market Economies: Perspectives and Best Practices*, Kluwer Academic Publishers, Boston, MA, pp. 141–56.

Gioia, D.A. and Corley, K.G. 2002, 'Being Good versus Looking Good: Business School Rankings and the Circean Transformation from Substance to Image', *Academy of Management Learning & Education*, vol. 1, pp. 107–20.

Glick, W.H. 2008, 'Rain Man or Pied Piper? Moving Business Schools Beyond Media Rankings with Mass Customization and Stakeholder Education', *Academy of Management Perspectives*, vol. 22, pp. 18–22.

GMAC 2010, *Corporate Recruiters Survey Report 2010*, Graduate Management Admission Council, accessed 10 March 2016 at http://bit.ly/124Fakk

Godfrey, P.C., Illes, L.M. and Berry, G.R. 2005, 'Creating Breadth in Business Education Through Service-Learning', *Academy of Management Learning & Education*, vol. 4, p. 309.

Graue, B. 2006, 'The Transformative Power of Reviewing', *Educational Researcher*, vol. 35, pp. 36–41.

Grey, C. 2002, 'What are Business Schools For? On Silence and Voice in Management Education', *Journal of Management Education*, vol. 26, pp. 496–511.

Gutek, B.A. 1997, 'Teaching and Research: A Puzzling Dichotomy', in R. Andre and P. Frost (eds), *Academics Hooked on Teaching*, SAGE, Thousand Oaks, CA, pp. 27–39.

Habermas, J. 1987, *Toward a Rational Society*, Polity Press, Cambridge, UK.

Hall, S. 2009, 'Ecologies of Business Education and the Geographies of Knowledge', *Progress in Human Geography*, vol. 33, pp. 599–618.

Halperin, M., Hebert, R. and Lusk, E.J. 2009, 'Comparing the Rankings of MBA Curricula: Do Methodologies Matter?', *Journal of Business & Finance Librarianship*, vol. 14, pp. 47–62.

Hamilton, D., McFarland, D. and Mirchandani, D. 2000, 'A Decision Model for Integration across the Business Curriculum in the 21st Century', vol. 24, pp. 102–26.

Harzing, A.-W. and Adler, N.J. 2009, 'When Knowledge Wins: Transcending the Sense and Nonsense of Academic Rankings', *Academy of Management Learning & Education*, vol. 8, pp. 72–95.

Herbert, D.L., Barnett, A.G. and Graves, N. 2013, 'Funding: Australia's Grant System Wastes Time', *Nature*, vol. 495, p. 314.

Hicks, D. 2012, 'Performance-based University Research Funding Systems', *Research Policy*, vol. 41, pp. 251–61.

Hodgkinson, G.P. and Rousseau, D.M. 2009, 'Bridging the Rigour–Relevance Gap in Management Research: It's Already Happening!', *Journal of Management Studies*, vol. 46, pp. 534–46.

Iñiguez de Onzoño, S. 2011, *The Learning Curve: How Business Schools are Re-inventing Education*, Palgrave Macmillan, Basingstoke, UK.

Jackson, K.T. 2006, 'Breaking Down the Barriers: Bringing Initiatives and Reality into Business Ethics Education', *Journal of Management Education*, vol. 30, pp. 65–89.

Jacobs, J.A. 2014, *In Defense of Disciplines: Interdisciplinarity and Specialization in the Research University*, University of Chicago Press, Chicago, IL.

Jacobs, J.A. and Frickel, S. 2009, 'Interdisciplinarity: A Critical Assessment', *Annual Review of Sociology*, vol. 35, pp. 43–65.

Jacques, R.S. 2006, 'History, Historiography and Organization Studies: The Challenge and the Potential', *Management & Organizational History*, vol. 1, no. 1, pp. 31–49.

Jarvis, W.P. 2009, 'Moral Accountability in the MBA: A Kantian Response to a Public Problem', University of Technology Sydney, Australia.

Jensen, M.C. and Meckling, W.H. 1976, 'Theory of the Firm: Managerial Behavior, Agency Costs and Ownership Structure', *Journal of Financial Economics*, vol. 3, pp. 305–60.

Judge, T.A., Cable, D.M., Colbert, A.E. and Rynes, S.L. 2007, 'What Causes a Management Article to be Cited: Article, Author, or Journal?', *The Academy of Management Journal*, vol. 50, pp. 491–506.

Julian, S.D. and Ofori-Dankwa, J.C. 2006, 'Is Accreditation Good for the Strategic Decision Making of Traditional Business Schools?', *Academy of Management Learning & Education*, vol. 5, p. 225.

Keenoy, T. 2005, 'Facing Inwards and Outwards at Once: The Liminal Temporalities of Academic Perfomativity', *Time & Society*, vol. 14, no. 2–3, pp. 303–21.

Khurana, R. 2007, *From Higher Aims to Hired Hands: The Social Transformation of American Business Schools and the Unfulfilled Promise of Management as a Profession*, Princeton University Press, Princeton, NJ.

Kieser, A. and Leiner, L. 2011, 'On the Social Construction of Relevance: A Rejoinder', *Journal of Management Studies*, vol. 48, pp. 891–8.

Kiyatkin, L., Reger, R. and Baum, J.R. 2011, 'Thought Leadership on Business and Social Issues', *Journal of Corporate Citizenship*, vol. 2011, no. 41, pp. 83–102.

Klein, J.T. 1990, *Interdisciplinarity: History, Theory, and Practice*, Wayne State University Press, Detroit, MI.

Knights, D. 2008, 'Myopic Rhetorics: Reflecting Epistemologically and Ethically on the Demand for Relevance in Organizational and Management Research', *Academy of Management Learning & Education*, vol. 7, p. 537.

Knights, D. and Clarke, C.A. 2014, 'It's a Bittersweet Symphony, this Life: Fragile Academic Selves and Insecure Identities at Work', *Organization Studies*, vol. 35, no. 3, pp. 335–57.

Knights, D. and Willmott, H. 1997, 'The Hype and Hope of Interdisciplinary Management Studies', *British Journal of Management*, vol. 8, pp. 9–22.

Kogan, M. 2007, 'The Academic Profession and its Interface with Management', in M. Kogan and U. Teichler (eds), *Key Challenges to the Academic Profession*, Kassel, Germany, pp. 159–74, accessed 10 March 2016 at http://bit.ly/RzB81C

Kuhn, T.S. 1962, *The Structure of Scientific Revolutions*, University of Chicago Press, Chicago, IL.

Kumar, R. and Usunier, J.-C. 2001, 'Management Education in a Globalizing World: Lessons from the French Experience', *Management Learning*, vol. 32, pp. 363–91.

Latham, G., Latham, S.D. and Whyte, G. 2004, 'Fostering Integrative Thinking: Adapting the Executive Education Model to the MBA Program', *Journal of Management Education*, vol. 28, pp. 3–18.

Latham, M.E. 2000, *Modernization as Ideology: American Social Science and "Nation-building" in the Kennedy Era*, University of North Carolina Press, Chapel Hill, NC.

Latour, B. and Woolgar, S. 1979, *Laboratory Life: The Social Construction of Scientific Facts*, vol. 80, SAGE Publications, Beverly Hills, CA.

Leme Fleury, M.T. and Wood Jr, T. 2011, 'Creating a Business School Model Adapted to Local Reality: A Latin American Perspective', in M. Morsing and A.S. Rovira (eds), *Business Schools and their Contribution to Society*, SAGE, London, pp. 16–23.

Lerner, J., Li, Y., Valdesolo, P. and Kassam, K. 2015, 'Emotion and Decision Making', *Annual Review of Psychology*, vol. 66, pp. 799–823.

Lorsch, J.W. 2009, 'Regaining Lost Relevance', *Journal of Management Inquiry*, vol. 18, pp. 108–17.

Lowrie, A. and Willmott, H. 2009, 'Accreditation Sickness in the Consumption of Business Education: The Vacuum in AACSB Standard Setting', *Management Learning*, vol. 40, pp. 411–20.

Malhotra, D. and Wang, L. 2011, 'Economics Education and Greed', *Academy of Management Learning & Education*, vol. 10, pp. 643–60.

Martin, R.L. 2009, *The Design of Business*, Harvard Business School Publishing, Harvard, MA.

McCabe, D.L., Butterfield, K.D. and Trevino, L.K. 2006, 'Academic Dishonesty in Graduate Business Programs: Prevalence, Causes, and Proposed Action', *Academy of Management Learning & Education*, vol. 5, p. 294.

Méon, P.-G. and Sekkat, K. 2005, 'Does Corruption Grease or Sand the Wheels of Growth?', *Public Choice*, vol. 122, pp. 69–97.

Mingers, J. and Willmott, H. 2013, 'Taylorizing Business School Research: On the "One Best Way" Performative Effects of Journal Ranking Lists', *Human Relations*, vol. 66, no. 8, pp. 1051–73.

Mintzberg, H. 2004, *Managers not MBAs: A Hard Look at the Soft Practice of Managing and Management Development*, Berrett-Koehler, San Francisco, CA.

Mitev, N. 2009, 'In and Out of Actor-Network Theory: A Necessary but Insufficient Journey', *Information Technology & People*, vol. 22, pp. 9–25.

Mo, P.H. 2001, 'Corruption and Economic Growth', *Journal of Comparative Economics*, vol. 29, pp. 66–79.

Myers, L.L. and Tucker, M.L. 2005, 'Increasing Awareness of Emotional Intelligence in a Business Curriculum', *Business Communication Quarterly*, vol. 68, pp. 44–51.

Navarro, P. 2008, 'The MBA Core Curricula of Top-Ranked U.S. Business Schools: A Study in Failure?', *Academy of Management Learning & Education*, vol. 7, p. 108.

Nicolai, A. and Seidl, D. 2010, 'That's Relevant! Different Forms of Practical Relevance in Management Science', *Organization Studies*, vol. 31, pp. 1257–85.

Nonis, S. and Swift, C.O. 2001, 'An Examination of the Relationship between Academic Dishonesty and Workplace Dishonesty: A Multicampus Investigation', *Journal of Education for Business*, vol. 77, pp. 69–77.

Norton, A. 2012, *Mapping Australian Higher Education*, Grattan Institute, Melbourne, VIC, Australia.

Olsen, J.P. and March, J.G. 1976, *Ambiguity and Choice in Organizations*, Universitetsforlaget, Bergen, Germany.

Orton, J.D. and Weick, K.E. 1990, 'Loosely Coupled Systems: A Reconceptualization', *The Academy of Management Review*, vol. 15, pp. 203–23.

Özbilgin, M.F. 2009, 'From Journal Rankings to Making Sense of the World', *Academy of Management Learning & Education*, vol. 8, no. 1, pp. 113–21.

Parker, M. 2014, 'University, Ltd: Changing a Business School', *Organization*, vol. 21, no. 2, pp. 281–92.

Parker, M. and Jary, D. 1995, 'The McUniversity: Organization, Management and Academic Subjectivity', *Organization*, vol. 2, pp. 319–38.

Parsons, T. 1951, *The Social System*, Routledge & Kegan Paul, London.

Paton, S., Chia, R. and Burt, G. 2013, 'Relevance or "Relevate"? How University Business Schools can Add Value through Reflexively Learning from Strategic Partnerships with Business', *Management Learning*, vol. 45, no. 3, pp. 267–88.

Pearce, J.L. and Huang, L. 2012, 'The Decreasing Value of Our Research to Management Education', *Academy of Management Learning & Education*, vol. 11, p. 247.

Pearse, M.E. 2010, 'The Management Rush: A History of Management in Australia', Doctoral dissertation, Macquarie University, Australia.

Peters, K. 2007, 'Business School Rankings: Content and Context', *The Journal of Management Development*, vol. 26, pp. 49–53.

Peters, T. and Bogner, W.C. 2002, 'Tom Peters on the Real World of Business', *The Academy of Management Executive (1993–2005)*, vol. 16, pp. 40–44.

Pfeffer, J. 2007, 'A Modest Proposal: How We Might Change the Process and Product of Managerial Research', *The Academy of Management Journal*, vol. 50, pp. 1334–45.

Pfeffer, J. and Fong, C.T. 2004, 'The Business School "Business": Some Lessons from the US Experience', *Journal of Management Studies*, vol. 41, pp. 1501–20.

Radder, H. 2010, 'The Commodification of Academic Research', in H. Radder (ed.), *The Commodification of Academic Research: Science and the Modern University*, The University of Pittsburgh Press, Pittsburgh, pp. 1–23.

Raelin, J.A. 2007, 'Toward an Epistemology of Practice', *Academy of Management Learning & Education*, vol. 6, p. 495.

Raelin, J.A. 2008, 'Refereeing the Game of Peer Review', *Academy of Management Learning & Education*, vol. 7, p. 124.

Rafols, I., Leydesdorff, L., O'Hare, A., Nightingale, P. and Stirling, A. 2012, 'How Journal Rankings can Suppress Interdisciplinary Research: A Comparison between Innovation Studies and Business & Management', *Research Policy*, vol. 41, pp. 1262–82.

Reeves-Ellington, R. 2004, 'What is Missing from Business Education? Meeting the Needs of Emerging Market Business Education', in I. Alon and J.R. McIntyre (eds), *Business Education and Emerging Market Economies: Perspectives and Best Practices*, Kluwer Academic Publishers, Boston, MA, pp. 27–48.

Rhodes, C. 2001, *Writing Organization: (Re)Presentation and Control in Narratives at Work*, vol. 7, John Benjamins Publishing, Amsterdam, NL.

Rittel, H.W.J. and Webber, M.M. 1973, 'Dilemmas in a General Theory of Planning', *Policy Sciences*, vol. 4, pp. 155–69.

Roberts, J. 1996, 'Management Education and the Limits of Technical Rationality: The Conditions and Consequences of Management Practice?', in R. French and C. Grey (eds), *Rethinking Management Education*, SAGE, London, pp. 54–75.

Ross, J. 2012, 'Short Sweeter for Student Visitors', *The Australian*, p. 31.

Rousseau, D.M. 2006, '2005 Presidential Address: Is there Such a Thing as "Evidence-Based Management"?', *The Academy of Management Review*, vol. 31, pp. 256–69.

Rutherford, M.A., Parks, L., Cavazos, D.E. and White, C.D. 2012, 'Business Ethics as a Required Course: Investigating the Factors Impacting the Decision to Require Ethics in the Undergraduate Business Core Curriculum', *Academy of Management Learning & Education*, vol. 11, pp. 174–86.

Ryan, S. and Guthrie, J. 2009, 'Collegial Entrepreneurialism: Australian Graduate Schools of Business', *Public Management Review*, vol. 11, no. 3, pp. 317–44.

Ryan, S. and Neumann, R. 2011, 'Interdisciplinarity in an Era of New Public Management: A Case Study of Graduate Business Schools', *Studies in Higher Education*, vol. 38, pp. 1–15.

Safón, V. 2009, 'Measuring the Reputation of Top US Business Schools: A MIMIC Modeling Approach', *Corporate Reputation Review*, vol. 12, pp. 204–28.

Schulz, M. 1998, 'Limits to Bureaucratic Growth: The Density Dependence of Organizational Rule Births', *Administrative Science Quarterly*, vol. 43, pp. 845–76.

Schulze, G.G. and Frank, B. 2000, 'Does Economics Make Citizens Corrupt?', *Journal of Economic Behavior & Organization*, vol. 43, pp. 101–13.

Simon, H.A. 1957, *Models of Man, Social and Rational: Mathematical Essays on Rational Human Behaviour in a Social Setting*, Wiley, New York.

Sinclair, A. 1995, 'Sex and the MBA', *Organization*, vol. 2, no. 2, pp. 295–317.

Spicer, A. 2006, 'Beyond the Convergence-Divergence Debate: The Role of Spatial Scales in Transforming Organizational Logic', *Organization Studies*, vol. 27, pp. 1467–83.

Starbuck, W.H. 2003, 'Turning Lemons into Lemonade: Where is the Value in Peer Reviews?', *Journal of Management Inquiry*, vol. 12, pp. 344–51.

Starbuck, W.H. 2005, 'How Much Better are the Most-Prestigious Journals? The Statistics of Academic Publication', *Organization Science*, vol. 16, pp. 180–200.

Starkey, K. and Madan, P. 2001, 'Bridging the Relevance Gap: Aligning Stakeholders in the Future of Management Research', *British Journal of Management*, vol. 12, pp. S3–S26.

Starkey, K. and Tempest, S. 2008, 'A Clear Sense of Purpose? The Evolving Role of the Business School', *Journal of Management Development*, vol. 27, pp. 379–90.

Starkey, K., Hatchuel, A. and Tempest, S. 2004, 'Rethinking the Business School', *Journal of Management Studies*, vol. 41, pp. 1521–31.

Steiner, S.D. and Watson, M.A. 2006, 'The Service Learning Component in Business Education: The Values Linkage Void', *Academy of Management Learning & Education*, vol. 5, p. 422.

Stichweh, R. 2001, 'Scientific Disciplines, History of', in N.J. Smelser and P.B. Balter (eds), *International Encyclopedia of the Social and Behavioral Sciences*, Elsevier, New York.

Sturdy, A. and Gabriel, Y. 2000, 'Missionaries, Mercenaries or Car Salesmen? MBA Teaching in Malaysia', *Journal of Management Studies*, vol. 37, pp. 979–1002.

Syed, J., Mingers, J. and Murray, P.A. 2010, 'Beyond Rigour and Relevance: A Critical Realist Approach to Business Education', *Management Learning*, vol. 41, pp. 71–85.

ten Bos, R. 2000, *Fashion and Utopia in Management Thinking*, John Benjamins, Amsterdam, NL.

Thomas, A., Whitley, R. and Marceau, J. 1981, *Masters of Business?: Business Schools and Business Graduates in Britain and France*, Tavistock Publications, New York.

Thompson, T.A. and Purdy, J.M. 2009, 'When a Good Idea isn't Enough: Curricular Innovation as a Political Process', *Academy of Management Learning & Education*, vol. 8, p. 188.

Trank, C.Q. and Rynes, S.L. 2003, 'Who Moved our Cheese? Reclaiming Professionalism in Business Education', *Academy of Management Learning & Education*, vol. 2, p. 189.

Trounson, A. 2012, 'Academic "Golden Age" a Lazy Privileged Men's Club – Bradley', *The Australian*, 24 November, accessed 31 July 2014 at http://bit.ly/1zyiyZ4

Tushman, M.L., O'Reilly, C.A., Fenollosa, A., Adam, M.K.A.M. and McGrath, D. 2007, 'Relevance and Rigor: Executive Education as a Lever in Shaping Practice and Research', *Academy of Management Learning & Education*, vol. 6, p. 345.

Vaara, E. and Faÿ, E. 2011, 'How Can a Bourdieusian Perspective Aid Analysis of MBA Education?', *Academy of Management Learning & Education*, vol. 10, p. 27.

Vaara, E. and Faÿ, E. 2012, 'Reproduction and Change on the Global Scale: A Bourdieusian Perspective on Management Education', *Journal of Management Studies*, vol. 49, pp. 1023–51.

Vince, R. 2010, 'Anxiety, Politics and Critical Management Education', vol. 21, no. s1, pp. s26–s39.

Weatherbee, T., Dye, K. and Mills, A.J. 2008, 'There's Nothing as Good as a Practical Theory: The Paradox of Management Education', *Management & Organizational History*, vol. 3, pp. 147–60.

Weber, J.W. and Englehart, S.W. 2011, 'Enhancing Business Education through Integrated Curriculum Delivery', *Journal of Management Development*, vol. 30, pp. 558–68.

Weber, M. 1920 [2005], *The Protestant Ethic and the Spirit of Capitalism*, Routledge, London.

Wedlin, L. 2007, 'The Role of Rankings in Codifying a Business School Template: Classifications, Diffusion and Mediated Isomorphism in Organizational Fields', *European Management Review*, vol. 4, pp. 24–39.

Wedlin, L. 2011, 'Going Global: Rankings as Rhetorical Devices to Construct an International Field of Management Education', *Management Learning*, vol. 42, p. 199.

Weick, K.E. 1976, 'Educational Organizations as Loosely Coupled Systems', *Administrative Science Quarterly*, vol. 21, pp. 1–19.

Weick, K.E. 1982, 'Management of Organizational Change among Loosely Coupled Elements', in P.S.G.A. Associates (ed.), *Change in Organizations*, Jossey-Bass, San Francisco, CA, pp. 375–408.

Weick, K.E. 2001, 'Gapping the Relevance Bridge: Fashions Meet Fundamentals in Management Research', *British Journal of Management*, vol. 12, pp. S71–S75.

Weller, A.C. 2001, *Editorial Peer Review: Its Strengths and Weaknesses*, Information Today, Medford, NJ.

Weller, M. 2011, *The Digital Scholar: How Technology is Transforming Academic Practice*, A&C Black, London.

Wensley, R. 2010, 'Beyond Rigour and Relevance: A Critical Realist Approach to Business Education', *Management Learning*, vol. 41, no. 1, pp. 71–85.

Willmott, H. 1995, 'Managing the Academics: Commodification and Control in the Development of University Education in the UK', *Human Relations*, vol. 48, pp. 993–1027.

Wilson, D.C. and McKiernan, P. 2011, 'Global Mimicry: Putting Strategic Choice Back on the Business School Agenda', vol. 22, no. 3, pp. 457–69.

Wilson, D.C. and Thomas, H. 2012, 'The Legitimacy of the Business of Business Schools: What's the Future?', *The Journal of Management Development*, vol. 31, pp. 368–76.

Wittgenstein, L. 1958, *Philosophical Investigations*, trans. G.E.M. Anscombe, Blackwell, Oxford, UK.

Wood, C.M. 2004, 'Usefulness of Micro-Business Models in Developing Countries', in I. Alon and J.R. McIntyre (eds), *Business Education and Emerging Market Economies: Perspectives and Best Practices*, Kluwer Academic Publishers, Boston, MA, pp. 183–200.

Yeung, B. and Kulwant, S. 2011, 'The Changing Role of Business Schools as Key Social Agents in Asia', in M. Morsing and A.S. Rovira (eds), *Business Schools and their Contribution to Society*, SAGE, London, pp. 24–36.

Ylijoki, O.-H. 2005, 'Academic Nostalgia: A Narrative Approach to Academic Work', *Human Relations*, vol. 58, no. 5, pp. 555–76.

Zammuto, R.F. 2008, 'Accreditation and the Globalization of Business', *Academy of Management Learning & Education*, vol. 7, p. 256.

Zell, D. 2001, 'The Market-Driven Business School: Has the Pendulum Swung Too Far?', *Journal of Management Inquiry*, vol. 10, no. 4, pp. 324–38.

Index

Printed and bound by CPI Group (UK) Ltd, Croydon, CR0 4YY

23/04/2025

14660959-0001